THE LEGEND OF BASIL THE BULGAR-SLAYER

The reign of Basil II (976–1025), the longest of any Byzantine emperor, has long been considered a "golden age," in which Basil's greatest achievement was the annexation of Bulgaria. This, we have been told, was achieved through a long and bloody war of attrition which won Basil the grisly epithet *Voulgartoktonos*, "the Bulgar-slayer."

In this new study Paul Stephenson argues that neither of these beliefs is true. Instead, Basil fought far more sporadically in the Balkans and, like his predecessors, considered this area less prestigious than the East. Moreover, his reputation as "Bulgar-slayer" emerged only a century and a half later, the creation of a martial regime immersed in bellicose panegyric. Thereafter the "Bulgar-slayer" was periodically to play a galvanizing role for the Byzantines. Fading from view during the period of Ottoman rule, Basil returned to center stage as the Greeks struggled to establish a modern nation state. As Byzantium was embraced as the Greek past by scholars and politicians, the "Bulgar-slayer" became an icon in the struggle for Macedonia (1904–8) and the Balkan Wars (1912–13).

THE LEGEND OF BASIL THE BULGAR-SLAYER

PAUL STEPHENSON

University of Wisconsin-Madison and Dumbarton Oaks

CAMBRIDGE UNIVERSITY PRESS

CAMBRIDGE UNIVERSITY PRESS
Cambridge, New York, Melbourne, Madrid, Cape Town, Singapore,
São Paulo, Delhi, Dubai, Tokyo, Mexico City

Cambridge University Press
The Edinburgh Building, Cambridge CB2 8RU, UK

Published in the United States of America by Cambridge University Press, New York

www.cambridge.org
Information on this title: www.cambridge.org/9780521158831

First published 2003
First paperback edition 2010

A catalogue record for this publication is available from the British Library

Library of Congress catalogue card number: 74-16991

ISBN 978-0-521-81530-7 Hardback
ISBN 978-0-521-15883-1 Paperback

Additional resources for this publication at www.cambridge.org/9780521158831

In memory of SWS, IPS, GHS, DHS,
and for my sisters

Μελετῶ ἄλλη ἐποχή, ἀρκετὰ γνωστή, τοῦ Ἀλεξίου Κομνηνοῦ, κ' ἐδῶ ἡ φαντασία δὲν μπορεῖ πιὰ νὰ γεμίσει τὰ χάσματα, ὅπως στὸν καιρὸ τοῦ Βουλγαροκτόνου ποὺ τόσο λίγο γνωρίζομε.

Penelope Delta to Kostis Palamas, February 1912

But Christian Spain badly needed some relics and a shrine to boost its campaign to drive out the Moors. That's how Saint James became the patron saint of Spain, and "*Santiago!*" the Spanish battle-cry. According to another legend, he appeared in person at the crucial battle of Clavijo in 834 to rally the wilting Christian army, and personally slew seventy thousand Moors. The archdiocese of Santiago had the face to lay a special tax on the rest of Spain as a thank you to St James, though in fact there is no evidence that the battle of Clavijo ever took place, with or without his intervention. In the churches along the Camino you see statues of "*Santiago Matamoros*", St James the Moorslayer, depicting him as a warrior on horseback, wielding his sword and trampling the corpses of swarthy, thick-lipped infidels. They could become an embarrassment if Political Correctness ever gets a hold in Spain.

David Lodge, *Therapy*, London 1995

Contents

Illustrations

a Greek soldier is depicted blinding a Bulgarian. Historical and
Ethnological Society of Greece.

MAPS

Preface

The Greeks have often been accused of dwelling on the past, to the detriment of both the present and the future. Indeed, one critical philhellene coined the term *progonoplexia*, or "ancestoritis," to describe this apparent obsession. But using history, recreating the past to comprehend and shape the present and future, is neither inherently wrong, nor is it uniquely Greek. Every generation must rewrite the past to give it meaning, and in doing so ask new questions of the evidence at hand. This was especially true in the nineteenth century, an era of nation formation, when many new materials were made available for study. Students of medieval history now rarely discover new sources, but constantly discover new questions to ask of those they have, revealing new levels of meaning pertinent to both past and present societies. Most historians, and even some politicians, now regret the "abuse" of the past for nationalist ends. This is especially true in Greece, where for more than twenty years critical historians have offered a counterbalance to nationalist rhetoric. But elsewhere, scholars continue to produce "history" in the service of the nation state. We should condemn this, especially when it leads to the manipulation and falsification of evidence, as it often does. But the fact remains that few educational systems emphasize any aspect of history over the history of the nation. The Greek passion for Byzantium, as a period of Greek cultural history, is and will remain of the greatest benefit to the vitality of Byzantine studies. Therefore, I offer this study to Greeks and philhellenes alike in all humility.

In researching and writing this book I have incurred many debts of gratitude. I am particularly grateful to my good friend Despina Christodoulou, who gave me a base in Athens for three summers, and took the opportunity to correct, encourage and facilitate my research at all stages. Also in Athens, in 2000, I was privileged to be invited by the late Lenos Mavrommatis to present the kernel of my ideas at the EIE conference, *Vyzantio kai Voulgaroi, 1018–1185*. I benefited then, as before, from broader discussions with Telemachos Lounghis, and also with Paschalis Kitromilides. At a late stage,

I presented a paper on the revival of interest in the Bulgar-slayer at the annual Monemvasia symposium, and for that opportunity I am grateful to Chryssa Maltezou and Haris Kalligas. J. C. Mazarakis-Aenian, secretary-general of the Historical and Ethnological Society of Greece, generously provided color transparencies of several images.

This project is not about Bulgaria, and it attempts to keep Bulgar-slaying to a minimum. To that end, I am grateful to two very lively Bulgarians, Dorotei Getov and Elka Bakalova, for their helpful comments and criticisms. I was also enlightened by visiting and speaking with members of the Macedonian community of Perth, Western Australia, and am grateful to John Melville-Jones for that opportunity. In addition, papers with variations on the name of this book were given by invitation at a number of institutions, including: The Queen's University, Belfast; The School of Slavonic and East European Studies, University College London; The University of Florida, Gainesville. I am grateful to Margaret Mullett, Wendy Bracewell, Alex Drace-Francis, Florin Curta, Will Hasty and Tom Gallant for the invitations and excellent critical feedback. At Cambridge University Press, William Davies has provided the same impeccable service and unstinting support that he did for my last effort. Byzantine historians owe him a great debt.

I will not mention every Byzantinist who has helped at various stages of the project, so that they may have a chance to review the book! They know who they are. However, I must express my gratitude to foundations and institutions that have supported my research since 1998. Initial forays were undertaken at the University of Oxford, and there I was guided in various directions by Averil Cameron, Peter Mackridge and Richard Clogg. Catherine Holmes generously read draft chapters, and offered copies of her papers prior to their publication. The Alexander von Humboldt-Stiftung made it possible for me to enjoy two stints at the Seminar für Byzantinistik at the Johannes Gutenberg-Universität Mainz, where the idea to produce a short book was conceived. Under the diligent and kindly eye of Günter Prinzing I produced two preliminary papers. These were both published in *Byzantine and Modern Greek Studies*, and I am grateful to the editor John Haldon for permission to reproduce much of the text, albeit substantially reorganized. Little research was undertaken, but much fun was had at University College Cork, Ireland, thanks to Donnchadh Ó Corráin, Jennifer O'Reilly, Damian Bracken, Dermot Keogh, Joe Lee and especially Gillian Smith. Bill Courtenay, David Morgan, Michael Chamberlain and Mike Clover were instrumental in bringing me from Cork to the University of Wisconsin-Madison, where the Graduate School has generously sponsored two summers of research overseas. My second home, Dumbarton Oaks, has proved the perfect place to complete the project, while honing other necessary skills. I am immensely grateful to the Director, Edward Keenan, who glanced over a draft of the book; to the Director of the program in Byzantine Studies, Alice-Mary Talbot, for her guidance in matters philological; and to the Byzantine Librarian (retired), Irene Vaslef, without whom the library, the heart of an august institution, would be a lesser resource. Our senior and most erudite Research Associate, Irfan Shahîd, generously translated Arabic material where existing translations were unclear or inaccurate. Without the generosity of John and Jeanne Rowe, this project would not yet have reached an end, but more stout would have been taken.

Annotation and transliteration

I have attempted to cite all literature in the fullest form both in footnotes and bibliography. Since the manuscript was prepared for publication at Dumbarton Oaks Research Library and Collection, I have adopted the style employed in *Dumbarton Oaks Papers*. This has required that I, somewhat more reluctantly, adopt American English spelling.

It was my original intention to use original alphabets whenever possible. However, after some reflection, I have chosen to employ Latin transliterations far more frequently. It seemed an excessive burden on the reader to present her with three alphabets – Latin, Greek and Cyrillic – on any given page. (Transliterated Arabic terms are far less frequent.) When transliterating from Cyrillic I have used a modified version of the Library of Congress system, omitting some diacritics. However, where a work has been published with a transliterated title, I have employed that for the sake of clarity. For example, I cite the work in Russian by V. R. Rozen according to the transliterated title offered by the editor of the reprinted edition: *Imperator Vasilij Bolgarobojca. Izvlečenija iz Letopisi Jaxi Antioxijskago* (St. Petersburg, 1908; repr. London, 1972). Similarly, I have not altered an author's preferred transliteration of his or her name, so I refer to I. Dujčev not Duichev, and V. Šandrovskaya not Shandrovskaia.

I have been deliberately inconsistent in my transliteration of Greek. Because so many Byzantine Greek terms will be familiar to the intended readership, to retain the Greek letters would be both awkward and pedantic. Moreover, the *ODB* now offers a model to follow, and in all cases I have sought to do so: hence Theophylaktos, not Theophylact of Ohrid, but John, not Ioannes or Ioannis Komnenos. The Byzantine Greek term for general, στρατηγός, is commonly transliterated as *strategos* (see *ODB*, III, 1964). However, if this were used in a Modern Greek context, I would prefer *stratigos*, to represent better the sound of the eta. For similar reasons, the reader will find references to Lambros, not Lampros, but *basileus* not *vasilefs*. This is not to suggest that the words would have been pronounced so differently, but merely to follow established conventions. The one notable exception is *Voulgaroktonos*, not *Boulgaroktonos*, which I have employed throughout.

Abbreviations

ArtB	*The Art Bulletin*, New York 1913–
BCH	*Bulletin de correspondance hellénique*, Athens and Paris 1877–
BMGS	*Byzantine and Modern Greek Studies*, Oxford 1975–83, Birmingham 1984–
BSl	*Byzantinoslavica*, Prague 1929–
ByzF	*Byzantinische Forschungen*, Amsterdam 1966–
ByzSt	*Byzantine Studies/Etudes byzantines*, Pittsburgh 1974–6, Phoenix, 1981–5, Bakersfield 1986, Shepherdstown 1996–
BZ	*Byzantinische Zeitschrift*, Leipzig and Munich 1892–
CFHB	*Corpus Fontium Historiae Byzantinae*, Washington, DC et al. 1967–
CSHB	*Corpus Scriptorum Historiae Byzantinae*, Bonn 1828–97
DOP	*Dumbarton Oaks Papers*, Cambridge, MA and Washington, DC, 1941–
DOS	*Dumbarton Oaks Studies*, Washington, DC
EEBS	Ἐπετηρὶς Ἑταιρείας Βυζαντινῶν Σπουδῶν, Athens 1924–
EHR	*The English Historical Review*, London 1886–
EO	*Echos d'Orient*, Paris 1897–1932, Istanbul 1933–7, Bucharest 1938–42
HUS	*Harvard Ukrainian Studies*, Cambridge, MA 1977–
JHS	*The Journal of Hellenic Studies*, London 1880–
JMGS	*Journal of Modern Greek Studies*, Baltimore 1983–
JÖB	*Jahrbuch der Österreichischen Byzantinistik*, Vienna, Cologne and Graz 1969–
MGH	*Monumenta Germaniae Historica*, Hanover et al. 1824–1934
Neos Ellin.	Νέος Ἑλληνομνήμων, Athens 1904–27

ODB   *The Oxford Dictionary of Byzantium*, eds. A. Kazhdan,
A.-M. Talbot, A. Cutler, T. E. Gregory and N. P.
Ševčenko, 3 vols., Oxford and New York 1991

PG   *Patrologia Cursus Completus, series Graeco-Latina*, ed. J. P.
Migne, Paris 1857–66, 1880–1903

PL   *Patrologia Cursus Completus, series Latina*, ed. J. P. Migne,
Paris 1844–1974

REB   *Revue des études byzantines*, Bucharest and Paris 1944–

REG   *Revue des études grecques*, Paris 1888–

RESEE   *Revue des études sud-est européennes*, Bucharest 1963–

SEER   *The Slavonic and East European Review*, London 1922–

Skylitzes   *Ioannis Scylitzes Synopsis Historiarum*, ed. J. Thurn,
CFHB 5, Berlin and New York 1973

SüdostF   *Südost-Forschungen*, Munich 1936–

TM   *Travaux et Mémoires. Centre de recherche d'histoire et
civilisation byzantines*, Paris 1965–

VV   *Vizantiiskii vremennik*, St. Petersburg 1894–1927,
Moscow 1947–

ZRVI   *Zbornik Radova Vizantološkog Instituta*, Belgrade 1952–

Basil the Bulgar-slayer: an introduction

The principal historians of the Byzantine empire writing in the first half of the twentieth century agreed that the reign of the emperor Basil II (976–1025) marked the apogee of the medieval Byzantine state, the culmination of a recovery initiated with the establishment on the throne of the Macedonian dynasty by his grandfather's grandfather, Basil I.[1] The fullest account of Basil II's life and deeds can be found in the grand narrative of the French Byzantinist Gustave Schlumberger.[2] In recent years serious critical historians have questioned Schlumberger's interpretation, although it still features in popular literature.[3] This book does not offer a new account of Basil's reign, although it does suggest many revisions to the traditional narrative of his activities in Bulgaria. Rather it is a survey, from the time of his death to the present, of Basil's reputation as the "Bulgar-slayer," which challenges the notion that his reign was the culmination of a "golden age."[4]

---

[1] A. A. Vasiliev, *Histoire de l'empire byzantin*, 2 vols. (Paris, 1932), I, 397, originally published in Russian in 1917; C. Diehl, *Histoire de l'empire byzantin* (Paris, 1919), 90–1, 106–8; S. Runciman, *Byzantine civilisation* (London, 1933), 48–9; N. Iorga, *Histoire de la vie byzantine. Empire et civilisation, II. L'empire moyen de civilisation hellénique* (Bucharest, 1934), 201; G. Ostrogorsky, *History of the Byzantine state*, tr. J. Hussey, 2nd English ed. (Oxford, 1968), 298–9, 315, originally published in German in 1940; L. Bréhier, *Le monde byzantin, I. Vie et mort de Byzance* (Paris, 1948), 212–13, 238.

[2] G. Schlumberger, *L'épopée byzantine à la fin du dixième siècle, II. Basile II le tueur des Bulgares* (Paris, 1900).

[3] In fact, the first notable dissenting voice was that of A. Toynbee, *The Place of mediaeval and modern Greece in history. Inaugural lecture of the Koraes Chair of Modern Greek and Byzantine Language, Literature and History* (London, 1919), 22–3, who maintained that Basil's campaigns overstretched the empire. For a recent, and far fuller analysis in the same vein, see M. Angold, *The Byzantine empire, 1025–1204: a political history*, 2nd ed. (London, 1997), 24–34, on Basil's tainted legacy. A forceful endorsement of Basil's civilian successors was offered by P. Lemerle, *Cinq études sur le XIe siècle byzantin* (Paris, 1977), 249–312, who questioned the correlation between military expansion and the notion of apogee. Similar sentiments are implicit in the analysis by A. Ducellier, *Byzance et le monde orthodoxe* (Paris, 1986), 140–50, esp. 148: "A la mort de Basile II il *semblait* que l'Empire eût atteint le sommet de sa puissance militaire et politique" (my italics).

[4] For a fresh account of Basil's eastern policy, administration and principal historian (Skylitzes) see now C. J. Holmes, "Basil II and the government of empire (976–1025)," D.Phil. dissertation, University of Oxford (Oxford, 1999). I have published my first thoughts on Basil's Bulgarian campaigns

Basil II's reign, the longest of any medieval East Roman emperor, witnessed a number of episodes and events of enduring importance. The formal conversion in 988/9 to Orthodox Christianity of the ruler of the Rus' of Kiev, Vladimir Sviatoslavich, must be singled out, not least because its significance remains the subject of intense discussion.[5] However, it is generally agreed that Basil's greatest achievement was the annexation of Bulgaria to the Byzantine empire, following a protracted and bloody war. Since the sixth century the Balkan peninsula had been occupied by Slavic-speaking peoples, who, following the arrival of the Turkic Bulgars in 680, had increasingly recognized the authority of the Bulgar khan. Attempts by Byzantine emperors to repeal Bulgar hegemony in the northern Balkans generally ended prematurely, in failure, or occasionally in disaster. On 26 July 811 a Byzantine army led by Emperor Nikephoros I was trapped in a mountain pass between wooden barricades erected by the troops of Khan Krum. The Bulgars fell on the Byzantine encampment, slaughtering many including the emperor.[6] The story of this defeat would long haunt Byzantine emperors who engaged battle with the Bulgars. Its memory was expunged almost exactly 203 years later in the most notorious, although far from the last, act in Basil's Bulgarian war.

The battle of Kleidion ("the little key"), also called the battle of Belasica, took place on 29 July 1014. This has been singled out as the decisive moment in Basil's campaigns, and the reason for his receiving the epithet "Bulgar-slayer."[7] The earliest extant account of the battle of Kleidion is contained in the *Synopsis historion* of John Skylitzes.

The emperor [Basil] did not relent, but every year he marched into Bulgaria and laid waste and ravaged all before him. [The Bulgarian ruler] Samuel was not able to resist openly, nor to face the emperor in open warfare, so, weakened from all sides, he came down from his lofty lair to fortify the entrance to Bulgaria with ditches and fences. Knowing that the emperor always made his incursions through so-called

---

in P. Stephenson, *Byzantium's Balkan frontier: a political study of the northern Balkans, 900–1204* (Cambridge, 2000), 58–79.

[5] A. Poppe has addressed the issue on several occasions and at length: "The political background to the baptism of Rus'. Byzantine–Russian relations between 986–89," *DOP* 30 (1976), 195–244; "Two conceptions of the conversion of Rus' in Kievan writings," *HUS* 12/13 (1988/1989), 488–504 (a volume devoted to *Proceedings of the international congress commemorating the millennium of Christianity in Rus'-Ukraine*); "The Christianization and ecclesiastical structure of Kyivan Rus' to 1300," *HUS* 21 (1997), 311–92. Most recently, see J. Korpela, *Prince, saint and apostle. Prince Vladimir Svjatoslavič of Kiev, his posthumous life, and the religious legitimization of the Russian great power* (Wiesbaden, 2001).

[6] See I. Dujčev, "La chronique byzantine de l'an 811," *TM* 1 (1965), 205–55; P. Niavis, *The reign of the Byzantine emperor Nicephorus I (AD 802–811)* (Athens, 1987), 221–53.

[7] Vasiliev, *Histoire de l'empire byzantin*, 423; Diehl, *Histoire de l'empire byzantin*, 104; Runciman, *Byzantine civilisation*, 49; Iorga, *Histoire de la vie byzantine*, II, 200; Ostrogorsky, *Byzantine state*, 310.

"Kiava Longon"[8] and [the pass known as] "Kleidion," he undertook to fortify the difficult terrain to deny the emperor access. A wall was built across the whole width [of the pass] and worthy defenders were committed to it to stand against the emperor. When he arrived and made an attempt to enter [Bulgaria], the guards defended the wall manfully and bombarded and wounded the attackers from above. When the emperor had thus despaired of gaining passage, Nikephoros Xiphias, the *strategos* of Philippopolis, met with the emperor and urged him to stay put and continue to assault the wall, while, as he explained, he turned back with his men and, heading round to the south of Kleidion through rough and trackless country, crossed the very high mountain known as Belasica. On 29 July, in the twelfth indiction [1014, Xiphias and his men] descended suddenly on the Bulgarians, from behind and screaming battle cries. Panic-stricken by the sudden assault [the Bulgarians] turned to flee, while the emperor broke through the abandoned wall. Many [Bulgarians] fell and many more were captured; Samuel barely escaped from danger with the aid of his son, who fought nobly against his attackers, placed him on a horse, and made for the fortress known as Prilep. The emperor blinded the Bulgarian captives – around 15,000 they say – and he ordered every hundred to be led back to Samuel by a one-eyed man. And when [Samuel] saw the equal and ordered detachments returning he could not bear it manfully nor with courage, but was himself struck blind and fell in a faint to the ground. His companions revived him for a short time with water and smelling salts, and somewhat recovered he asked for a sip of cold water. Taking a gulp he had a heart attack and died two days later *on 6 October*.[9]

Skylitzes was writing most probably between 1079 and 1096, thus already up to eighty years after the battle. His synoptic history does not present a full record of events in Basil's reign, but rather is characterized by elaborate set pieces, largely military encounters, conjoined by short summarizing sentences. It is, therefore, typical that Skylitzes should state that Basil invaded Bulgaria each year before 1014, but provide no further information to support this short sentence. And while he provides no details of any encounters between 1005 and 1014, Skylitzes' testimony has been taken as

---

[8] Various readings have been advanced by those seeking to identify this location. Thurn's critical edition of Skylitzes offers «διὰ τοῦ λεγομένου Κίαβα Λόγγου», where Κίαβα is offered in recensions A, C, V and B. Four alternative readings are: Κίαμβα (E); Κίσβα (U); Κίμβα (M, N, H); Κιμβαλόγγου (D). The last two have often been favored and translated into Latin as "campus longus," and English as "long field" or "long plain." An alternative suggestion identifies in Κία(μ)βα the latinate Vlach word *kamba*, which allows for the translation "long rock," or by extension "long, rocky defile." A summary of suggestions is provided by N. Moutsopoulos, "Le tombeau du Tsar Samuil dans la Basilique de Saint Achille à Prespa," *Etudes Balkaniques* 3 (1984), 114–26 at 117.

[9] Skylitzes, 348–9. The date, in italics, is supplied in a gloss to one of the extant manuscripts of Skylitzes, U, attributed to a certain Michael of Devol. See J. Prokić, *Die Zusätze in der Handschrift des Johannes Skylitzes, codex Vindobonensis hist. graec. LXXIV. Ein Beitrag zur Geschichte des sogennanten westbulgarischen Reiches* (Munich, 1906), 30; J. Ferluga, "John Skylitzes and Michael of Devol," *ZRVI* 10 (1967), 163–70.

proof that Basil fought an arduous and protracted war intending to conquer Bulgaria.

In his set piece description Skylitzes states that 15,000 Bulgarians were blinded: such a large number has to be questioned, although an independent source of the same period, Kekaumenos, provides some corroboration.[10] We know that the Bulgarians fought on for four more years, so their forces cannot have been so depleted. Moreover, Skylitzes qualifies his own account with the aside "they say" (*phasi*), which is an indication that the huge figure was drawn from a popular story and was subject to scrutiny even by contemporaries. The figure also approximates the size of a field army, whereas Basil's troops fell on a garrison guarding a pass, albeit one presently overseen by the tsar himself. It is conceivable then, that as news of Basil's victory was circulated and entered the popular imagination, "army" replaced "garrison," and an approximate figure, fourteen or fifteen thousand, was added for clarification.

It is likely, therefore, that Skylitzes was reporting a story which had remained in circulation since the episode, and which had been modified and exaggerated in the telling. So much is also suggested in the *Life of St. Nikon*, composed in southern Greece around 1050, which celebrated the life of a saint who lived much of his life in Sparta. Here Basil is considered "the most fortunate of all emperors . . . [whose] life was famous and time of his rule the longest, and his trophies over opponents quite numerous." It is further noted that by his hand "the nation of the numberless Bulgarian phalanx was struck down and humbled, as the story about him shows in fuller detail."[11] This must refer to the story of the blindings at Kleidion. The story echoed and inverted that of Krum's victory in 811. Furthermore, the story recalled and inverted an equally familiar account of a battle fought in a northern Greek mountain pass some fifteen centuries earlier, in which Spartans took the lead. There are obvious parallels between the events at Kleidion and those at Thermopylae as recorded by Herodotus, in which Xerxes' vast army of Persians – Herodotus estimated 2.3 million, although the Spartans later claimed to have fought 4 million – is unable to displace a far smaller body of Greek troops defending a wall across a mountain pass. The Persian ruler, therefore, secures a local guide to lead his forces across the mountain by a track, and falls on the Greeks from behind. Three hundred Greeks, Spartans and their Thespian allies stay to fight to the

[10] *Cecaumeni Strategicon*, eds. B. Wassiliewsky and P. Jernstedt (St. Petersburg, 1896), 18; *Sovety i rasskazy Kekavmena. Sochinenie vizantiiskogo polkovodtsa XI veka*, ed. G. G. Litavrin (Moscow, 1972), 152, provides the figure 14,000.

[11] D. F. Sullivan, ed. and tr., *The life of St. Nikon* (Brookline, 1987), 140–3, 148–51.

Figure 1   Two contiguous miniatures from an illustrated manuscript of the Slavic version of the Chronicle of Constantine Manasses: Cod. Vat. Slav. II, fol. 184 v. The battle of Kleidion, and the death of Tsar Samuel. Vatican Library.

death under their ruler Leonidas, unable to prevent a Persian invasion of lands to the south.[12] At Kleidion the roles are reversed: Byzantine troops confront the forces of Tsar Samuel; the Bulgarians do not fight to the death, but surrender and consequently are blinded; Samuel does not die with his men, but flees, yet later dies as a consequence of seeing his mutilated men. Skylitzes would certainly have been familiar with Herodotus' account, and makes allusions to this elsewhere in his text.[13]

The battle of Kleidion, we may conclude, although a significant Byzantine victory, was imbued with far greater significance after the fact. The story mirrored and inverted familiar stories of past defeats. Moreover, through time the story became the centerpiece of a broader revival and reworking of Basil II's reputation. That is, Basil's actions at Kleidion were linked to his receiving the nickname Bulgar-slayer, despite the fact that no mention is made of this in contemporary sources. We must wait until the early fourteenth century for this connection to be made explicitly, by the verse chronicler Ephraim.[14] Yet the story and the epithet have become inextricably entwined in the historical imagination and record. The immediate and obvious flaw in associating the epithet Bulgar-slayer with events at Kleidion is that Basil did not slay, but blinded the captured Bulgarians. Blinding was considered a more humane punishment, which would eliminate a large number of enemy troops without taking a large number of Christian lives.[15] This was not the first, nor would it be the last time that Basil blinded enemies. In 989 he had blinded the pretender Bardas Skleros, who was thus led before him no longer a threat: a blind man, like a eunuch, was incomplete, and rendered incapable of performing the imperial role.[16] Shortly after Kleidion, in the aftermath of a Byzantine defeat, all Bulgarians captured in the vicinity of Pelagonia were blinded as a deterrent to further resistance or treachery.[17] There are no similar reports of Basil slaying thousands of captives. One purpose of this book, therefore, is to restore Kleidion to the historical record as one in a series of confrontations and compromises between Basil and the Bulgarians. A second is to explore how and why the epithet Bulgar-slayer was first applied more than a century after Basil's death, and subsequently

---

[12] Herodotus, *Histories*, VII, 199–228; tr. A. de Selincourt (Harmondsworth, 1954), 484–94. Tom Gallant drew this to my attention.

[13] See, for example, Skylitzes, 455, his own brief "Scythian excursus." See also E. Malamut, "L'image byzantine des Petchénègues," *BZ* 88 (1995), 105–47 at 121–2.

[14] *Ephraem Aenii historia chronica*, ed. O. Lampsides, CFHB 27 (Athens, 1990), 109.

[15] J. Herrin, "Blinding in Byzantium," in ΠΟΛΥΠΛΕΥΡΟΣ ΝΟΥΣ. *Miscellanea für Peter Schreiner zu seinem 60. Geburtstag*, eds. C. Scholz and G. Makris (Leipzig, 2000), 56–68.

[16] Skylitzes, 338–9; Herrin, "Blinding," 61.   [17] Skylitzes, 353.

was invoked in a number of martial scenarios in the twelfth to twentieth centuries.

The first chapters of this book will comprise an exploration of the history and medieval historiography of Basil's Bulgarian wars. I will suggest, in chapter two, that Basil was not committed to a thirty-year war of attrition against Samuel's Bulgaria, and was even willing to recognize an independent Bulgarian realm centered on Prespa and Ohrid. If, between 1005 and 1014, his large standing army was kept in the field, and its attention directed seasonally at Samuel's realm – neither being certain – Basil demonstrated no desire to conquer nor annex Bulgaria to the empire, which would at one stroke eliminate a most convenient "punching bag." This changed with the death of Tsar Samuel in October 1014, which led to a competition between Samuel's son, his nephew and other magnates. The power struggle presented Basil with an unprecedented opportunity to gain territory and clients, while simultaneously presenting pretenders to Samuel's realm with a reason to demonstrate martial ability; in order, that is, to galvanize support for themselves. The period of intensified warfare, between 1014 and 1018, is presented in far greater detail by Skylitzes than the preceding decade. Skylitzes will, therefore, provide the framework for my account of these campaigns, augmented by occasional, but vital alternative readings from Latin and Arabic sources, and from the archaeological, numismatic, and sigillographic record. Moreover, we may be certain that earlier written accounts once existed, and that Skylitzes used them. It is likely, for example, that Basil employed writers to compose battle reports to convey the news to his subjects, and that these provided details employed in subsequent written and oral accounts. I will suggest, in chapter three, that Basil had a particular interest in circulating news of his "atrocities" to instill fear in his opponents, and to bolster the image he had chosen for himself, as a tireless warrior emperor, ever vigilant in the service of his subjects. This sentiment was recorded in Basil's own epitaph. It can also be seen clearly in the illustration Basil commissioned to adorn his personal psalter. This image, and others generally associated with Basil's victory in Bulgaria, will be considered in chapter four.

Unfortunately, no official battle reports or eyewitness accounts have survived from Basil's reign.[18] If they had, this study may have taken a different tack. Georges Duby, in interpreting the significance of the battle

---

[18] We have at least one such document and copious related panegyrical compositions from the later twelfth century: *Nicetae Choniatae orationes et epistolae*, ed. J.-L. van Dieten, CFHB 3 (Berlin and New York, 1972), 6–12; Stephenson, *Byzantium's Balkan frontier*, 292.

of Bouvines (27 July 1214), was able to offer telling insights into the sociology of war in the thirteenth century. He could do so thanks to the survival of a contemporary, official account of the encounter produced by William the Breton, which Duby considered "a detailed, precise, clear account, not overcluttered with rhetoric or with attempts at pleasing or showing off the author's classical erudition."[19] Moreover, between 1214 and 1300, thus in approximately the time that elapsed between the battle of Kleidion and the composition by Skylitzes of our first surviving account, ninety-two extant historical sources from across western Europe made mention of the battle of Bouvines. Thirty-three of these sources were produced in Francia, and most of these in or near Flanders, the location of the battle. Remarkably, the ninety-two sources account for only one-third of those available to Duby, meaning two-thirds of sources which may have mentioned the battle of Bouvines did not.[20] Quite how different the nature and volume of source material is for the historian of Basil's confrontation with Samuel will become apparent in chapter five.[21]

Even allowing for the greater rates of survival of historical documents in western European contexts, we must surmise that Bouvines had a greater immediate political and historiographical impact than Kleidion. The two were also quite distinct in the medium term. Whereas after 1300 "the name 'Bouvines' becomes rapidly erased from memory... to remain almost invisible for a long time to come,"[22] Kleidion emerges as the centerpiece of Basil's reputation and legacy over a century after his death.[23] This emergence will be the subject of chapter six, where it will be related to changes during the twelfth century in the way Byzantines viewed Bulgarians, and in the way Byzantine emperors were portrayed and praised. From that time, we shall see, Basil was always known as the Bulgar-slayer. However, while fuller elaboration of Basil's reputation suited the particular circumstances of the later twelfth and thirteenth centuries, it was of lesser importance afterwards, and particularly so following the fall of Constantinople to the Ottoman Turks in 1453.[24] Thereafter, I will argue in chapter seven, Basil

---

[19] G. Duby, *The legend of Bouvines. War, religion and culture in the Middle Ages*, tr. C. Tihanyi (Cambridge, 1990), 9.

[20] Duby, *Legend of Bouvines*, 143–4.

[21] The historian of the baptism of Vladimir of Kiev must similarly deal with a dearth of contemporary source material, and the nature of later interpretations: Korpela, *Prince, saint and apostle*, 35–46. The opposite is true for the legend of Charlemagne: R. Folz, *Le souvenir et la légende de Charlemagne dans l'empire germanique médiéval* (Paris, 1950).

[22] Duby, *Legend of Bouvines*, 167.

[23] As we will see below, pp. 29–30, there is no justification in the claim that Kleidion, as Kliuch, is mentioned specifically in a Cyrillic inscription dated to 1015/16.

[24] This may usefully be contrasted with the image of Charlemagne, which was regularly recreated during the Middle Ages to suit changing circumstances: Folz, *Le souvenir et la légende de Charlemagne*, 563–9.

had no role to play until the efforts to construct the modern Greek state began in the later eighteenth, and accelerated through the nineteenth century. At this time, although intially it had been scorned in favor of the classical past, Greek intellectuals, scholars and politicians began a systematic effort to recover the Byzantine past and insert it within a continuum of Greek ethnic and national history. In this, they were provoked or assisted by scholars in Germany, France and Britain, as well as notable Russians, who all contributed to the emergence of modern Byzantine studies.

In the later nineteenth century, scholars outside the nascent Greek state concurred that the Byzantine millennium was an important period in the cultural history of Eastern Europe, the Mediterranean and the Middle East. The prevailing view in Greece, however, following the definitive formulation by Konstantinos Paparrigopoulos, was to regard Byzantium primarily, if not solely, as the past of modern Greeks, and testament to the transformative power of Hellenism. For the first time it became clear to statesmen and school-children alike that the reign of Basil II, the Bulgar-slayer, was a crucial period in the narrative of Hellenic history. For at that time, it was held, an Hellenic empire achieved its greatest territorial extent for five centuries and Greek culture washed over a sea of Slavs in the wake of Basil's victories in the Balkans. And so, according to prevailing Greek sentiments, it should be again. This was particularly true in that region where Basil was believed to have fought the medieval Bulgarians to a bloody standstill, Macedonia.[25] Chapter eight, therefore, will comprise a study of the role played by the Bulgar-slayer in the struggle for Macedonia between Greek- and Slavic-speaking peoples and governments after 1870. Here I will present neither a comprehensive nor a balanced overview of the so-called "Macedonian Question," which, judging from the vastness and occasional vitriol of modern scholarship, cannot easily be achieved. Nor should the fact that in this chapter I focus on, and criticize, mainly Greek interpretations, be considered in any way partisan.

The subject of this final chapter, as of the others, is Basil II and his legend, and it is in the Greek-speaking milieu that Basil takes center stage. The chapter, indeed this book, could be expanded to consider more fully the image of Basil in Slavic literatures (although it is far less significant than in the Greek). Moreover, an equally interesting study could be written

---

[25] The Byzantine administrative district of Macedonia did not, during Basil II's reign, correspond to the geographical region known today, and in antiquity, as Macedonia. This has been pointed out by numerous scholars in a recent edited volume, where one might start with the erudite paper by J. Koder, "Macedonia and Macedonians in Byzantine spatial thinking," in J. Burke and R. Scott, eds., *Byzantine Macedonia. Identity, image and history*, Byzantina Australiensia 13 (Melbourne, 2000), 12–28.

on Tsar Samuel from at least two, possibly three Slavic perspectives, but that is not the task I have set myself, and indeed it is beyond my ability. An historian inclined to undertake such an endeavour may find, as did I, inspiration and instruction in Duby's study, for that Frenchman writes elegantly and critically of French approaches to a legend, particularly as it was taught to French school-children who grew up to fight in wars during the fifty years either side of 1900. This approach, so damaging before 1945 and quietly abandoned since, may be summed up in a single phrase, taken from C. Calvet's 1903 primer of French history for schools: "This was our first victory over the Germans."[26]

[26] Duby, *Legend of Bouvines*, 173.

2

Basil and Samuel

The *Life of St. Achilleios*, bishop of Larissa during the reign of Constantine the Great, relates that a casket containing the saint's ashes was concealed soon after his death and lay hidden for many years. At an unspecified time this holy treasure was uncovered and began promptly to discharge *myron*, the blessed unguent which cured the diseases of the faithful Larisseans. Despising such signs of grace, the Devil stirred war in the region between the Romans, as the Byzantines called themselves, and the Bulgarians, as the Romans called the followers of Samuel Kometopoulos.[1] Consequently, the ashes were seized and taken from Larissa into Bulgarian lands, where they were deposited at Samuel's island compound in Lake Prespa.[2] Samuel later built a basilica church dedicated to St. Achilleios to house the saint's remains, and also, possibly, his own. Excavations at the basilica in the 1960s uncovered four graves, one of which housed the skeleton of a seventy-year-old man adorned in gilded bronze chain mail and a vestment of rich cloth woven from gold and silk thread. The cloth bore a pattern of medallions, within each of which perched two birds, possibly eagles or griffins, possibly parrots. The man's left elbow had been fractured and badly set some years before his death, perhaps by a sword blow from a right-handed warrior. The grave was enthusiastically proclaimed to be Samuel's.[3]

---

[1] The relevant excerpt is presented at: Ch. Loparev, "Opisanie nekotorykh grecheskykh zhit'ii sviat'ikh," *VV* 4 (1897), 337–401 at 363–4; reproduced at *Fontes Graeci historiae Bulgaricae* eds. G. Cankova-Petkova, I. Dujčev, L. Jončev, V. Tăpkova-Zaimova and P. Tivčev [= Fontes historiae Bulgaricae, XI] (Sofia, 1965), 7.

[2] Skylitzes, 330. See also J. Ferluga, "Vreme podizanje Crkve Sv. Ahileja na Prespi," *Zbornik za likovne umetnosti* 2 (1966), 3–7; repr. in J. Ferluga, *Byzantium on the Balkans. Studies on the Byzantine administration and the southern Slavs from the VIIth to the XIIth centuries* (Amsterdam, 1976), 355–60.

[3] N. Moutsopoulos, "Le tombeau du Tsar Samuil dans la Basilique de Saint Achille à Prespa," *Etudes Balkaniques* 3 (1984), 114–26. The full excavation reports are available: N. Moutsopoulos, *Anaskafi tis vasilikis tou agiou Achilleiou*, 5 vols. (Thessaloniki, 1966–72). The silk fragment is now on display in the Museum of Byzantine Culture in Thessaloniki, where, despite Moutsopoulos' attribution, no mention of Samuel is made.

Figure 2   Church of St. Achilleios at Prespa. Photo: Sharon Gerstel, in the Dumbarton
Oaks Byzantine Photograph and Fieldwork Archives, Washington, DC.

Samuel claimed to rule Bulgaria, an independent realm in the northern
Balkans free of Byzantine suzerainty, as the successor to Symeon and Peter,
emperors of the Bulgarians. In the reign of Symeon (c. 894–927) the frontier
between Byzantium and Bulgaria, as marked by boundary stones, ran some
22 km north of Thessalonika.[4] Symeon's son, Peter (927–69), continued to
rule an extensive empire effectively, at least until the later 960s.[5] However,
by the end of 972, much, although certainly not all of this territory was in
Byzantine hands for the first time in three centuries, following decisive campaigns by the emperor John I Tzimiskes (969–76). The extent of Tzimiskes'
reconquest, and the nature of Byzantine rule thereafter is the subject of
much discussion which cannot be reprised here.[6] In any event Byzantine
control of the northern Balkans was short-lived: Tzimiskes' advances were

[4] I have taken the opportunity here to revise and expand ideas first presented in my *Byzantium's
Balkan frontier*. See also J. Shepard, "Bulgaria: the other Balkan 'empire'," in T. Reuter, ed., *The new
Cambridge medieval history, III, c. 900–c. 1024* (Cambridge, 1999), 567–85. S. Runciman, *A history of
the first Bulgarian empire* (London, 1930), remains the best sustained narrative in English.

[5] J. V. A. Fine, Jr., "A fresh look at Bulgaria under Tsar Peter (927–69)," *ByzSt* 5 (1978), 88–95;
J. V. A. Fine, Jr., *The early medieval Balkans: a critical survey from the sixth to the late twelfth century*
(Ann Arbor, 1983), 160–71.

[6] V. Tăpkova-Zaimova has written extensively on this. See her monograph: *Dolni Dunav – granichna
zona na vizantiiskiia zapad* (Sofia, 1976). Several of her papers are conveniently collected in *Byzance*

eradicated while the new young emperors, the *porphyrogennetoi* Basil and Constantine, under the tutelage of Basil the *parakoimomenos*, fought a civil war with various Byzantine aristocratic families led by Bardas Phokas and Bardas Skleros. The struggle for mastery of the empire took place in Anatolia. Bulgaria and the lands beyond were neglected, and in the absence of any firm imperial interest a revolt by the four sons of count (*komes*) Nicholas, a regional potentate or army officer based in Macedonia, secured control over certain lands west of Thrace. The brothers were called David, Moses, Samuel and Aaron, and by the collective name Kometopouloi, "sons of the count."[7]

During the revolt, the Bulgarian imperial brothers, Boris and Romanos, sons of the late Tsar Peter, were allowed to flee Constantinople, where they had been held hostage since 969.[8] Boris was killed by a Bulgarian sentry, apparently by mistake, but Romanos reached the Kometopouloi. Although

---

et les Balkans à partir du VIe siècle (London, 1979). Important papers published since then include: "Les frontières occidentales des territoires conquis par Tzimiscès," in H. Ahrweiler, ed., *Géographie historique du monde méditerranéen*, Byzantina Sorbonensia 7 (Paris, 1988), 113–18; "Quelques nouvelles données sur l'administration byzantine au Bas Danube (fin du Xe–XIe s.)," *BSl* 54 (1993), 95–101. The study of the region was transformed by N. Oikonomides' discovery of the *Escorial Taktikon*. Oikonomides published numerous important articles, most recently "A propos de la première occupation byzantine de la Bulgarie (971–ca 986)," in ΕΥΨΥΧΙΑ. *Mélanges offerts à Hélène Ahrweiler*, ed. M. Balard et al., Byzantina Sorbonensia 16, 2 vols. (Paris, 1998), II, 581–9.

7 Skylitzes, 328. An Armenian writer of the early eleventh century, Asołik, also known as Stephen of Taron (*Des Stephanos von Taron armenische Geschichte*, tr. H. Gelzer and A. Burckhardt (Leipzig, 1907), 185–6), refers to just two brothers, and names only Samuel as the elder. The episode refers to the situation in 986, when only two brothers were still alive: Samuel and his younger sibling Aaron. On this see W. Seibt, "Untersuchungen zur Vor- und Frühgeschichte der 'bulgarischen' Kometopulen," *Handes Amsorya. Zeitschrift für armenische Philologie* 89 (1975), 65–98 at 93–4. On the name "Kometopoulos" see *ibid.* 65–6 and 82–3, where "Komsajagk'n", the literal Armenian translation offered by Asołik is explained (see below at p. 72). The names of Nicholas and his wife Ripsime, or Ripsimia, are provided in an interpolation by Michael of Devol. See J. Prokić, *Die Zusätze in der Handschrift des Johannes Skylitzes, codex Vindobonensis hist. graec. LXXIV. Ein Beitrag zur Geschichte des sogennanten westbulgarischen Reiches* (Munich, 1906), 28. For the fullest analysis of the alleged Armenian origins of the Kometopouloi, and of the value of Asołik, see N. Adontz, "Samuel l'Arménien, roi des Bulgares," in his *Etudes armeno-byzantines* (Lisbon, 1965), 347–407.

8 The date of the insurrection is disputed, and has been linked to the notion that the Kometopouloi ruled an independent "western Bulgaria" from 963 (swiftly disproven) or 969, which was favored by V. Zlatarski, *Istoriia na bulgarskata durzhava prez srednite vekove*, 3 vols. (Sofia, 1927), I/ii, 590; S. Antoljak, *Samuel and his state* (Skopje, 1985), 22–8. In contrast, G. Ostrogorsky, *History of the Byzantine state*, tr. J. Hussey, 2nd ed. (Oxford, 1968), 302, n. 1, maintained there is no indication in the sources that the Kometopouloi had established control of "western Bulgaria" between 969 and 976. Seibt, "Untersuchungen," 77, agrees that a rebellion before 976 "cannot really be imagined." J. Ferluga, "Le soulèvement des Cometopoules," *ZRVI* 9 (1966), 75–84, insists that the revolt commenced in 976. T. Wasilewski, "La genèse de l'empire de Samuel," in M. Apostolski, S. Antoljak and B. Panov, eds., *Iljada godini od vostanieto na komitopulite i sozdavanjeto na Samoilovata drzava: zbornik na materijali od naucnata sredba odrzana vo Prespa od 10 do 15 oktombri 1969 godina* (Skopje, 1971), 249–52, also argues for the period 976–9, despite presenting his paper at a conference to commemorate the 1000th anniversary in 1969! For the latest, sensible analysis, see S. Pirivatrić, *Samuilova drzava. Obim i karakter* (Belgrade, 1997), 44–57. Asołik, tr. Gelzer and Burckhardt, 186, suggests that the Kometopouloi had

Byzantine sources are silent about his role or title until 1004 (when he reappears as governor of Skopje), it seems clear that Romanos gained support for the four brothers when they turned their attention to the lands between the Haimos and the lower Danube.[9] Control of this region, as elsewhere in the northern Balkans, lay with the local and regional potentates. Romanos' presence provided an additional reason to transfer loyalty to the Kometopouloi, besides their impressive military record. Thus, the heartland of the former Bulgarian empire fell under their control, including the capital and seat of the Byzantine *strategos*, Preslav.[10]

With the loss of Preslav affairs beyond the Haimos had reached a critical juncture for the young Byzantine emperors. While Constantine took a back seat, Basil turned away from domestic disputes to focus on Bulgaria. At this time, according to an Armenian historian, Basil proposed a peace treaty, offering his sister as a wife for one of the brothers. The offer was rejected, and the ambassador, the Metropolitan of Sebasteia, was murdered, when it became apparent that the woman with him was not Anna *porphyrogennete*, but an impostress.[11] A fanciful tale perhaps, although Anna was at that time unmarried and soon to be despatched to Kiev. If we may detect a kernel of truth in the story, it is not unlikely that Basil would have proposed such an alliance, inexperienced as he was in warfare. However, since peace was not to be had, Basil launched his first campaign in the Balkans in 986. His march to Sardika (modern Sofia) ended in a humiliating retreat, and worse still, a crushing defeat following an ambush near the so-called "Trajan's Gates." Basil was almost captured and in his flight abandoned the imperial tent and much baggage.[12] The emperor's departure tacitly acknowledged

previously served the Byzantine emperor, but had switched allegiance to the Bulgarian ruler, "who was a eunuch." This is clearly Romanos, and suggests that the Kometopouloi had changed sides before Romanos was taken hostage. This would allow them to act independently after 969, but not to seek to extend their authority until after the death of John Tzimiskes in 976.

[9] The date of Romanos' capture is disputed, although Skylitzes (346) provides the date 1004. For commentary on the revolt of the Kometopouloi, and the extension of their authority, see now Pirivatrić, *Samuilova država*, 73–96; Fine, *Early medieval Balkans*, 188–97.

[10] I am not convinced by a recent suggestion that, since the numismatic and sigillographic profile of the city is apparently unaffected, Preslav remained in Byzantine hands. See P. Doimi de Frankopan, "The workings of the Byzantine provincial administration in the 10th–12th centuries: the example of Preslav," *Byzantion* 71 (2001), 73–97. Frankopan appears not to have noticed Skylitzes' explicit testimony that Preslav was recovered by Byzantine generals in 1000/1. The issue is surely what is meant by "loss" and "recovery" of the city, since moderately peaceful handovers by local potentates would not impact significantly on the material record.

[11] Asołik, tr. Gelzer and Burckhardt, 185–6. Runciman, *First Bulgarian empire*, 223, dismissed the episode as "a complete legend."

[12] *Leonis Diaconi Caloensis historiae libri decem*, ed. C. B. Hase, CSHB (Bonn, 1828), 171–3, henceforth Leo the Deacon, provides an eye-witness account of this rout. See also *Histoire de Yahya-Ibn-Saïd d'Antioche*, fasc. 2, ed. and tr. I. Kratchkovsky and A. Vasiliev, Patrologia Orientalis 23/2 (Paris, 1932),

Figure 3   Cyrillic inscription dated 993, discovered at the village of German, near Prespa, in the 1880s. Now housed in the National Archaeological Museum, Sofia, Bulgaria. Reproduced from C. Jireček and V. Jagić, "Die cyrillische Inschrift vom Jahre 993," *Archiv für slavische Philologie* 21 (1899).

the dominance of the Kometopouloi and, more significantly, obliged local and regional potentates to do so explicitly.

At this time, one brother, Samuel Kometopoulos, took measures to improve his personal standing. Two of his brothers were already dead: David had been killed between Kastoria and Prespa early in 976; Moses had died during the siege of Serrai (modern Serres) later that same year. After the victory at "Trajan's Gates" Samuel put to death his third brother, Aaron, on 13 June 987 or 988.[13]

The deaths of Samuel's eldest brother David, and also his father and mother, count Nicholas and his wife Ripsimia, appear to be commemorated on an inscribed stone, discovered at the village of German near Prespa in c. 1880.[14] The date of the discovery has given scholars reason to question the authenticity of the inscription, occurring as it did at the height of

418–19, henceforth Yahya, PO, I; *Yahyā al-Antakī, Cronache dell'Egitto fātimide e dell'impero bizantino 937–1033*, tr. B. Pirone (Milan, 1997), 193, §10.141; Asołik, tr. Gelzer and Burckhardt, 186–7, also records Basil's defeat, and the capture of the imperial tent, attributing the emperor's rescue to his Armenian infantry. John Geometres, PG 106, 934, mourns the episode in a poem.

[13] Skylitzes, 329; Seibt, "Untersuchungen," 90–4.

[14] First noted in 1883, and mentioned in a Bulgarian journal of 1891, the full inscription was published in 1899 by scholars of the Russian Archaeological Institute in Constantinople: *Izvestiia Russkogo arkheologicheskogo instituta v Konstantinopolie* 4 (1899), 1–20. It was swiftly analyzed and republished by C. Jireček and V. Jagić, "Die cyrillische Inschrift vom Jahre 993," *Archiv für slavische Philologie* 21 (1899), 543–57, and its authenticity accepted by, for example, Prokić, *Die Zusätze*, 19–20. See also

the struggle for "national consciousness" in Macedonia.[15] The inscription, which is placed to the side and at a right angle to three gouged crosses, reads:

In the name of the Father, the Son and the Holy Spirit. I Samuel, servant of God, place these crosses in memory of my father, mother and brother. Their names were [Ni]kola, the servant of God, [. . .]a, David. Written in the year from the creation of the World 6501, in the sixth indiction [i.e. 993].

By 993 Samuel had ruled alone for at least five years, and from his base at Prespa he launched regular attacks on surrounding lands, focusing his attention on Thessalonika, the great Byzantine stronghold and rich trading center, and Larissa, the metropolitan see of Thessaly, whence were taken the remains of St. Achilleios.[16] Repeated raiding also led to the abandonment of the Gomaton monastery, near Hierissos on Mount Athos, which was merged with the Great Lavra by order of the patriarch, Nicholas Chrysoberges, in 988.[17]

Samuel's invasions, which reached as far south as the isthmus of Corinth, engendered great fear among the populations of Hellas and Peloponnesos, and so much is reflected in the *Life of St. Nikon*, which was written within living memory of Samuel's campaigns. The saint is credited with alleviating the suffering and anxiety of the *praitor* and *strategos* of Corinth, Basil Apokaukos, who faced Samuel's advance, and with prophesying the eventual elimination of the Bulgarian menace. But this was for the future, and for now Samuel was considered "invincible in power and unsurpassed in

---

Seibt, "Untersuchungen," 97. See now P. Malingoudis, *Die mittelalterlichen kyrillischen Inschriften der Hämus-Halbinsel, I. Die bulgarischen Inschriften* (Thessaloniki, 1979), 39–42.

[15] For similar reasons, an inscription "discovered" at Edessa in northern Greece in 1997 was dismissed as a forgery by the director of the Bulgarian National Historical Museum, Bozhidar Dimitrov. This was reported in the Sofia newspaper, *Kontinent*, 6 October 1997. An authoritative analysis of the German inscription, although with a call for further study, was presented by M. Pavlović, "Nadgrobnata plocha najdena vo selo German kaj Prespa", *Iljada godini*, 73–93. Pavlović argued that the inscription could not be genuine on both philological and palaeographic grounds. He was followed by M. Loos, "Symposium historique «l'insurrection des comitopules de la création de l'Etat de Samuel.» Prespa, 10–15 Octobre 1969," *BSl* 31 (1970), 292–4 at 292; and Antoljak, *Samuel and his state*, 17, 143–4, n. 70. Both Moutsopoulos, "Le tombeau du Tsar Samuil," 115–16, and Pirivatrić, *Samuilova država*, 24, 59–62, note the skepticism, but treat the inscription as if it were genuine.

[16] *Cecaumeni Strategicon*, eds. B. Wassiliewsky and P. Jernstedt (St. Petersburg, 1896), 65–6; *Sovety i rasskazy Kekavmena. Sochinenie vizantiiskogo polkovodtsa XI veka*, ed. G. G. Litavrin (Moscow, 1972), 250–2.

[17] *Actes de Lavra, première partie des origines à 1204*, eds. P. Lemerle, A. Guillou, N. Svoronos and D. Papachryssanthou, Archives de l'Athos V (Paris, 1970), 117, nr. 8; I. Dujčev, "Recherches sur le Moyen Age bulgare [sommaire par V. Grumel]," *REB* 7 (1949), 129–32 at 129; C. J. Holmes, "Basil II and the government of empire (976–1025)," unpublished D.Phil. dissertation, University of Oxford (Oxford, 1999), 264.

strength."[18] Similar comment was made in Constantinople, where John Kyriotes Geometres penned a poem offering a punning comparison between the Kometopoulos and a comet which appeared in 989. It begins "Above the comet scorched the sky, below the comet[opoulos] burns the West."[19]

Basil, thus far unable to best Samuel on the battlefield, reverted to diplomacy, and, clearly familiar with precedents for dealing with a recalcitrant ruler in Bulgaria, entered into negotiations with the Serbs. A document dated September 993 from the Lavra monastery contains a reference to an earlier Serbian embassy which was forced to travel to Constantinople by sea to avoid the lands dominated by Samuel. The unfortunate envoys were captured and taken prisoner on the island of Lemnos by Arab pirates.[20]

In spring 991, the Byzantine emperor led an army against Bulgaria. We know practically nothing of what ensued, having only a passing reference to a four-year campaign by Yahya, a Christian Arabic author writing in distant Antioch.[21] Skylitzes merely notes that a Fatimid attack on Antioch and Aleppo forced the emperor to march east in 995, leaving his confidant Nikephoros Ouranos in command.[22] Ouranos' forces enjoyed a spectacular victory at the river Spercheios, wounding both Samuel and his son, Gabriel Radomir, before they escaped. They evaded capture by hiding among the corpses of the slain, while 12,000 of their men are said to have been captured.[23]

The Kometopoulos was bowed, and his ability to launch major invasions curtailed. Moreover, he temporarily lost control of Dyrrachion (modern

---

[18] D. F. Sullivan, ed. and tr., *The life of St. Nikon* (Brookline, 1987), 2–7 (for the date of composition, shortly after 1042), 140–2 (Basil Apokaukos), 148–9 (judgment on Samuel). See also C. Stavrakos, "Die Vita des hl. Nikon Metanoeite als Quelle zur Prosopographie der Peloponnes im späten 10. Jahrhundert," *SüdostF* 58 (1999), 1–7, esp. 2–4.

[19] PG 106, 920. G. Schlumberger, *L'épopée byzantine à la fin du dixième siècle, I. Jean Tzimiscès; les jeunes années de Basile II, le tueur de Bulgares (969–989)* (Paris, 1896), 643–4, provides a French translation. See also K. Argoe, "John Kyriotes Geometres, a tenth century Byzantine writer," Ph.D. thesis, University of Wisconsin (Madison, 1938), 140–41, argues for 989, against Runciman, *First Bulgarian empire*, 222–3, who proposed 985. Certainly, the sequence of tenses and the use of the singular construction in the second line, Κάτω κομήτης πυρπολεῖ τὴν Ἑσπέραν, suggests a date after the death of Samuel's last brother in 986.

[20] *Actes de Lavra*, I, ed. P. Lemerle et al., 124, nr. 12; G. Ostrogorsky, "Une ambassade Serbe auprès de l'empereur Basile II," *Byzantion* 19 (1949), 187–94.

[21] Yahya, PO, I, 430; *Yahyā al-Antakī, Cronache*, tr. Pirone, 201, §10:173, from which we learn Basil captured "Barija." See also Asołik, tr. Gelzer and Burckhardt, 198, who suggests an Armenian, the *magistros* Gregory, was installed at "Veriay." This is surely Veria (in northern Greece), and not Sofia as is suggested by Antoljak, *Samuel and his state*, 56, n. 411. See now Pirivatrić, *Samuilova država*, 95–7, 100.

[22] Skylitzes, 340–2.

[23] Skylitzes, 341–2. For the date, casualties and further commentary see Pirivatrić, *Samuilova država*, 103–4. Perhaps Samuel received a blow to his left elbow on this occasion.

Durrës in Albania), a major Adriatic port, which was also the gateway to the Via Egnatia, the great land road which passed through his lands as far as Thessalonika and from there ran on to Constantinople. Samuel had gained control in Dyrrachion by marrying a daughter of the leading man, Chryselios.[24] After Spercheios he entrusted the city to his son-in-law, Ashot, a Byzantine captive whom he had recently married to his daughter Miroslava.[25] However, Ashot fled on a Byzantine ship, bearing a letter from Chryselios promising to cede the city to the emperor. Clearly Samuel's charisma and credibility were damaged by the defeat at Spercheios. Yet, in 997 he still held most of the lands that had been ruled by Tsar Symeon at the height of his power, from the lower Danube to the Adriatic, and in that year had himself crowned as tsar of Bulgaria. It was the mission and greatest achievement of Emperor Basil II, we are told, to humble the tsar and recover Bulgaria for Byzantium between 1000 and 1018.

Basil's first advance towards Sardika (modern Sofia) in 1001 divided Samuel's realm in two. It is, therefore, both convenient and appropriate to treat the campaigns in two parts: those to the northeast and those to the northwest. Success in the northeast was swift, as Basil's generals Theodorokanos and Nikephoros Xiphias easily recovered Preslav, "Little Preslav" (Presthlavitza) and Pliska.[26] The speed of the Byzantine advance illustrates how control of the whole region rested with a few strongholds, within which Samuel had only nominal support. Much of the interior region, between the lower Danube and Haimos mountains, remained unoccupied and uncultivated and the population was concentrated in settlements on the river Danube and Black Sea. The so-called Mysian plain was not brought under cultivation until the advent of widespread irrigation in the nineteenth century.[27]

Basil's forces reoccupied fortresses which had been captured and, in some cases, redeveloped by Tzimiskes after his earlier reconquest of Bulgaria. The *Escorial Taktikon* (or *Taktikon Oikonomides*), the modern name given to a

[24] Skylitzes, 349. The date at which this took place is uncertain, although Skylitzes implies it followed the defeat at Spercheios. Pirivatrić, *Samuilova država*, 82–3, discusses the possibility that the marriage took place as early as 976.

[25] Skylitzes, 342–3.   [26] Skylitzes, 343–4.

[27] For perceptive commentary on the region into the early Byzantine period, see A. Poulter, "Town and country in Moesia Inferior," in A. Poulter, ed., *Ancient Bulgaria. Papers presented to the International Symposium on the Ancient History and Archaeology of Bulgaria, University of Nottingham, 1981*, 2 vols. (Nottingham, 1983), II, 74–118. For a more recent survey of archaeological excavations see G. von Bulow and A. Milcheva, eds., *Der Limes an der unteren Donau von Diokletian bis Heraklios. Vorträge der internationalen Konferenz Svishtov, Bulgarien (1.–5. September 1998)* (Sofia, 1999). For comments on patterns of settlement in the Balkans drawing on written sources see M. Hendy, *Studies in the Byzantine monetary economy, 300–1450* (Cambridge, 1985), 78–90.

precedence list drawn up in Constantinople, certainly after 971, and probably between 975 and 979, gives some indications of Tzimiskes' arrangements, and we can surmise that Basil's were not identical.[28] For example, a command known as Mesopotamia of the West was created in the lands of the Danube delta by Tzimiskes, which appears not to have survived into Basil's time.[29] However, we cannot be certain of this, and the *Escorial Taktikon* must be handled with care, for it does not appear to be a full list of commands created by Tzimiskes, nor does it provide evidence for the nature of Byzantine administration in annexed territories.[30] We may turn, however, for further insights to lead seals, which demonstrate that officers from the Byzantine field army were installed as garrison commanders in several localities known from the *Escorial Taktikon*. The first *strategoi* of Preslav were a certain *protospatharios* named John, and the more senior *protospatharios epi tou Chrysotriklinou* Constantine Karantinos.[31] The commander appointed at Dristra was the *primikerios* Theodore.[32] Contemporary *strategoi* at Presthlavitza were Leo Pegonites,[33] and John Maleses, also known as Malesios (and possibly Melias).[34]

N. Oikonomides identified Presthlavitza, the Little Preslav, as Nufǎru on the St. George arm of the Danube delta.[35] The material evidence uncovered by extensive excavations at the site appears to confirm this. Archaeologists have discovered the foundations of ramparts on a promontory overlooking the river. The adjacent site is littered with fragments of pottery and other everyday utensils, and more than 1,250 stray finds of coins have been discovered which date from c. 971 to c. 1092.[36] Upstream from Presthlavitza,

---

[28] *Les listes de préséance byzantines des IXe–Xe siècles*, ed. N. Oikonomides (Paris, 1972).

[29] *Listes de préséance*, 268–9; N. Oikonomides, "Recherches sur l'histoire du Bas-Danube au Xe–XIIe siècles: Mésopotamie d'Occident," *RESEE* 3 (1965), 57–79. The latest research is summarized insightfully by A. Madgearu, "The military organization of Paradunavon," *BSl* 60 (1999), 421–46.

[30] Holmes, "Basil II and the government of empire," 286–8.

[31] I. Iordanov, *Pechatite ot strategiiata v Preslav (971–1088)* (Sofia, 1993), 146–9; *idem*, "Neizdadeni vizantiiski olovni pechati ot Silistra (II)," *Izvestiia na Narodniia Muzei Varna* 21 [36] (1985), 98–107 at 102, nr. 6.

[32] I. Iordanov, "Neizdadeni vizantiiski olovni pechati ot Silistra (I)," *Izvestiia na Narodniia Muzei Varna* 19 [34] (1983), 97–110 at 109, nr. 16.

[33] I. Iordanov, "Neizdadeni (I)," 104–5, nr. 10 (from Silistra); *idem*, *Pechatite*, 153–4 (from Preslav); N. Bǎnescu and P. Papahagi, "Plombs byzantins découverts à Silistra," *Byzantion* 10 (1935), 601–6 (from Silistra); V. Šandrovskaya, "Iz istorii Bolgarii X–XII vv. po dannym sfragistiki," *Byzantinobulgarica* 7 (1981), 455–67 at 462 (now in St. Petersburg).

[34] Šandrovskaya, "Iz istorii Bolgarii," 463–4 (now in St. Petersburg); I. Iordanov, "Neizdadeni vizantiiski olovni pechati ot Silistra (IV)," *Izvestiia na Narodniia Muzei Varna* 28 [43] (1992), 229–45 at 232 (from Silistra); Iordanov, *Pechatite*, 154 (Melias, from Preslav).

[35] N. Oikonomides, "Presthlavitza, the Little Preslav," *SüdostF* 42 (1983), 1–9. An alternative hypothesis maintains that Presthlavitza is identical with Preslav, for which see P. Diaconu, "De nouveau à propos de Presthlavitza," *SüdostF* 46 (1987), 279–93.

[36] For further references to the excavations see S. Baraschi and O. Damian, "Considérations sur la céramique émaillée de Nufǎru," *Dacia* 37 (1993), 237–77.

the *kastron* of Noviodunum dominated the Danube at one of its principal fords. It had been the base of the Roman fleet of the Danube (*Classis Flavia Moesica*), and shows signs of substantial renovations in the period after 971, and continuous occupation thereafter. Similarly, at Dinogetia (modern Garvăn) the original walls of the *kastron*, which were destroyed by an invasion of Koutrigours in around 560, were rebuilt and a whole new gate complex was added under Tzimiskes.[37] Two small fortresses at Capidava and Dervent were occupied from 971 until their destruction by the Pechenegs in or shortly after 1036. At Dervent a further seal of the aforementioned "John Maleses, *patrikios* and *strategos*" has been discovered.[38]

Stray finds of anonymous *folles* at all of these sites – Preslav, Dristra, Nufăru, Dinogetia, Noviodunum, Capidava and Dervent – suggest that they were reoccupied by Byzantine troops during Basil's reign.[39] Of the 1,254 coins discovered during excavation at Nufăru 163 were struck by Basil; at Dinogetia more than a quarter of the total finds (211 of 748) were his; and at Capidava more than half (43 of 85).[40] However, given the relative length of Basil's reign compared to those of his immediate successors, the numbers of finds are not large. Therefore, we may surmise that the absence of a real threat to the region at this time allowed Basil to commit far more of his resources to recovering and occupying outlying regions in the northwestern Balkans, to which we will turn shortly. Of particular note is the apparent redundance as a military installation of the most impressive project undertaken by Tzimiskes in the region. The mighty naval complex on an island known today as Păcuiul lui Soare, opposite Dervent and just a few miles downstream from Dristra, was of little use once the threat of a further attack by the Rus' along the river had disappeared.[41]

---

[37] I. Barnea, "Dinogetia et Noviodunum, deux villes byzantines du Bas-Danube," *RESEE* 9 (1971), 343–62; I. Barnea, "Les sceaux byzantins mis au jour à Noviodunum," in N. Oikonomides, ed., *Studies in Byzantine sigillography*, II (Washington, DC, 1990), 153–61.

[38] I. Barnea, "Sceaux de deux gouverneurs inconnus du thème de Paristrion," *Dacia* 8 (1964), 239–47 at 245–7, which is dated c. 1000–1036. The latest research suggests that Capidava may have been occupied until 1048: see Madgearu, "Military organization," 435.

[39] Pace J. Haldon, *Warfare, state and society in the Byzantine world, 565–1204* (London, 1999), 64, who posits the abandonment of the defensive system at the lower Danube by Basil II. Total coin finds for several sites in Romania are conveniently tabulated in G. Mănucu-Adameşteanu, "Aspecte privind circulaţia monetară la Mangalia în secolele X–XI (969–1081)," *Pontica* 28–9 (1995–6), 287–300 at 294–9. For further references to individual sites and graphs illustrating coin finds to 1991 see P. Stephenson, "Byzantine policy towards Paristrion in the mid-eleventh century: another interpretation," *BMGS* 23 (1999), 43–66.

[40] Mănucu-Adameşteanu, "Aspecte privind circulaţia monetară," 297–9; G. Custarea, "Catalogul monedelor bizantine anonime descoperite la Capidava," *Pontica* 28–9 (1995–6), 301–7. Slightly different figures are given in G. Custarea, *Circulaţia monedei bizantine în Dobrogea (sec. IX–XI)* (Constanţa, 2000).

[41] P. Diaconu and D. Vîlceanu, *Păcuiul lui Soare, cetatea bizantină*, I (Bucharest, 1972), 27–46. The island appears to have flourished as a trading center in the middle of the eleventh century.

Turning to the northwestern Balkans, as early as 1002 Basil II had cast his gaze upon the Danubian lands upstream of Dristra. In that year he personally conducted an eight-month siege of Vidin.[42] Shortly afterwards a chieftain known as Achtum (in Hungarian, Ajtóny), whose lands stretched north to the river Körös (Caraş), was received by imperial officials at the recently recovered *kastron*. He was baptized according to the Orthodox rite, and subsequently founded a monastery in honor of St. John the Baptist at Morisena on the river Maros (Mureş).[43] There is evidence for the promotion of Orthodoxy in and around Szeged in the first quarter of the eleventh century, and we know from a rare charter that the monastery of St. Demetrios at Sirmium owned land in that district.[44] The fullest account of Achtum's activities is contained in the *Vita Maior* of St. Gerard, which reveals further that he controlled the passage of salt along the Maros and Tisza (Tisa, Theiss) to Szeged.[45]

The established view of Basil's activities after the siege of Vidin sees the emperor constantly in the field waging a bloody war of attrition to wear down the manpower and defenses of Samuel's Bulgaria.[46] This is based largely on a single sentence in Skylitzes, which claims that Basil "did not relent, but every year marched into Bulgaria and laid waste and ravaged all before him".[47] However, alternative views have also been advanced, including my own suggestion that Basil had no intention of conquering Bulgaria before 1014, and may even have signed a peace treaty with Samuel in 1005 recognizing the limits of his independent realm based on Ohrid and

---

[42] Skylitzes, 346.

[43] C. Bálint, *Südungarn im 10. Jahrhundert* (Budapest, 1991), 115–17; G. Kristó, "Ajtony and Vidin," in G. Káldy-Nagy, ed., *Turkic-Bulgarian-Hungarian relations (VIth–XIth Centuries)*, Studia Turco-Hungarica 5 (Budapest, 1981), 129–35; F. Makk, "Relations Hungaro-Bulgares au temps du Prince Géza und du Roi Etienne 1er," in *Szegedi Bolgarisztika*, Hungaro-Bulgarica 5 (Szeged, 1994), 25–33. Achtum's "ethnicity" is disputed by historians of Transylvania. For a critical overview of the region at this time, see now F. Curta, "Transylvania around A.D. 1000," in P. Urbanczyk, ed., *Europe around the year 1000* (Warsaw, 2001), 141–65.

[44] G. Györffy, "Das Güterverzeichnis des Klosters zu Szávaszentdemeter (Sremska Mitrovica) aus dem 12. Jahrhundert," *Studia Slavica* 5 (1959), 9–74 at 47; A. Kubinyi, "Handel und Entwicklung der Städte in der ungarischen Tiefebene im Mittelalter," in *Europa Slavica – Europa Orientalis. Festschrift für K. Ludat*, ed. K. D. Grothusen and K. Zernack (Berlin, 1980), 423–44 at 427.

[45] *Legenda Sancti Gerhardi Episcopi*, ed. I. Madzsar, in E. Szentpétery, ed., *Scriptores Rerum Hungaricarum*, 2 vols. (Budapest, 1937–8), II, 461–506 at 490. The short and long Lives of Gerard (in Hungarian, Gellért) have received much attention in Hungary, but the best English introduction remains C. A. Macartney, "Studies on the earliest Hungarian historical sources, I: the Lives of St. Gerard," *Archivum Europae Centro-Orientalis* 18 (1938), 1–35; repr. in his *Early Hungarian and Pontic history*, eds. L. Czigány and L. Péter (Aldershot, 1999).

[46] Antoljak, *Samuel and his state*, 78–80. This view has been restated, albeit briefly and cautiously by Pirivatrić, *Samuilova država*, 119–20, and it is fundamental to his vision of Samuel's state being forged in continual war. See also M. Whittow, *The making of Orthodox Byzantium, 600–1025* (London, 1996), 386–9; Holmes, "Basil II and the government of empire," vii, 264–5.

[47] Skylitzes, 348. See above at p. 2.

Prespa.[48] My suggestion follows the statement by Yahya of Antioch that Basil was victorious after four years of fighting.[49] This corresponds exactly with the notion that the campaigns which began in 1001 were brought to an end by the events of 1005. It is perfectly possible that Basil was satisfied with his achievements to date, which included the recovery of the key coastal stronghold of Dyrrachion, the reopening of the Via Egnatia and consolidation of his control north of Thessalonika. He was, therefore, content to leave Samuel with a realm based around Prespa and Ohrid, from which he could dominate the southern Slavs in Duklja and southern Dalmatia, but was denied access to the lands north and east of Sardika, and to Thessaly and the *themata* of Hellas and Peloponnesos. Samuel must also have kept his imperial title. Indeed, with the caution appropriate to any argument from silence, it is possible that Basil's agreement with Samuel has been erased from the written record to conceal the fact that the proud warrior emperor was previously a peacemaker. On my reading of the evidence, Basil recognized an independent realm known as Bulgaria. This leaves us with the possibility that a peace treaty was signed which lasted for ten years (1005–14). But we cannot travel further down this road without further evidence: I believe we may find it in the *notitiae episcopatuum*, notices of bishoprics subject to the patriarch of Constantinople.

Although these notices are notoriously difficult to date, making an absolute chronology impossible to establish, a firm relative chronology has been constructed. According to *notitia* 7, compiled at the beginning of the tenth century, the archbishopric of Dyrrachion had slipped to forty-second in the precedence list of metropolitan sees subject to Constantinople. The list of bishops suffragan to Dyrrachion had been reduced to just four: Stefaniaka (exact location unknown, but near Valona in Albania), Chounabia (exact location unknown, but between Dyrrachion and the river Mat), Kruja (modern Krujë) and Alessio (modern Lesh) (see map 1).[50] According to *notitia* 9 – first completed in 946, and revised between 970 and 976 – the status of Dyrrachion remained the same throughout the tenth century.

---

[48] Stephenson, *Byzantium's Balkan frontier*, 66–77. The argument is developed in P. Stephenson, "The Byzantine frontier in Macedonia," *Dialogos* 7 (2000), 23–40.

[49] Yahya, PO, I, 461; *Yahyā al-Antakī, Cronache*, tr. Pirone, 226, §12:33. See also V. R. Rozen, *Imperator Vasilij Bolgarobojca. Izvlečenija iz Letopisi Jaxi Antioxijskago* (St. Petersburg, 1908; repr. London, 1972), 42, 338, n. 283, for translation and commentary, and 411 for these four years in a chronological survey of Basil's reign. That the war initially lasted but four years is also noted by Whittow, *The making of Orthodox Byzantium*, 389, 423; W. Treadgold, *A history of Byzantine state and society* (Stanford, 1997), 525.

[50] *Notitiae episcopatuum ecclesiae Constantinopolitanae*, ed. J. Darrouzès (Paris, 1981), 272, 286. This seventh extant notice is generally attributed to the patriarch of Constantinople Nicholas I Mystikos (901–7, 912–25).

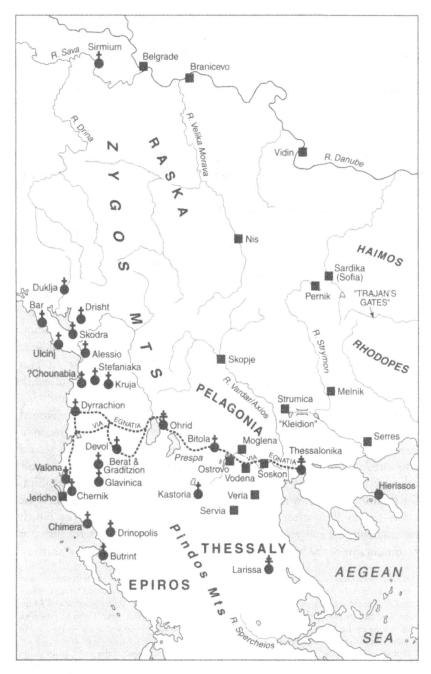

Map 1   Map of western Balkans at the time of Basil II.

However, its standing improved suddenly in *notitia* 10, when it was granted eleven more suffragan sees, bringing the total under the metropolitan to fifteen. These were Stefaniaka, Chounabia, Kruja, Alessio, Duklja, Skodra, Drisht, Polatum, Glavinica, Valona, Ulcinj, Bar, Chernik and Berat (with Graditzion).[51] The date of *notitia* 10 cannot be ascertained precisely, but it certainly postdates *notitia* 9, and must pre-date additional documents issued by Basil II in 1020, which stripped Dyrrachion of all the additional sees and granted them to Ohrid. (By 1020 Basil had recovered Ohrid and the surrounding territories for the empire.) Therefore, *notitia* 10 must date from the final years of the tenth, or, more likely, the first years of the eleventh century.[52]

The reason for the short-lived promotion of the metropolitan of Dyrrachion has been the subject of speculation. However, if we accept that between 1005 and 1014 Basil acknowledged Samuel's political and ecclesiastical control over Ohrid, the brief promotion of Dyrrachion makes perfect sense: it was to serve as the center of Byzantine ecclesiastical authority in the lands to the west of Samuel's realm, and as a check to encroachments from Ohrid. A complementary, but equally controversial feature of *notitia* 10, recension *a* (but not *c*), is the apparent consolidation of the authority of the bishop of Larissa in Thessaly.[53] Larissa temporarily acquired five additional sees: Vesaine, Gardikion, Lestinos, Charmenoi and Peristerai. These are also recorded as suffragans of Larissa in a separate manuscript of the fifteenth century (Cod. Par. gr. 1362), which, Darrouzès suggests, was conflating information from several earlier documents which are now lost. Samuel had captured Larissa in 986 and for that reason the temporary extension of that see's authority, after its recovery in the early eleventh century, would have acted as a complement to that of Dyrrachion, guarding against possible encroachments to the south from Ohrid. Therefore, the geographical distribution of the sees subject to both Dyrrachion and Larissa may be considered an illustration of the limits of Basil's political authority, which was concentrated in the coastal lands north and south of Dyrrachion, in the mountains to the west of Prespa and Ohrid and in the lands southwest

---

[51] *Notitiae episcopatuum*, 113–14, 330. The additional sees are recorded in two of the four recensions of *notitia* 10, being *a* (the oldest) and *c* (the most numerous). They are not recorded by recensions *b* and *d*. According to Darrouzès (*Notitiae episcopatuum*, 117) contradictions between *ac* and *bd* are the most historically significant, and therefore one must choose which version is to be preferred. In coming to the choice presented here I have followed his advice that one must regard *a* as the "conservateur" and the other recensions as "évolutif."

[52] *Notitiae episcopatuum*, 103, 116–17, suggests in or after the later years of the tenth century, but Darrouzès sees no grounds to be more precise. The context for compilation suggested here would allow greater precision.

[53] *Notitiae episcopatuum*, 110–11, 326–7, 339.

of Thessalonika.[54] In addition, the Byzantine military governor of Larissa briefly acquired authority over the Byzantine *thema* of Macedonia, which at this time lay to the east of Samuel's realm.[55] That is, according to an inscription, the *patrikios* Gregory, "*strategos* of Larissa and Macedonia," founded a church in 1006/7 in Tao, the recently acquired region which lay east of Trebizond on the Black Sea coast. This temporary extension of the scope of the *strategos* of Larissa's military authority, over lands to the south and east of Samuel's realm, may well reflect the acknowledged loss of direct imperial control over lands around Ohrid and Prespa.

So much then for the relative limits of Basil's and Samuel's political and ecclesiastical authority. My suggestions are contentious because they rest on an argument from silence (because there is no account of the annual campaigns which Basil is alleged to have launched against Samuel between 1005 and 1014), an episcopal notice (*notitia* 10) of uncertain date and questionable authority and an inscription from distant Tao. J. Shepard has advanced a nuanced interpretation which, while discounting the notion of a treaty, also stresses the difference between Basil's rhetoric of conquest and the apparent political and military realities he faced. Shepard suggests that Basil treated the Bulgars as a convenient "punching bag" against which to flex his army's muscles, demonstrate his own military leadership and provide his troops with sources of loot and slaves. Full-scale conquest was his publicly stated aim, but his real aim was political and military stability in the face of his large standing army and the machinations of his own generals. The rhythm of maneuvers and campaigning helped maintain equilibrium in Constantinople and Anatolia.[56] This changed in the second half of 1014, by chance not design.

In summer 1014 – perhaps at the expiration of a ten-year treaty – Basil determined to march against Bulgaria. This does not demonstrate his intention to conquer Bulgaria, but rather a desire to exercise his troops and

---

[54] V. von Falkenhausen, "Bishops," in G. Cavallo, ed., *The Byzantines* (Chicago, 1997), 172–96 at 173: "the organization of the ecclesiastical geography and hierarchy [was], almost inevitably, a reflection of secular organization."

[55] J. Koder, "Macedonia and Macedonians in Byzantine spatial thinking," in J. Burke and R. Scott, eds., *Byzantine Macedonia. Identity, image and history*, Byzantina Australiensia 13 (Melbourne, 2000), 12–28. See also: "Larissa," *ODB* II, 1180; "Macedonia," *ibid.*, 1261–2, citing K. N. Yuzbashian, *Ellinisticheskii blizhnii Vostok, Vizantiia i Iran* (Moscow, 1967), 115. We can dismiss, therefore, Oikonomides' (*Listes de préséance*, 358) suggestion that we should consider a second Larissa, a *tourma* in Sebasteia.

[56] Shepard, "Byzantium expanding, 944–1025," in Reuter, ed., *New Cambridge medieval history*, III, 586–604 at 599–601. Shepard will expand upon this in his forthcoming monograph *Byzantium between neighbours*. To be fair, Pirivatrić, *Samuilova država*, 206–7, also notes that pitched battles were rare, and that Basil benefited greatly politically from the prolonged clashes.

to accrue booty and prestige. This would better explain his first reaction on meeting solid resistance in 1014, which was to return home: hardly the action of a man bent on the annihilation of an independent Bulgarian realm. However, a ruse by a general, perhaps one familiar with Herodotus' histories, saw the emperor achieve a significant victory on 29 July 1014 at the pass known as Kleidion.[57] Almost immediately afterwards the emperor suffered a dramatic reverse, and once again Skylitzes is our only source of information. From Kleidion, Basil marched against the adjacent stronghold of Strumica and a nearby fortress called Matzoukion. He also despatched an advance force under the command of Theophylaktos Botaneiates, which was intended to clear a passage through the hills above Strumica for the emperor's own forces to proceed onto Thessalonika. After initial success, while seeking to return to the emperor, Botaneiates was ambushed. Skylitzes provides a gory account of Botaneiates' demise, alongside most of his troops, in a narrow pass, and notes that Basil was so disheartened that he turned back, pausing only to secure the powerful fortress of Melnik before pressing on to Mosynopolis, halfway back to Constantinople. Here, however, he received the news that Samuel had died, and changed his mind once again. He determined to press his advantage by marching back to Thessalonika, and thence back to Pelagonia, "destroying nothing in the vicinity except a [Bulgarian] imperial foundation of Gabriel's in Bitola."[58] This appears to have been a base for Samuel's son, Gabriel Radomir, who had succeeded his father, but had yet to establish authority over his father's subordinates. Basil was able, in spring 1015, to strike at two major fortresses guarding access to Bulgarian strongholds: Vodena and Moglena. The citizens of Vodena (modern Edessa), who had previously sworn faith to Basil, had risen against him, so their city was besieged, a new oath extracted and troublesome occupants relocated to Voleron. In addition Basil constructed two new fortresses to secure the area. The emperor then turned his attention to Moglena, which was besieged and captured by sapping the walls. The *kavkhan* Dometian, a senior Bulgarian official and close associate of Gabriel Radomir, and Ilica, the governor of the city, surrendered. Those able to bear arms were transferred to Vaspurakan, in Armenia, while others were enslaved. Instead of rebuilding, Basil razed Moglena, and garrisoned a nearby fortress called Enotia.[59] At this point Basil contacted, or was contacted by a pretender to the Bulgarian imperial title, John Vladislav, son of Samuel's murdered brother Aaron. Uncertainty arises from the fact

---

[57] See above at pp. 2–6.   [58] Skylitzes, 350–1.
[59] Skylitzes, 352; Pirivatrić, *Samuilova država*, 123. See also V. Kravari, *Villes et villages de Macédoine occidentale*, Réalitiés byzantines (Paris, 1989), 68–70 (Vodena), 82–3 (Moglena).

that we now have a second account of affairs, and are not wholly reliant on Skylitzes' abbreviated testimony.

The *Chronicle of the Priest of Duklja* (*Letopis' Popa Dukljanina*, henceforth *LPD*), written in Bar (in modern Montenegro) in the late twelfth century, but preserved only in sixteenth- and seventeenth-century redactions, provides unique information on Basil's campaigns in Bulgaria between 1014 and 1018. Although the veracity of the information must be questioned, the *LPD* provides the only detailed account of Basil's activities in Bulgaria from a non-Byzantine perspective, and for that reason it demands our careful attention.[60] The *LPD* states that after 1014 the Bulgarian ruler, Gabriel Radomir, "waged numerous wars against the Greeks during the reign of the Greek emperor Basil, and conquered all the lands as far as Constantinople." This does not tally with Skylitzes' version of affairs, which places Basil on the offensive, and shows him to be largely successful in 1015. But the *LPD*'s account of Basil's solution does echo Skylitzes': Gabriel Radomir was to be murdered by his cousin, John Vladislav.

Fearing the loss of his empire, the emperor Basil secretly sent ambassadors to Vladislav, Radomir's cousin, who asked: "Why do you not avenge the blood of your father? Take our gold and silver, as much as you desire to be at peace with us, and take Samuel's kingdom because he killed your father, his own brother. If you get the upper hand, kill his son Radomir, who now rules the kingdom." Vladislav consented to these words, and on an appointed day while Radomir was out hunting, he rode out with him and struck him dead. In this way Radomir died, and Vladislav, his murderer, ruled in his stead.[61]

This passage is contained in a section of the *LPD* which incorporates an independent *vita* of St. Vladimir.[62] For that reason it has often been afforded greater credibility than the rest of the text. As with all hagiography, details presented as historical background demand critical scrutiny, but may preserve useful insights. For example, Basil's offer to Vladislav is claimed also to have included control over the city of Dyrrachion.[63] Given Samuel's commitment to controlling that city, and the close family connections he enjoyed, such an offer is likely. However, the emperor

[60] *Letopis Popa Dukljanina*, ed. F. Šišić, Posebno Isdanje Srpske kr. akademije, knj. 67 (Belgrade and Zagreb, 1928). On the value of the chronicle in general see now: L. Steindorff, "Die Synode auf der Planities Dalmae. Reichseinteilung und Kirchenorganisation im Bild der Chronik des Priesters von Diocleia," *Mitteilungen des Instituts für Österreichische Geschichtsforschung* 93 (1985 [1986]), 279–324; L. Steindorff, "Deutungen des Wortes *Dalmatia* in der mittelalterlichen Historiographie. Zugleich über die Synode auf der *Planities Dalmae*," in N. Budak, ed., *Etnogeneza Hrvata* (Zagreb, 1996), 250–61.

[61] *LPD*, ed. Šišić, 336.

[62] N. W. Ingham, "The martyrdom of Saint John Vladimir of Dioclea," *International Journal of Slavic Linguistics and Poetics* 35–6 (1987), 199–216.

[63] *LPD*, ed. Šišić, 341.

reneged on this last promise, forcing Vladislav into a siege of the city. And here Vladislav fell, suffering retribution for his sins, struck down by a vision of St. Vladimir. The *LPD* then informs us that "after the death of Vladislav, emperor of the Bulgars, the emperor Basil mustered a mighty army and a powerful fleet, which he set to attacking the land until he captured the whole of Bulgaria, Raška [central Serbia] and Bosnia, and the whole of Dalmatia and the maritime cities as far as the border of Dalmatia Inferior."[64]

Skylitzes presents a different version of events, attributing the initial approach to Vladislav, via a one-armed Roman messenger who brought news that Gabriel Radomir was already dead, murdered at Petrich.[65] Consequently, Vladislav is said to have been ready to recognize Basil's authority, but reneged on this. Skylitzes makes no mention of a deal to recognize Vladislav's control of Dyrrachion. He does, however, provide a vignette centered on the city, where the heroic Byzantine *strategos* Pegonites meets Vladislav in single combat before the city's walls. Michael of Devol adds the additional information that two foot soldiers struck the fatal blows to Vladislav's stomach.[66] Although highly stylized and incorporating a later interpolation, we should prefer this version to the Priest of Duklja's. Moreover, Pegonites' presence appears to be corroborated by an inscription now in the Istanbul Archaeological Museum, which notes that before the arrival of a certain "[Peg]onites," Epidamnos (the ancient name for Dyrrachion) had been entrusted to a series of incompetent *strategoi*, allowing the previously accessible city to become isolated, and her riches lost. This surely refers to the city's capture by Samuel, and the consequent loss of revenues associated with trade along the Via Egnatia.[67]

Before the episode at Dyrrachion, Skylitzes provides details of Basil's campaigns in the lands Vladislav sought to control. Thus we learn that Basil returned swiftly to the offensive after his deal with Vladislav went awry. By way of exacting revenge, and deterring future acts of treachery, he laid waste the lands around Ostrovo, Soskon and the Pelagonian plain, and blinded all Bulgarians captured there. After this initial, brutal

---

[64] *LPD*, ed. Šišić, 344.

[65] Runciman, *First Bulgarian empire*, 244, locates Petrich, as Petriskos, on the Lake of Ostrovo. It is not to be confused with Petrich in the Strymon valley. Zlatarski, *Istoriia na bulgarskata durzhava*, I/ii, 850–3, discusses a document dated 1479 from the Rila Monastery which locates Gabriel Radomir's death at Soskon.

[66] Skylitzes, 357.

[67] C. Mango, "A Byzantine inscription relating to Dyrrhachium," *Archäologischer Anzeiger* 3 (1966), 410–14.

Figure 4 Cyrillic inscription dated, possibly, 1015/16, discovered in Bitola in the 1950s. Now housed in the Historical Museum, Ohrid, Republic of Macedonia. Reproduced from I. Zaimov, *Bitolski nadpis na Ivan Vladislav samodrzhets bulgarski* (Sofia, 1970).

success, however, Basil's battles against Vladislav were largely unsuccessful. Although the emperor seized Ohrid, sacking royal residences (but not the citadel), Vladislav installed himself in Bitola, where he strengthened fortifications and resisted Byzantine encroachments.[68] Here he sought to project an imperial image for himself, and thereby secure the support of those who had followed Samuel, or Samuel's son Gabriel Radomir. In this context we may understand the so-called "Bitolski Nadpis," a partial inscription discovered in Bitola during the demolition of a mosque in the 1950s.

[In the year 1015/16(?) this fortress was] built anew by John, emperor of the Bulgarians, with the help and prayers of our Virgin Mary and through the representation of the twelve supreme apostles. This fortress was constructed as a haven for the salvation of the Bulgarians. The fortress of Bitola was started on 20 October, and

---

[68] See Antoljak, *Samuel and his state*, 121, 19. See also Kravari, *Macédoine occidentale*, 311–13; I. Mikulčić, *Srednovekovni gradovi i tvrdini vo Makedonija* (Skopje, 1996), 139–43, on the fortifications of medieval Bitola.

was completed in the month of... This emperor was Bulgarian by birth, grandson of..., son of Aaron, who is [brother to] S[amuel, the emperor]... where they took... And this same tsar in the year 6522 [i.e. 1014–15] from the beginning of the world...[69]

Vladislav's styling himself "emperor of the Bulgarians," "Bulgarian by birth," as well as "son of Aaron," would appear to be the epigraphical protests of an individual whose claims to rule Samuel's Bulgarian realm were subject to scrutiny.[70] Indeed, rather than view Vladislav uncritically as the last independent Bulgarian tsar, as he clearly would have wished to be regarded, it is possible that he was never able to command the universal support of Samuel's magnates.

Seeking to take advantage of the political fragmentation and factionalism that followed Samuel's death, Vladislav killed Gabriel Radomir. This was both an act of vengeance and an attempt at usurpation, which led not to Vladislav's general recognition, but rather to further competition between magnates. Several potentates, staking claims to territory and fortifications in their possession, appeared to have enjoyed some parity with Vladislav. Thus, one Krakras, who had defended the fortress of Pernik against a Byzantine siege in 1002, was probably still commander in 1016 when Basil set a second siege. After eighty-eight days the fortress had not fallen, and Basil withdrew to Mosynopolis having "realized that he had embarked upon an impossible task."[71] The following year, the same Krakras "gathered many people" to join Vladislav and an army of Pecheneg mercenaries planning to attack Basil. The implication is that Krakras acted independently. Vladislav, then, was most likely acknowledged as *primus inter pares*, but could not dominate the regional magnates as had Samuel, and in such circumstances a cohesive independent Bulgaria could not survive. Immediately after Vladislav was killed at Dyrrachion in February 1018, Krakras and others realized they

---

[69] I. Zaimov, *Bitolski nadpis na Ivan Vladislav samodrzhets bulgarski* (Sofia, 1970), 33–4, 155. Zaimov provides a fuller and more creative translation than is presented here, drawing on information provided far later by Skylitzes or Michael of Devol to fill in several substantial lacunae. He provides, where the writing is lost: a solid date for the inscription of 1015–16; the names of Nikola and Ripsimia; additional imperial titles for Samuel; the names Samuel and Basil; names and details of the battles of Shtipon and Kleidion (Kliuch). Such suggestions must be treated with extreme caution.

[70] Despite suggestions that the inscription is a modern forgery, there is little doubt, given the circumstances and date of its discovery, plus its epigraphical and palaeographical qualities, that it is genuine. However, the references to Bulgaria and Bulgarians, smacking as they do of political hyperbole, do not provide irrefutable confirmation of "the ethnical [sic] nature of Macedonia at the beginning of the eleventh century" as Zaimov maintains. Cf. J. Zaimov, "Eindeutige und umstrittene Stellen in der Bitolja-inschrift des bulgarischen Selbstherrschers Ivan Vladislav (11. Jh.)," *Zeitschrift für Balkanologie* 13 (1977), 194–204.

[71] Skylitzes, 355.

could not stand against Basil. While Vladislav's widow entered into disputes over his succession with Samuel's descendants, Krakras surrendered, as did numerous other warlords and potentates, meeting Basil as he marched east at the head of a large army.[72] With this surrender, the independent realm known as Bulgaria came to an end.

[72] Skylitzes, 357–60.

3

Basil annexes Bulgaria

Traditional accounts of Basil's victory in Bulgaria emphasize the emperor's military prowess, and fail to mention three crucial factors which secured the Byzantine victory in 1018: luck, fear and diplomacy. Basil was lucky. The geopolitical position in the second part of his reign allowed him to make the best use of substantial but limited military resources. It has been estimated that at the end of his second Dacian war, Trajan could muster some 400,000 troops, and stationed half of these on the middle and lower Danube. Basil's total forces never numbered more than 110,000 across the whole empire.[1] Therefore, despite commanding the largest standing army of the middle Byzantine period, it was impossible for Basil to fight simultaneously on both eastern and western fronts. His Balkan campaigns after 1000 were facilitated by the remarkable stability of the empire's eastern frontier. The disintegration of the Buyid position in Baghdad after 983 meant that for the first time since the seventh century no great power sat beyond Armenia and the Transcaucasus. An alliance with the Fatimid Caliph al-Hakim in 1000 or 1001 brought to an end a period of fierce conflict centered on Aleppo. The treaty was renewed in 1011, and although conflict recommenced in 1016, the rivalry thereafter did not attain the intensity nor scale of earlier years. Basil was also able, through a personal arrangement with the *kouropalates* David in 990, to annex the Caucasian principality of Upper Tao upon David's death in 1000.[2]

---

[1] K. Strobel, *Untersuchungen zu den Dakerkriegen Trajans. Studien zur Geschichte des mittleren und unteren Donauraumes in der hohen Kaiserzeit* (Bonn, 1984), 153–4; J. Haldon, *Warfare, state and society in the Byzantine world, 565–1204* (London, 1999), 103.

[2] J. H. Forsyth, "The Byzantine-Arab chronicle (938–1034) of Yahyā b. Saʿid al-Antākī," Ph.D. thesis, University of Michigan, 2 vols. (Ann Arbor, 1977), I, 513–15; W. A. Farag, "Byzantium and its Muslim neighbours during the reign of Basil II (976–1025)," Ph.D. thesis, University of Birmingham (Birmingham, 1976), 188–92 (Aleppo), 263–4 (treaty, dated to 1001); C. J. Holmes, "Basil II and the government of empire (976–1025)," D.Phil. dissertation, University of Oxford (Oxford, 1999), 276–85, 314 n. 122, 355.

Furthermore, Basil benefited from a change in the situation north of the Black Sea. Whereas Tzimiskes' campaigns north of the Haimos had been inspired by a Rus' invasion along the lower Danube, Basil's closer relationship with the Rus' after 988/9 limited this threat. That is, the marriage to Basil's sister, and conversion to Orthodox Christianity of the Kievan Prince Vladimir (978–1015) may have had a pacifying influence in his dealings with Byzantium. However, a greater boon to Basil's expansion into the northern Balkans was the intensification in hostilities between the Rus' and Pechenegs recorded in the *Russian primary chronicle*.[3] Constant warfare between these peoples during Vladimir's reign prevented either from harboring designs on the lower Danube. Excavations appear to have confirmed the *Chronicle's* testimony that Vladimir undertook extensive construction work to defend Kiev. He built long lines of earthworks known as the "Snake Ramparts" to the south and west of the city, including a continuous wall on the left bank of the Dnieper. Fortifications were erected along the Dnieper's tributaries, which Vladimir garrisoned with local men.[4] We cannot completely discount the possibility that a strategy of "divide and rule," famously outlined in the mid-tenth-century text known as the *De Administrando Imperio,* was employed to foment tension between the Rus' and Pechenegs.[5] However, luck clearly played a large role in allowing Basil to concentrate his forces against Samuel.

The second feature of Basil's reign, and a major weapon in his armory, was his ability to inspire fear in those who threatened to defy him. To that end, Basil performed occasional acts of great brutality. The most notorious atrocity was that at the pass of Kleidion in 1014, where the emperor is said to have blinded up to 15,000 of Samuel's men, leaving a single eye to one in each hundred who might thereby lead his comrades home.[6] It has often been noted that Basil could not have blinded so many troops, who were in any event merely a division guarding a pass, since this would sorely have depleted the Bulgarian army; an army which fought on for four years after Kleidion, and Samuel's death. However, whether or not Basil

---

[3] *Povest' vremennykh let. Po Lavrent'evskoj letopisi 1377 goda,* eds. D. S. Likhachev and V. Adrianova-Perets, I (Moscow and Leningrad, 1950), 83; *The Russian primary chronicle,* tr. S. H. Cross and O. Sherbowitz-Wetzor (Cambridge, MA, 1953), 119.

[4] S. Franklin and J. Shepard, *The emergence of Rus, 750–1200* (London and New York, 1996), 169–80; J. Shepard, "The Russian steppe frontier and the Black Sea zone," *Archeion Pontou* 35 (1979), 218–37.

[5] *Constantine Porphyrogenitus De Administrando Imperio,* ed. G. Moravcsik, tr. R. J. H. Jenkins, CFHB 1 (Washington, DC, 1967).

[6] Skylitzes, 348–9, quoted in full in translation, above at pp. 2–3. See also *Cecaumeni Strategicon,* eds. B. Wassiliewsky and P. Jernstedt (St. Petersburg, 1896), 18; *Sovety i rasskazy Kekavmena. Sochinenie vizantiiskogo polkovodtsa XI veka,* ed. G. G. Litavrin (Moscow, 1972), 152. Henceforth: Kekaumenos.

truly did mutilate that number of men is less significant than the fact that he was believed to have done so. Moreover, shortly afterwards Basil committed a similar act, blinding all those whom he captured in the region of Ostrovo, Soskon and the Pelagonian plain. On this occasion, according to Skylitzes, Basil was provoked by the treachery of John Vladislav, and his action can thus be seen as both a punishment and deterrent to further acts of treachery.[7] There can be no doubt that stories of Basil's victories and atrocities circulated widely during his reign, as the emperor wished, and remained in circulation for years after, as the *Life of St. Nikon* demonstrates.[8]

The third crucial element in Basil's policy, subsumed beneath the rhetoric of military conquest, is diplomacy. Some of Basil's luck was the result of diplomatic endeavors, as was, for example, his closer relationship with the Rus' by virtue of the marriage of his sister to the Kievan Prince Vladimir. When the Pechenegs did turn away from the Rus' and advance upon the lower Danube in 1017, the threat was averted by negotiation. Basil despatched one Tzotzikios the Iberian, who convinced the nomads to remain north of the Danube, and no attacks were launched across the river until 1027, two years after Basil's death.[9] Similarly, good relations with those settled across the Danube at Vidin and in Transylvania were ensured diplomatically, by the baptism of Achtum and the promotion of Orthodox Christianity in his territories. Basil later secured a military alliance with King Stephen of Hungary, who is said to have provided troops to assist in the recovery of Ohrid in 1018.[10]

Imperial diplomacy was not reserved for dealings with "external" powers, but used to equal effect within the empire. Thus, Basil's advance in the northern Balkans is marked not so much by a trail of blood as of alliances. It is evident from reading Skylitzes' abbreviated account of Basil's early campaigns, in 1001–5, that control was achieved by securing the support of the leading man (*proteuon*) in a *kastron*, and the ruler (*archon*) of a district.[11] And in this struggle Basil's greatest weapon was his capacity to award lofty imperial titles, with their associated insignia, stipends and prestige. Thus,

---

[7] Skylitzes, 353.   [8] See above at pp. 4, 16.   [9] Skylitzes, 356.
[10] G. Györffy, "Zur Geschichte der Eroberung Ochrids durch Basileios II.," in *Actes du XIIe Congrès international des études byzantines, Ochride, 10–16 septembre 1961*, II (Belgrade, 1964), 149–54; F. Makk, "Relations Hungaro-Bulgares au temps du Prince Géza und du Roi Etienne 1er," in *Szegedi Bolgarisztika*, Hungaro-Bulgarica 5 (Szeged, 1994), 25–33 at 30–1.
[11] For a provisional list of Bulgarian aristocrats who fought or negotiated with Basil, see G. Nikolov, "The Bulgarian aristocracy in the war against the Byzantine empire (971–1019)," in M. Salamon and G. Prinzing with P. Stephenson, eds., *Byzantium and East-Central Europe*, Byzantina et Slavica Cracoviensia 3 (Cracow, 2001), 141–58.

crucially, Dyrrachion, the great stronghold on the Adriatic, was returned
to Byzantine suzerainty by the leading family, the Chryselioi, who had
previously acknowledged Samuel. Since Samuel was married to a daughter
of John Chryselios, the leading man (*proteuon*) of Dyrrachion, the change
in loyalty was even more remarkable. Chryselios did so in exchange for
imperial recognition for himself and his two sons as *patrikioi*.[12] Similarly,
Veria came with the loyalty of Dobromir, who was also a relative of Samuel
by marriage, and who received the rank of *anthypatos*. Servia was handed
over by the commander Nikolitzas, who was taken to Constantinople and
given the rank of *patrikios*. Unlike Dobromir, he proved fickle, and fled
back to Samuel. A further prize, Skopje, came with Romanos, the son of the
former Bulgarian Tsar Peter, whom Samuel had installed there as governor.
Romanos, who had taken the name Symeon, was promoted to the rank of
patrikios praipositos and given an imperial command in the city of Abydos on
the Hellespont. The policy was repeated following the renewal of intensive
campaigning in 1014, and the death of Vladislav in 1018. Thus, as we have
seen, the warlord Krakras surrendered Pernik, which could not be taken by
siege, as well as thirty-five surrounding fortresses, in exchange for the rank
of *patrikios*. Similarly, a certain Dragomouzos ceded Serrai and the region
of Strumica, also in exchange for the title *patrikios*, releasing the former
doux of Thessalonika John Chaldos in the process.[13]

At his encampment outside Ohrid, Basil received the various wives and
children of Samuel, Gabriel Radomir and John Vladislav. At Prespa he set
up a dais from which to receive the submission of Vladislav's remaining
sons, Prusjan (Prousianos), Alusjan (Alousianos) and Aaron; the first was
named *magistros*, the other two became *patrikioi*.[14] Here Basil also received
Ivatzes, the last Bulgarian potentate to offer serious resistance, blinded
by a ruse of Eustathios Daphnomeles, *strategos* of Ohrid.[15] An important
sentiment can be discerned in Skylitzes' account of Eustathios' entreaty to
Ivatzes' followers, who threatened to kill their master's attacker: "As you are
fully aware, you men assembled here, there is no hatred between your lord
and me because he is a Bulgarian and I am a Roman. Indeed, I am not a
Roman from Thrace or Macedonia, but from Asia Minor far from here, as
some of you know."[16] Tensions between Bulgarians and Romans who lived

---

[12] Skylitzes, 342–3, recorded out of sequence.
[13] Skylitzes, 357–60. Chaldos is said to have been imprisoned at Strumica for twenty-two years, although
an interpolation by Michael of Devol suggests that he was captured by Samuel in 1002, for which
see Skylitzes, 347.
[14] Skylitzes, 360.   [15] Skylitzes, 360–3.
[16] Skylitzes, 362, 391–4. G. Schlumberger, *L'épopée byzantine à la fin du dixième siècle, II. Basile II le
tueur des Bulgares* (Paris, 1900), offers a French translation of this portion of Skylitzes.

side by side in the Balkans are also mentioned by Yahya, in his description of the Bulgarians' general surrender.

The Bulgarian chiefs wrote to the emperor Basil to surrender to him, explaining their wish that he take possession of the fortresses and lands they held and asking him for permission to present themselves before him and take his orders. Thus, all the Bulgarian chieftains came to meet Basil, and brought with them the wife and children of the Bulgarian ruler Aaron. The emperor took possession of their fortresses, but showed himself to be well disposed towards them by awarding each an appropriate title. He preserved intact powerful fortresses, installing in them Roman governors, and razed others. He re-established order in Bulgaria, naming *vasilikoi*, functionaries charged with the administration of finances and state revenues (*al-a'māl wa l-amwâl*). In this way the kingdom of Bulgaria was annexed to the empire of *rūm* and transformed into a *katepanate*. This was in the forty-fourth year of his reign. The emperor returned to Constantinople. He married Roman sons to Bulgarian daughters, and Bulgarian sons to Roman daughters; in uniting one with the other he brought to an end the ancient animosity which had existed between them.[17]

It has generally been assumed that *vasilikoi* were imperial functionaries sent out from Constantinople, who were charged with supervising the fiscal administration of a region. However, a closer reading of Yahya's text demonstrates that he uses the term *vasilikoi* to refer to native potentates who had been charged by the emperor with certain duties in their own districts, which may have included, but were not exclusively concerned with, taxation.[18] Thus, in 975 a certain Christian Arab called Kouleïb (Kulayb) surrendered the fortresses of Barzouyah (Barzūyah) and Saoune (Sihyawn) in northern Syria, and was named in return *patrikios* and *vasilikos* of Antioch. There he remained until he committed himself to support Bardas Skleros against Basil. Yet, despite this apparent treachery, Kouleïb reappears

---

[17] *Histoire de Yahyā ibn Sa'īd d'Antioche*, fasc. 3, ed. I. Kratchkovsky, tr. F. Micheau and G. Tropeau, Patrologia Orientalis 47/4, no. 212 (Turnhout, 1997), [112–15], 406–7. Henceforth, Yahya, PO, II. Yahya here confuses John Vladislav with his father, Aaron. Cf. *Yahyā al-Antakī, Cronache dell'Egitto fātimide e dell'impero bizantino 937–1033*, tr. B. Pirone (Milan, 1997), 284, §13:46–7, who misleadingly offers the singular *vasilikos*. I am grateful to Irfan Shahîd for confirming the correct reading. See also; V. R. Rozen, *Imperator Vasilij Bolgarobojca. Izvlečenija iz Letopisi Jaxi Antioxijskago* (St. Petersburg, 1908; repr. London, 1972), 59, 362–6; Schlumberger, *Basile II le tueur des Bulgares*, 419–20, with the unsupported claim that "Here the Syrian author is wrong. The violent hatred between the two races survived the conquest."

[18] This point is eloquently made by Holmes, "Basil II and the government of empire," 330–42, who concludes for the empire's eastern lands that "underneath a thin veneer of centrally appointed officials . . . the quotidian administration of the frontier remained in the hands of indigenous officials." See now C. Holmes, "Byzantium's eastern frontier in the tenth and eleventh centuries," in N. Berend and D. Abulafia, eds., *Medieval frontiers: concepts and practices* (Aldershot, 2002), 83–104 at 94–5.

as *vasilikos* of Melitene, a post he still held in 987.[19] Clearly, this regional potentate enjoyed such authority that he could not easily be replaced. The same can be said for a second Christian Arab, Obeïdallah (Ubayd Allāh), who was *vasilikos* of Melitene in 976, and succeeded Kouleïb as governor of Antioch in 987/8. He appears to have been granted this title for life.[20] Thus, the natural interpretation of Yahya's comments on Basil's arrangements in Bulgaria would be that he granted powerful native aristocrats the title *vasilikos*, allowing them to retain authority in certain districts, subject to supervision by Byzantine military officers.[21] This fits very nicely with his further comment that Basil's intention was to diminish "ancient animosity."

Just as it has been assumed that, between 1001 and 1018, Basil was consumed entirely with efforts to conquer Bulgaria, so it has been asserted that immediately upon achieving this goal he created a series of administrative districts (*themata*) which stretched across all former Bulgarian lands from the Adriatic to the mouth of the Danube.[22] In fact, all evidence points to a rather looser, *ad hoc* series of arrangements which utilized established power structures to generate revenue and thus pay for the occupation.[23] Basil levied taxes in kind, not cash. An army could best be provisioned by raising taxes in this manner, and there is every indication that initial efforts to integrate Bulgaria into the empire involved little more than military occupation of key towns, fortresses and other strategic locations, bolstered by appropriate marriages between children of Byzantine

---

[19] Yahya, PO, II, 369, 373, 420; *Yahyā al-Antakī, Cronache*, tr. Pirone, 155, §9.24–5; 159, §10.9–11; 194, §10.146.

[20] Yahya, PO, II, 375–7; *Yahyā al-Antakī, Cronache*, tr. Pirone, 159–62, §10.10, 10.15–23.

[21] Cf. K. N. Yuzbashian, "L'administration byzantine en Arménie aux XIe et XIIe siècles," *Revue des études arméniènnes* 10 (1973–4), 139–83 at 179–81, which refers to various "tanutēr-s" known from inscriptions (dated 1059–67) on Ani Cathedral, who were there identified as representatives of their communities in fiscal affairs responsible to the Byzantine military official, the *katepano*. All held Byzantine court titles, and may be regarded as equivalents to *vasilikoi*.

[22] For example, G. Ostrogorsky, *History of the Byzantine state*, tr. J. Hussey, 2nd English ed. (Oxford, 1968), 311: "As a component of the Byzantine empire, the newly-conquered region was divided into *themata*, like any other Byzantine territory." The traditional interpretation is stated succinctly by V. Kravari, *Villes et villages de Macédoine occidentale*, Réalitiés byzantines (Paris, 1989), 36. Schlumberger, *Basile II le tueur des Bulgares*, 418, stated "We possess, alas! scarcely any information on the reorganisation by the Bulgar-slayer of the government of the newly-reconquered provinces of Bulgaria." However, he also noted astutely (p. 422) that "Bulgaria was not immediately transformed into a *thema* proper . . . but remained a conquered territory organised militarily with the fewest possible changes to the old order of affairs which had existed during its independence."

[23] On such practical appointments, see H. Ahrweiler, "Recherches sur l'administration de l'empire byzantin aux IX–XI siècles," *BCH* 84 (1960), 1–109 at 47–8; repr. in her *Études sur les structures administratives et sociales de Byzance* (London, 1971), no. VIII. L. Maksimović, *The Byzantine provincial administration under the Palaiologoi* (Amsterdam, 1988), 43–46, makes similar suggestions for the thirteenth-century Byzantine recovery of districts in Thrace and Macedonia, as reported by Akropolites.

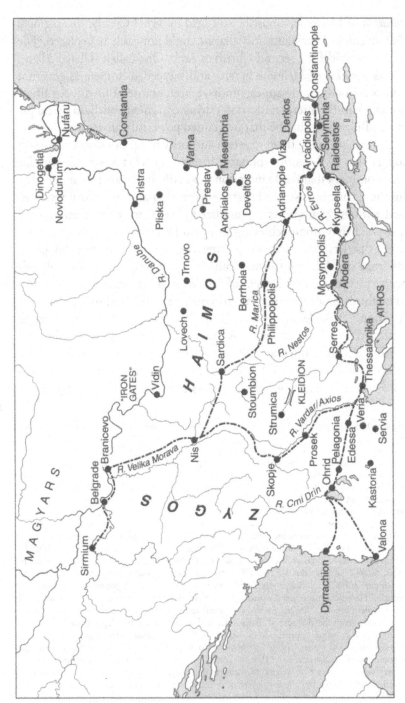

Map 2   Map of the northern Balkans in the eleventh century.

and Bulgarian aristocrats. Supreme authority over the armed forces in the northern Balkans rested with the *strategos autokrator* of Bulgaria. The first such officer was the *patrikios* David Arianites, whom Michael of Devol describes also as *katepano* of Bulgaria.[24] Subordinate *strategoi* stationed in key cities enjoyed control over imperial forces in their vicinity, and were responsible for liaising with and monitoring local potentates who retained political authority. One important subordinate military officer was the former *doux* of Thessalonika, the *patrikios* Constantine Diogenes, who in 1018 was designated commander in Sirmium (modern Sremska Mitrovica) and the neighboring territories.[25] There is no evidence that these lands comprised one large composite *thema* of Western Paristrion, nor a *thema* of Sirmium-Serbia stretching from the Danube into the highlands west of the river Velika Morava. However, it is perfectly possible that Diogenes' title at this time was *strategos* of Serbia.[26] Similarly, there is no conclusive evidence that a unified command of Paristrion was created during Basil's reign linking the various small *themata* bordering the lower Danube.[27] The failure to create such a unified command may reflect the relative peace and stability which prevailed in this recently volatile region. It would also suggest that the commanders of the lower Danube region were, at least for a time, militarily subordinated to the *strategos autokrator* of Bulgaria, based in Skopje. The first indication of an independent command structure at the northeastern frontier comes in the context of the Pecheneg wars fought in

[24] Skylitzes, 358.

[25] Skylitzes, 365–6. *Pace* T. Wasilewski, "Le thème de Sirmium-Serbie au XIe et XIIe siècles," *ZRVI* 8 (1964), 465–82 at 474. Wasilewski correctly maintained that the southern Serbian lands remained in the hands of the native rulers. However, he also suggested that a large *thema* comprising Sirmium, "Paristrion braničévien," and northern Serbia was entrusted to Constantine Diogenes after 1018. This rests on his translating τῶν ἐκεῖσε μερῶν ἔρχων as "archonte du Paristrion braničévien," when it surely means no more than the hinterland of Sirmium.

[26] J. Nesbitt and N. Oikonomides, *Catalogue of Byzantine seals at Dumbarton Oaks and in the Fogg Museum of Art, I: Italy, north of the Balkans, north of the Black Sea* (Washington, DC, 1991), 102, nr. 34.1. This is surely the same seal in the Fogg Collection noted by V. Laurent, "Le thème byzantin de Serbie au XIe siècle," *REB* 15 (1957), 185–95 at 190. So much was suspected by L. Maksimović, "Organizacija Vizantijske vlasti u novoosvojenim oblastima posle 1018. godine," *ZRVI* 36 (1997), 31–43 at 39, who otherwise maintains that two distinct *themata* of Sirmium and Serbia had been created. I have suggested previously that a seal apparently struck by Constantine Diogenes as "*strategos* of Serbia" may well relate to his being in command of the fortified city of Servia in northern Greece in 1001. This, however, must be incorrect since the city of Servia was almost always known in the neuter plural form, τὰ Σέρβια, and never as a feminine singular noun. Cf. P. Stephenson, *Byzantium's Balkan frontier: a political study of the northern Balkans, 900–1204* (Cambridge, 2000), 66.

[27] For example, H.-J. Kühn, *Die byzantinische Armee im 10. und 11. Jahrhundert. Studien zur Organisation der Tagmata* (Vienna, 1991), 223–5, reflects this belief, assuming that the *strategos* of Dristra was in command of a "ducate of Paristrion." The next recorded incumbents of that office in Kühn's list date from the 1040s. For the transition from *strategos* to *doux* see J.-C. Cheynet, "Du stratège du thème au duc: chronologie de l'évolution au cours du XIe siècle," *TM* 9 (1985), 181–94.

the reign of Constantine IX Monomachos (1042–55), when an individual took command of the forces stationed in "Paradounavon," literally "[lands] beside the Danube." We have the seals of several *katepanoi* of Paradounavon, which have all been dated later than c. 1045. A seal of one Michael *vestarches*, *katepano* of Paradounavon was probably struck by Michael Dokeianos, a general who was captured and killed by the Pechenegs.[28] Several seals struck by the *katepano* of Paradounavon Demetrios Katakalon, *patrikios*, *anthypatos* and *vestes* have been discovered at Dristra. This character may be the court dignitary not named by the historian Attaleiates who achieved significant victories over the Pechenegs at Arkadiopolis and Rentakion.[29] However, Attaleiates may also be referring to a contemporary commander in the region, the *vestes* Symeon, who is known from seals with the legend "*vestes* and *katepano* of Paradounavon."[30]

In reviewing the copious earlier literature on this matter, Ostrogorsky noted astutely that "... the mention of a *strategus* in any particular town by no means implies that this town was the centre of a theme."[31] We may take this a stage further, as did Ahrweiler, and argue that the presence of a *strategos* need not imply the establishment of a *thema*, except in so far as that term may signify military control of a locality or region, and should note that Skylitzes uses the term in exactly this limited sense.[32] The Byzantine annexation of Bulgaria, therefore, involved establishing an army of occupation to oversee the activities of established potentates. There was no immediate change in civil administration. Support for this contention can be found in two areas. First, seals which pertain to former Bulgarian lands in this period are struck almost exclusively by military officers and churchmen. Very few seals were struck by ostensibly civilian

---

[28] *Michaelis Attaliotae historia*, ed. I. Bekker, CSHB (Bonn, 1853), 34; G. Zacos and J. Nesbitt, *Byzantine lead seals*, II (Berne, 1984), 300; I. Iordanov, *Pechatite ot strategiiata v Preslav (971–1088)* (Sofia, 1993), 143–4, favors an otherwise unattested Michael in the 1060s.

[29] Iordanov, *Pechatite*, 143–4.

[30] With such a title, he cannot have held this command in the 1020s as was claimed by N. Bănescu, *Les duchés byzantins de Paristrion (Paradounavon) et de Bulgarie* (Bucharest, 1946), 70. See now A. Madgearu, "The military organization of Paradunavon," *BSl* 60 (1999), 421–46 at 426–9, who also argues that a further supposed governor of Paradounavon, Basil Apokapes, was in fact the commander of an eastern army transferred to Paristrion; contra Bănescu, *Les duchés*, 84–8, who made the connection between Apokapes and Basil, *magistros tou Paradounabi*, mentioned in the will of Eustathios Boilas. See now M. Grünbart, "Die Familie Apokapes im Licht neuer Quellen," in N. Oikonomides, ed., *Studies in Byzantine sigillography*, V (Washington, DC, 1998), 29–41 at 37–40. Several of Basil Apokapes' seals have been published, for example: I. Iordanov, "Neizdadeni vizantiiski olovni pechati ot Silistra (III)," *Izvestiia na Narodniia Muzei Varna* 24 [39] (1988), 88–103 at 89–92.

[31] Ostrogorsky, *History of the Byzantine state*, 311 n. 2.

[32] Skylitzes, 363, l. 51; Ahrweiler, "Recherches," 48–52, 78–9.

functionaries, and those which were had associations with the raising of taxes in kind and provisioning of the military.[33] Second, Basil's efforts to consolidate military control have left clear traces in the archaeological record. At Sirmium renovations were undertaken on the walls, and a garrison installed. Occupation was limited to a small area near the southern ramparts, where twenty-six class A2 anonymous bronze *folles*, small denominations struck by Basil, have been discovered. These coins probably reached the site in the purses of troops.[34] On the opposite bank of the Sava, at modern Mačvanksa Mitrovica, a new episcopal church was built, the third on the site, presumably to cater to the new Christian garrison.[35] Similarly, a sixth-century church was renovated alongside the antique fortress of Taliata, known as Veliki Gradac (and today as Donji Milanovac), some way to the east of Sirmium.[36] The restoration of ramparts, and a relatively large number of class A2 *folles* found there, suggest that Basil also installed a garrison at Belgrade.[37] Moreover, unpublished excavations at the ten-hectare site at Margum, near modern Morava at the confluence of the rivers Velika Morava and Danube, have turned up at least two seals and several coins. To this may be added a recently found hoard of fourteen class A2 anonymous *folles* struck by Basil II and Constantine VIII.[38] Besides, perhaps, the restoration of stretches of the late antique ramparts, Margum seems not to have been redeveloped. Instead, the new, smaller fortress at Braničevo, at the confluence of the rivers Mlava and Danube, grew in importance

---

[33] Holmes, "Basil II and the government of empire," 324–7, has conducted an analysis of seals from the eastern frontier lands, and draws similar conclusions. See especially the remarks on p. 325: "Instead of introducing alien administrative practices and practitioners into these newly-conquered regions, imperial authorities were willing to acknowledge the logic that in regions where the language of economic and fiscal exchange was not Greek, maximum benefit was likely to accrue from minimal administrative change." To this we simply might add the coda that rebellions are also less likely.

[34] V. Popović, "Catalogue des monnaies byzantines du musée de Srem," in C. Brenot, N. Duval and V. Popović, eds., *Etudes de numismatique danubienne: trésors, l'ingots, imitations, monnaies de fouilles IVe–XIIe siècle*, Sirmium 8 (Rome and Belgrade, 1978), 179–93 at 189–93.

[35] V. Popović, "L'évêché de Sirmium," in S. Ercegović-Pavlović, ed., *Les nécropoles romains et médiévales de Mačvanska Mitrovica*, Sirmium 12 (Belgrade, 1980), i–iv.

[36] M. Janković, *Srednjovekovno naselje na Velikom Gradcu u X–XI veku* (Belgrade, 1981), 21–3, 41–2, 75–8.

[37] V. Ivanišević, "Optičaj Vizantijski folisa XI. veka na prostoru centralnog Balkana," *Numizmatičar* 16 (1993), 79–92; M. Popović, *Beogradska tvrdjava* (Belgrade, 1982), 42–3.

[38] L. Maksimović and M. Popović, "Les sceaux byzantins de la région danubienne en Serbie, II," in N. Oikonomides, ed., *Studies in Byzantine sigillography*, III (Washington, DC, 1993), 113–42 at 127–9. A seal struck by a *strategos* of Morava has been attributed to the commander of Margum: Nesbitt and Oikonomides, *Catalogue of seals*, I, 195. See also S. Pirivatrić, "Vizantijska tema Morava i 'Moravije' Konstantina VII Porfirogeneta," *ZRVI* 36 (1997), 173–201. For the coin hoard found in 1984 see V. Ivanišević and V. Radić, "Četiri ostave vizantijskog novca iz zbirke Narodnog Muzeja u Beogradu," *Numismatičar* 20 (1997), 131–46 at 133–4, 141.

through the eleventh century, and coins now in the national museum at Požerevac suggest a brief Byzantine military presence associated with Basil's campaigns.[39]

There are, in marked contrast, no clear indications that Basil established garrisons in the interior highlands south of the Danube and west of the Velika Morava, namely Raška and Bosnia. A seal struck by a *strategos* of Ras has been convincingly dated to Tzimiskes' reign, and may indicate that Basil's predecessor enjoyed a brief period of recognition in Raška.[40] This is apparently confirmed by the *Chronicle of the Priest of Duklja*.[41] Moreover, although a seal has demonstrated conclusively that a military district of Serbia existed briefly – perhaps, as we have seen above, relating to the recovery of Sirmium in 1018 – it never compromised the local Slavic power structure. N. Oikonomides suggested that we must see the *thema* of Serbia as having existed somewhere to the north of Bulgaria, but only briefly before authority passed swiftly back to the local aristocracy.[42] I would wish to modify this, and to state that if the idea of developing a *thema* of Serbia existed briefly, it was swiftly abandoned and the title *strategos* passed to the local aristocracy. In a charter issued in July 1039 the Slavic ruler of Zahumlje styled himself "Ljutovit, *protospatharios epi tou Chrysotriklinou*, *hypatos* and *strategos* of Serbia and Zahumlje."[43] Ljutovid's claim to be *strategos* not only of Zahumlje, but all Serbia suggests that he had been courted by the

[39] V. Ivanišević, "Vizantijski novac (491–1092) iz zbirke Narodnog Muzeja u Požarevcu," *Numizmatičar* 11 (1988), 87–99; M. Popović and V. Ivanišević, "Grad Braničevo u srednjem veku," *Starinar* 39 (1988), 125–79 at 130. The importance of Braničevo was linked to that of the Hungarian fortress of Haram on the opposite bank.

[40] Nesbitt and Oikonomides, *Catalogue of seals*, I, 101–2; J. Kalić, "La région de Ras à l'époque byzantine," in H. Ahrweiler, ed., *Géographie historique du monde méditerranéen*, Byzantina Sorbonensia 7 (Paris, 1988), 127–40.

[41] *Chronicle of the Priest of Duklja*, Latin version, ch. 30, where it is stated that Tzimiskes "conquered the whole of Bulgaria which he subjected to his imperial rule. He then returned to his palace and relinquished command of his army. However, those in charge led the army to capture the whole province of Raška." See *Letopis Popa Dukljanina*, ed. F. Šišić (Belgrade and Zagreb, 1928), 324. J. Ferluga, "Die Chronik des Priesters von Diokleia als Quelle für die byzantinische Geschichte," *Vyzantina* 10 (1980), 429–60, argues for the greater credibility of the Latin text after chapter 30, and for its utility for historians of the Byzantine Balkans. Ferluga has used the source frequently: see the index of his collected studies: *Byzantium on the Balkans. Studies on the Byzantine administration and the southern Slavs from the VIIth to the XIIth centuries* (Amsterdam, 1976), 458, "Priest of Dioclea, Chronicle of the."

[42] Nesbitt and Oikonomides, *Catalogue of seals*, I, 101.

[43] V. von Falkenhausen, "Eine byzantinische Beamtenurkunde aus Dubrownik," *BZ* 63 (1970), 10–23. This article puts beyond doubt – doubt expressed by many, including Laurent, "Le thème byzantin de Serbie," 185–95 – that the body of this charter and the titulature are authentic and belong together. Cf. E. Malamut, "Concepts et réalités: recherches sur les termes désignant les Serbes et les pays Serbes dans les sources byzantines des Xe-XIIe siècles," in *EYΨYXIA. Mélanges offerts à Hélène Ahrweiler*, ed. M. Balard et al. (Paris, 1998), 439–57 at 442, n. 33: "Cet article [par von Falkenhausen] ... met fin à la contestation de l'existence du stratège de Serbie."

emperor, and awarded nominal rights over neighboring lands, including Duklja, which was at the time at war with the empire. Moreover, if we can trust the *Chronicle of the Priest of Duklja*, our only narrative source, we must conclude that none of the Serbian lands was under direct Byzantine control in 1042.[44] In that year, we are told, the *ban* of Bosnia, the *župan* of Raška, and the Slavic *princeps* of Zahumlje (Chelmana), Ljutovid, received Byzantine ambassadors offering piles of imperial silver and gold to support imperial efforts against the ruler of neighboring Duklja, Stefan Vojislav.[45] The use of the Latin *princeps*, rather than *iupanus* or *banus*, to describe Ljutovid, supports the notion that he held the supreme authority among the Serbs at that time. However, this may merely reflect his closer association with Byzantium, which may in turn be a consequence of Zahumlje's proximity to Duklja.

Beyond Serbia authority was similarly exercised by local notables who were willing, at least in principle, to recognize Basil's overlordship. Thus, a seal has come to light which bears the legend "Leo, imperial *spatharokandidatos* and [...] of Croatia." Unlike in the case of Serbia, nobody has seriously suggested that a Byzantine *thema* of Croatia was created at this time, and the most likely reconstruction of the lacuna is *archon*.[46] The use of the name Leo may suggest that the Croat in question had taken a Byzantine name, or a bride, or been baptized by the emperor, or by one of his subordinates. We have examples of all such eventualities in the Balkan lands recovered by Basil.[47] Moreover, in a parallel situation to that of Ljutovid in Serbia, a certain Slav named Dobronja, who also went by the name Gregory, appears to have accepted Byzantine money and titles in recognition of his authority in the northern Dalmatian lands. Charters preserved in Zadar show that he had been granted the rank of *protospatharios* and the title *strategos* of all Dalmatia. Kekaumenos records that he traveled twice to Constantinople as *archon* and *toparch* of Zadar and Split before 1036, when he was taken prisoner and later died in the *praitorion*.[48] Dobronja's change

[44] *Pace* Laurent, "Le thème byzantin de Serbie," 191–2.

[45] *Chronicle of the Priest of Duklja*, Latin version, ch. 38: "Audiens praeterea Graecorum imperator quod evenerat, ira magna et tristis animo effectis, misit statim legatos cum auro et argento non modico, ut darent iupano Rassae et bano Bosnae et principi regionis Chelmanae, ut mitterent exercitum et gentem supra regem [Vojislav]." *Letopis Popa Dukljanina*, ed. Šišić, 346–7.

[46] Nesbitt and Oikonomides, *Catalogue of seals*, I, 48–9. For the seal of a further Slavic noble granted a Byzantine title and, apparently, a military command at this time, see G. Zacos and J. Nesbitt, eds., *Seals*, II, 460, nr. 1089: Vladtzertzes, *magistros* and *katepano* of Mesembria. This was certainly within lands now under direct Byzantine control. See also Bănescu, *Les duchés*, 136–7, for the seal of one Tzourvaneles, *patrikios*, *strategos* of Bulgaria.

[47] Stephenson, *Byzantium's Balkan frontier*, 74–7, 123–30.

[48] Kekaumenos, eds. Wassiliewsky and Jernstedt, 77–8; ed. Litavrin, 300–2.

of fortunes may have been a consequence of, or alternatively the cause of, the rebellion by a further native ruler who had recognized Byzantine over-lordship: that is, the aforementioned Stefan Vojislav of Duklja, who also went by the title *archon* and "*toparch* of the *kastra* in Dalmatia, Zeta and Ston."[49]

The affairs of the Dalmatians, Croats, Serbs and others, were overseen from both southwest and southeast by Byzantine *strategoi* in key outposts. The Byzantine military commanders in Skopje and Dyrrachion both took a keen interest in the activities of the Serbs, and both Dobronja and Vojislav had regular dealings with the *strategos* of Dubrovnik. On the occasion that this last office was held by a certain Katakalon, Vojislav took the opportunity of his own son's baptism to kidnap the *strategos*, who had come to act as Godfather, and his party.[50] This suggests a close, if formal, working relationship between native elites and Byzantine officers in this peripheral zone of the empire after Basil's reconquest. Moreover, a line of small watchtowers studded the passes through the Zygos mountains, marking the limits of direct Byzantine authority west of the Velika Morava corridor between Skopje and Niš. Excavations or surveys have identified several fortresses constructed or rebuilt in the eleventh century, including those at, from south to north, Lipljan, Zvečan, Galič, Jeleč, Ras and Brvenik.[51] It seems certain that this defensive line was established following Basil's campaigns to mark the internal frontier between Byzantine Bulgaria and semi-autonomous Serbia. The former was to be governed directly from Skopje and its subordinate command posts, the latter was to comprise a series of client "principalities" in the highlands between the productive interior and the external frontier at the Danube-Sava. In the later eleventh century we know that a no-man's-land stretched to the west of these fortresses, between the Serbian lands and the newly constituted *thema* of Niš-Braničevo.[52] This is first mentioned in the context of Alexios I's campaigns (1080s), although we have the earlier seal of one Nikephoros Lykaon (or Lalakon), *protospatharios* and *strategos* of Niš.[53]

David Arianites' successors as supreme commander in Bulgarian lands included the aforementioned Constantine Diogenes, who may have taken over as early as 1022. His subordinate was the previously unnoted

[49] Kekaumenos, eds. Wassiliewsky and Jernstedt, 27–8; ed. Litavrin, 170–2.   [50] *Ibid.*
[51] M. Popović, "Les fortresses du system défensif byzantin en Serbie au XIe–XIIe siècle," *Starinar* 42 (1991), 169–85; Stephenson, *Byzantium's Balkan frontier*, 125, 148–50.
[52] *Annae Comnenae Alexias*, eds. D. Reinsch and A. Kambylis, CFHB 40/1 (Berlin and New York, 2001), 266–7; *Anne Comnène, Alexiade*, ed. B. Leib, II (Paris, 1940), 166–7; English tr. E. R. A. Sewter, *The Alexiad of Anna Comnena* (Harmondsworth, 1969), 276.
[53] Nesbitt and Oikonomides, *Catalogue of seals*, I, 100.

Figure 5   Seals of Byzantine officials in the Western Balkans, c. 1000–1050. Photos: Dumbarton Oaks; by permissions of Dumbarton Oaks, Byzantine Collection, Washington, DC and the Harvard University Art Museums, Whittemore Collection.

"Christopher, *protospatharios, epi tou koitonos* and *katepano* of Bulgaria and Thessalonika."[54] This is almost certainly Christopher Burgaris (perhaps signifying that he was Bulgarian, but also known as Baragis), known from an inscription in the Church of Panagia Chalkeon in Thessalonika, who was transferred to Italy in 1027–8. Diogenes was still in overall command of both Sirmium and Bulgaria when he was sent against the Pechenegs in 1027, before Constantine VIII transferred him to Thessalonika (hence, coinciding with the departure of Christopher).[55] The discovery of his seal bearing the legend "Constantine Diogenes *anthypatos, patrikios* and *doux* of Thessalonika, Bulgaria and Serbia" suggests that he retained nominal control over his northern command, stretching south from Sirmium to Niš and Skopje, as well as in Thessalonika.[56] In effect, his grand title was an alternative to *strategos autokrator* of Bulgaria, meaning commander-in-chief of forces based in the northern Balkans. However, there is reason to believe that his withdrawal from Sirmium signaled that this region too

[54] Zacos and Nesbitt, eds., *Seals*, II, 429, nr. 969, who identify this man with the *katepano* of Langobardia in 1028, said to have come from Bulgaria in the *La cronaca Siculo-Saracena di Cambridge con doppio testo greco*, ed. G. Cozza-Luzi (Palermo, 1890), 86. Cf. V. von Falkenhausen, *La dominazione bizantina nell'Italia dal IX all'XI secolo*, 2nd ed. (Bari, 1978), 91, 201.

[55] Skylitzes, 376.

[56] I. Swiencickyj, "Byzantinische Bleisiegel in den Sammlungen von Lwow," *Sbornik v pamet na Prof. Nikov* (Sofia, 1940), 439–40, nr. 11. For the corrected reading see V. L[aurent], a short note in *BZ* 58 (1965), 220; Laurent, "Le thème byzantin de Serbie," 189.

would now be controlled by locals. For example, at Belgrade, twenty-one class A2 anonymous *folles* were discovered dating from Basil II's reign, but thereafter only two further coins for the whole eleventh century.[57] This suggests that the Byzantine troops had been withdrawn. Moreover, a saint's life similarly suggests that around 1030 the *kastron* at Belgrade was under the control of a local magnate (*princeps*) who prevented the blessed Symeon from proceeding on his planned pilgrimage to the Holy Land.[58]

The strong defensive line established by the garrisoned fortresses and a stretch of no-man's-land comprised an inner frontier in the northern Balkans, beyond which sat a ring of semi-autonomous clients. The stability this brought allowed the development of the institutions of the civilian and ecclesiastical administration in the secure *katepanate* of Bulgaria based on Skopje and Ohrid. But this came later, and attempts to posit a rapid transition from a war footing to a developed system of civilian provincial administration are flawed. They fail to take account of the degree to which Basil determined to operate through existing power structures, and present an unhelpful, rigid view of Byzantine administrative practices. Thus, Basil famously issued a series of three *sigillia* after c. 1020, which outlined how the ecclesiastical structure of the province was to be reorganized, based on the archbishopric at Ohrid.[59] A crucial point in understanding these documents is that they were not final, but interim judgments subject to modification as the situation developed. Clearly it did, and the same can be seen with regard to civilian administration. After 1042 an official known

---

[57] Popović, *Beogradska tvrdjava*, 42–3. *Pace* Stephenson, *Byzantium's Balkan frontier*, 177–8, Belgrade was probably back under direct Byzantine control at the time of the passage of the First Crusade, and subsequently a new stone fortress was constructed. On 1096, and the presence of a Byzantine general, Niketas Karikes, *doux* and *protoproedros*, see now G. Prinzing, "Zu Odessos/Varna (im 6. Jh.), Belgrad (1096) und Braničevo (um 1163). Klärung dreier Fragen aus Epigraphik, Prosopographie und Sphragistik," *BSl* 56 (1995), 219–25 at 220–4. Karikes is said to have consulted with notable locals, and was possibly still acting in the capacity of *doux* of Bulgaria, for which see the following note.

[58] *Ex miraculis Sancti Symeonis auctore Ebervino*, ed. G. Waitz, *MGH* Scriptores 8 (Hanover, 1868), 210. For the date of 1030 see W. Wattenbach, *Deutschlands Geschichtsquellen im Mittelalter*, II (Berlin, 1939), 174. A Byzantine governor may be referred to as *princeps*, as was Karikes in 1096 (see previous note). However, this appears to have been a Latin rendering of his rank (*proto)proedros*.

[59] H. Gelzer, ed., "Ungedruckte und wenig bekannte Bistümerverzeichnisse der orientalischen Kirche," *BZ* 2 (1893), 22–72. These three *sigillia* have only been preserved appended to a later chrysobull, apparently issued in 1272, and then only in one of four manuscripts containing the chrysobull (Cod. Sinait. 508 [976], 17th century). Two further manuscripts contain only a part of the first *sigillion*, and a third, a Slavonic translation of the chrysobull, nothing. The authenticity of Basil's arrangements has been questioned by two scholars: S. Antoljak, "Dali sa avtentički onie tri ispravi na tsarot Vasilij II izdadeni vo korist na Ohridsakata arhiepiskopija," in his *Srednovekovna Makedonija*, 3 vols. (Skopje, 1985), I, 69–108; E. Konstantinou Tegiou-Stergiadou, *Ta schetika tin Archiepiskopi Achridas sigillia tou Vasileiou II* (Thessaloniki, 1988).

as the *pronoetes* of (all) Bulgaria was installed in Skopje.[60] The first known *pronoetes*, the eunuch and monk Basil, even took command of the Bulgarian expeditionary force sent against the Pechenegs in 1048.[61] Subsequently a civilian administrator known as the *praitor* operated alongside the military commander, now known as the *doux* of Bulgaria. The *praitor* John Triakontaphyllos held the elevated rank of *protoproedros*, which was introduced c. 1060,[62] and he may well have been a contemporary of Gregory, *protoproedros* and *doux* of Bulgaria.[63] By this time the military commander of Bulgaria was no longer *strategos autokrator* of all imperial forces in the northern Balkans, but a more localized command. Other later eleventh-century *doukes* of Bulgaria include Nikephoros Vatatzes *proedros*, Niketas Karikes and Michael Saronites *vestarches*, known to have been *katepano* of Bulgaria in 1072.[64] Saronites was previously "*protospatharios* and *strategos* of Macedonia," and later "*magistros* and *doux* of the whole West."[65] There is also an unpublished seal in the Ashmolean Museum in Oxford which was struck by a certain Andronikos Philokales, *vestarches* and *katepano*, perhaps during his tenure as *katepano* of Bulgaria from c. 1065.[66] The transition to a peacetime footing, with concomitant introduction of many more fiscal and civilian officers, brought new problems to Bulgaria. Large rebellions occurred in the western Balkans in the 1040s, and these should be seen as a reaction to the increasing fiscalization of the region. Fiscalization itself was a response to cash shortages and demands to redirect both coinage and manpower to the northeastern Balkans, which lands were now threatened by the Pechenegs.[67]

---

[60] The exact meaning of *pronoetes* in this context is unclear. For suggestions see *ODB*, III, 1733; N. Oikonomides, "L'évolution de l'organisation administrative de l'empire byzantin au XIe siècle (1025–1118)," *TM* 6 (1976), 125–52 at 149–50.

[61] Kekaumenos, eds. Wassiliewsky and Jernstedt, 24; ed. Litavrin, 164, for Basil the *protonoetes Boulgaron*. Attaleiates, 37, calls Basil the *satrapes* of Bulgaria. Bănescu, *Les duchés*, 139–41; Kühn, *Die byzantinische Armee*, 229. See also G. Schlumberger, *Sigillographie de l'empire byzantin* (Paris, 1884), 740–1, for a seal of the *protonoetes pases Boulgarias*.

[62] Oikonomides, "L'évolution de l'organisation administrative," 126; *ODB*, III, 1727.

[63] Nesbitt and Oikonomides, *Catalogue of seals*, I, 94–5.

[64] Nesbitt and Oikonomides, *Catalogue of seals*, I, 94, nr. 29.3; H. Hunger, "Zehn unedierte byzantinischen Beamten-Siegel," *JÖB* 17 (1968), 179–95 at 186–7, nr. 9; Cf. J.-C. Cheynet, *Pouvoir et contestations à Byzance (963–1210)* (Paris, 1990), 409; Prinzing, "Klärung dreier Fragen," 223, n. 21.

[65] Nesbitt and Oikonomides, *Catalogue of seals*, I, 120–1, nr. 43.30; L. Mandić and R. Mihajlovski, "A XIth century byzantine seal from Heraclea near Bitola," *REB* 58 (2000), 273–7.

[66] See also Kekaumenos, eds. Wassiliewsky and Jernstedt, 72; ed. Litavrin, 264; Bănescu, *Les duchés*, 144; Kühn, *Die byzantinische Armee*, 230. Further seals struck by Philokales are noted by J.-C. Cheynet, in a review of my *Byzantium's Balkan frontier*, *REB* 59 (2001), 299. He also proposes the following additional Bulgarian commanders: Leo Drimys, Nikephoros *proteuon*, Romanos Diogenes, Nikephoros Melissenos, Nikephoros Botaneiates.

[67] P. Stephenson, "Byzantine policy towards Paristrion in the mid-eleventh century: another interpretation," *BMGS* 23 (1999), 43–66.

Basil II, therefore, achieved victory in Bulgaria by a combination of luck, diplomacy and force. His subsequent annexation and reorganization ensured the continued governance of established potentates, endowed with new titles and stipends, overseen by trusted military commanders. All was held together by fear of the emperor, which similarly prevented encroachments from beyond Bulgaria. Before 1025, the barbarian who rode his mount as far as the Danube was reminded that to pass beyond that line was to enter the realm of the warrior emperor Basil, and therefore was to risk his terrifying reprisal.[68] For this reason they turned back, in the words of Michael Psellos, "not daring to advance further into [Byzantine] lands."[69] Basil's "civilian" successors had equal diplomatic resources, but lacked Basil's luck with regard to the strategic situation beyond the frontiers. Moreover, by disbanding Basil's large standing army of occupation, and abandoning or downgrading far-flung fortifications such as Belgrade, they allowed the psychological deterrent to rebellion and invasion rapidly to evaporate. It was the task of a new military dynasty, the Komnenoi, to restore the prestige of the Byzantine military and with it the fear which kept subject-allies and neighbors in check. The Komnenoi would also be responsible for recreating the image of Basil II, as we shall see in chapter six. First, however, we must search for the Bulgar-slayer in the art and literature produced during Basil's reign and immediately after his death.

[68] See S. Mattern, *Rome and the enemy. Imperial strategy in the Principate* (Berkeley, 1999), 116–22, for the importance of reprisal, and fear of it, in defending the Roman frontier. See also W. Haase, " 'Si vis pacem, para bellum': Zur Beurteilung militärischer Stärke in der römischen Kaiserzeit," in J. Fitz, ed., *Limes. Akten des XI. Internationalen Limeskongresses (Székesfehérvár, 30.8.-6.9.1976)* (Budapest, 1977), 721–55.

[69] *Michaelis Pselli scripta minora*, eds. E. Kurtz and F. Drexl, 2 vols. (Milan, 1941), II, 239.

4

Victory and its representations

Other past emperors
previously designated for themselves other burial places.
But I Basil, born in the purple chamber,
place my tomb on the site of the Hebdomon
and take sabbath's rest from the endless toils
which I fulfilled in wars and which I endured.
For nobody saw my spear at rest,
from when the Emperor of Heaven called me
to the rulership of this great empire on earth,
but I kept vigilant through the whole span of my life
guarding the children of New Rome
marching bravely to the West,
and as far as the very frontiers of the East.
The Persians and Scythians bear witness to this
and along with them Abasgos, Ismael, Araps, Iber.
And now, good man, looking upon this tomb
reward it with prayers in return for my campaigns.

This, Basil II's verse epitaph, was originally an inscription associated with his sarcophagus, which was installed in the Church of St. John the Evangelist at the Hebdomon Palace.[1] The first point of note is that Basil made no explicit mention of Bulgaria, but alludes only to Scythians after the Persians. Scythian was the classicizing term used by Byzantine authors to refer to any northern Barbarian people, just as Persian was used for a range of eastern foes. It may be, indeed probably is used here to mean the Bulgarians, but this is not made clear. Clarification, or at least further information, is offered, for eastern peoples. Employing singular forms to fit the meter of the

---

[1] S. G. Mercati, "Sull'epitafio di Basilio II Bulgaroctonos," and "L'epitafio di Basilio Bulgaroctonos secondo il codice Modense Greco 144 ed Ottoboniano Greco 344," in his *Collectanea Byzantina*, 2 vols. (Bari, 1970), II, 226–31, 232–4. The latter provides several alternate readings, including a clarification of the verb in the first couplet. This perhaps confused J. Thibaut, "L'Hebdomon de Constantinople. Nouvel examen topographique," *EO* 21 (1922), 31–51 at 42, who provides an inaccurate French translation from an earlier, incomplete transcription by Du Cange.

poem, mention is made of the Abasgians (people of Abasgia, or Abkhazia, bordering the eastern shore of the Black Sea), Ismaelites (a generic term for Muslims), Arabs, and Iberians (people of the region around Tao, bordering Abkhazia). Like Bulgaria, both Abkhazia and Iberia were annexed to the empire by Basil II; unlike Bulgaria, these warrant special mention in his epitaph. Apparently, the "Bulgar-slayer," as had his predecessors, believed greater prestige accrued from success in the empire's eastern reaches, and to this he drew the attention of posterity.

The second point of note in Basil's epitaph is that the emperor wished his mortal remains to rest apart from those of his Macedonian predecessors, whose sarcophagi were to be found in the Church of the Holy Apostles, within the walls of Constantinople. His brother, Constantine VIII (d. 1028), was also to be buried at the Holy Apostles, his sarcophagus being the last to fit within the Mausoleum of Constantine the Great. If Yahya of Antioch is to be believed, this "sarcophagus [which] was of marble, extremely beautiful, of many colours and sporting exuberant carvings," was originally intended for Basil.[2] However, having commissioned the piece, Basil changed his mind, and asked Constantine to arrange for him to be laid to rest in simple clothing at the Church of St. John, known in Greek as the Theologian, at the Hebdomon Palace complex, outside the walls of Constantinople. He did so, Yahya suggests, to be amongst strangers, rather than emperors and kin.[3] Basil's burial at the Hebdomon is confirmed by Byzantine chroniclers, although no indication is given of why he chose this place.[4] However, we may add a further reason to Yahya's.

Both his epitaph and his selection of the Hebdomon demonstrate that Basil wished to be judged, in death as in life, by his military achievements.[5]

---

[2] *Histoire de Yahyā ibn Saʿīd d'Antioche*, fasc. 3, ed. I. Kratchkovsky, tr. F. Micheau and G. Tropeau, Patrologia Orientalis 47/4, no. 212 (Turnhout, 1997), [112–15], 480–3. Henceforth, Yahya, PO, II. Cf. *Yahyā al-Antakī, Cronache dell'Egitto fāṭimide e dell'impero bizantino 937–1033*, tr. B. Pirone (Milan, 1997), 336, §15:69; V. R. Rozen, *Imperator Vasilij Bolgarobojca. Izvlečenija iz Letopisi Jaxi Antioxijskago* (St. Petersburg, 1908; repr. London, 1972), 69, 383–4; G. Schlumberger, *L'épopée byzantine à la fin du dixième siècle, II. Basile II le tueur des Bulgares* (Paris, 1900), 622–4.

[3] Only Yahya refers to a small monastery at the site. I am grateful to Irfan Shahîd for clarifying the sense of the garbled Christian Arabic, which allows us to dispense with the supposition that Yahya is referring to a *xenodocheion*. See also R. Janin, *La géographie ecclésiastique de l'empire byzantin, I. Le siège de Constantinople et le patriarcat oecuménique, III. Les églises et les monastères* (Paris, 1953), 275–8, 426–9.

[4] Skylitzes, 368, "He asked his brother, whom he designated as successor to the throne, to bury him in the church of the Evangelist and Divine next to the Hebdomon, and thus it was done." Cf. the testimony of Theodore Skoutariotes: K. Sathas, ed., *Anonymou synopsis chroniki*, vol. VII of his *Mesaioniki vivliothiki* (Venice, 1894), 159, "At his death, the emperor Basil was buried in the church, that he had built, of the beloved St. John the Theologian in the Hebdomon."

[5] M. Lauxtermann, "Byzantine poetry and the paradox of Basil II's reign," in P. Magdalino, ed., *Byzantium in the year 1000* (Leiden, 2003), 199–216, makes similar claims, adding (at p. 210) that "Basil II is named in a number of run-of-the-mill verse inscriptions on city walls, ramparts and

The rhetoric of victory chimes well with Basil's policy of engendering fear and respect in enemies and subjects alike. In the metrical verse attention is drawn to his energy and martial prowess as a victorious general who fought at the empire's frontiers to both east and west. In his choice of burial place, Basil also made this point. The Hebdomon was so named because it lay seven Roman miles from the *milion*, the point in Constantinople from which mileage was measured. Here, since Valens in A.D. 364, emperors had been proclaimed prior to their entry into the city. More significantly for Basil, it adjoined the imperial parade ground, and was the point of departure for emperors celebrating triumphal entries into the city through the Golden Gate some two miles to the east.[6]

Basil entered Constantinople from the Hebdomon through the Golden Gate in 1019. First, however, he marked his victory over the Bulgarians with a march through northern Greece, culminating in his entrance into the city of Athens, where he presented votive offerings in the Church of the Virgin within the Parthenon. The emperor proceeded on to Constantinople, where he paraded prominent Bulgarian captives through the streets. Basil was not, on this occasion, as has often been written, acclaimed by the populace as "Bulgar-slayer."[7] Moreover, while it is likely that Basil commissioned works of art to mark this occasion, and we can be certain that Constantinople was decked out in silks and flowers as ceremonial demanded, two works traditionally associated with Basil's victory in Bulgaria have recently been shown to have no association with this occasion. These are the portrait of Basil on the frontispiece of his psalter, and a silk, now housed in Bamberg Cathedral, known as the Bamberger Gunthertuch.

The psalter of Basil II, to be found in the Marcian Library in Venice (Cod. Marc. gr. 17), contains on its frontispiece (fol. 3r) a very well known illumination of the emperor standing in the battledress of a Roman general holding in his right hand a lance and in his left a sheathed sword (plate 1). The emperor is shown wearing the crimson imperial boots, and being crowned with a *stemma* set with a red stone and a double row of pearls.[8] The

---

fortresses; as is only to be expected on works of fortification, these verse inscriptions emphasize the military aspect to the reign of Basil II."

[6] H. Glück, *Das Hebdomon und seine Reste in Makriköi* (Vienna, 1920), 2–3; C. Mango, "The triumphal way of Constantinople and the Golden Gate," *DOP* 54 (2000), 173–88 at 176.

[7] For example, G. Finlay, *A history of Greece from its conquest by the Romans to the present time, B.C. 146 to A.D. 1864*, 2nd ed., ed. H. F. Tozer, 7 vols. (Oxford, 1877), II, 383.

[8] Nikephoros III Botaneiates (1078–81) is portrayed wearing a similar *stemma*, set with a red stone, in Cod. Par. Coislin. 79, illustrated in H. C. Evans and W. D. Wixom, eds., *The glory of Byzantium: art and culture in the middle Byzantine era, A.D. 843–1261* (New York, 1997), 208. See also the miniature of Alexios I Komnenos (1081–1118) in Cod. Vat. gr. 666, fol. 2v, which is examined by I. Spatharakis, "Three portraits of the early Comnenian period," in his *Studies in Byzantine manuscript illumination and iconography* (London, 1996), 18–40 at 29–31.

coronation is performed by Gabriel, one of two archangels above his left and right shoulders, below each of whom are the busts of three military saints. Basil is standing, like a statue, on a small raised plinth (*suppedion*), behind and over eight prostrate figures performing *proskynesis*. Quite exceptionally, the four central figures have their palms placed downwards (not upwards, as was expected in *proskynesis*), supporting themselves as they kneel and bow low to the ground. The character to the fore in the bottom right corner has his hands clenched to form a loose grip, and his counterpart to the left, whose hands have mostly flaked away, may be similar. The hands of the two figures behind these are obscured. At the top center of the picture, immediately above Basil, a nimbate bust of Christ suspends a second crown over the emperor's head.[9] The portrait may usefully be compared to that of Basil I (Cod. Par. gr. 510, fol. Cv), crowned with the *stemma* by Archangel Gabriel and handed the *labarum* (not sword or lance) by his patron Saint Elijah. There, all three stand on a low, rectangular *suppedion*. A verse inscription around the border states that St. Elijah guarantees Basil victory, and Gabriel crowns him protector of the world.[10]

Basil II's psalter portrait has, since A. Grabar's definitive intervention in 1936, been regarded as portraying a triumphal ceremony to mark Basil's final victory over the Bulgarians.[11] That is, he is receiving the crown of victory and the submission of his defeated enemies, the Bulgarian chieftains, who are performing *proskynesis*. So much, it has been argued, is also suggested by the poem which accompanies the illumination:

---

[9] For a complete description see A. Cutler, "The psalter of Basil II," *Arte Veneta* 30 (1976), 9–19; "The psalter of Basil II (part II)," *Arte Veneta* 31 (1977), 9–15 at 9. Henceforth, all references will be to part II.

[10] See I. Spatharakis, "The portraits and the date of the Codex *Par. Gr. 510*," *Cahiers archéologiques* 23 (1974), 97–105; repr. in his *Studies in Byzantine manuscript illumination and iconography*, 1–12. It must be noted that Spatharakis here, and in a second paper, "A note on the imperial portraits and the date of Par. Gr. 510," *JÖB* 39 (1989), 89–93, identified this as pertaining to a particular victory, by Basil I in Germanikeia in 879. However, I. Kalavrezou-Maxeiner, "The portraits of Basil I in Paris gr. 510," *JÖB* 27 (1978), 19–24, has argued convincingly for a later date (880–3) not associated with a particular victory. L. Brubaker, *Vision and meaning in ninth-century Byzantium. Image as exegesis in the homilies of Gregory of Nazianzus* (Cambridge, 1999), 5–6, supports Kalavrezou's interpretation. For Basil I's victory celebrations, to which we will return below, see M. McCormick, *Eternal victory. Triumphal rulership in Late Antiquity, Byzantium and the early medieval West* (Cambridge and Paris, 1986), 154–7; H. Hunger, "Reditus Imperatoris," in G. Prinzing and D. Simon, eds., *Fest und Alltag in Byzanz* (Munich, 1990), 17–35 at 23–4, 28.

[11] A. Grabar, *L'empereur dans l'art byzantin* (Strasbourg, 1936), 86 n. 3, 86–7: "Since Kondakov, researchers have been unanimous in identifying here Bulgarian chieftains . . . It is almost certain that this image originally commemorated the definitive victory of Basil II over the Bulgars (1017) [sic], and was without doubt inspired by the famous triumph which was celebrated by the Bulgar-slayer." This has been repeated recently by, for example, T. Mathews, *Byzantium from Antiquity to the Renaissance* (New York, 1998), 36–8; P. Stephenson, *Byzantium's Balkan frontier: a political study of the northern Balkans, 900–1204* (Cambridge, 2000), 62. See also the frontispiece of K. Paparrigopoulos, *Istoria tou ellinikou ethnous*, ed. P. Karolides, revised ed. (Athens, 1925), IV, reproduced below as fig. 11.

A strange wonder is to be seen here: from Heaven, Christ with his life-bringing right [hand] extends the crown (στέμμα), the symbol of rulership to the faithful and mighty ruler Basil. Below are the first of the incorporeal beings, one of whom, taking [the crown] has brought it down and is joyfully crowning [the emperor]. The other, adding victories to rulership is placing the spear (ρομφαίαν), a weapon that scares the enemies (ἐναντίους) away, in the ruler's hand. The martyrs are his allies, for he is their friend. They cast down those lying at his feet.[12]

The scene and poem have found many commentators, including A. Cutler, who observed that art historians familiar with the illumination have dated the psalter to the first part of Basil's reign, considering it a close contemporary of Basil's *menologion*, to which it is stylistically very similar.[13] However, others, who had not seen the manuscript itself, were misled by a monochrome reproduction of the psalter illumination published by Labarte in 1864, where the flaking portrait of the emperor gives the impression that he has a long white beard. Arguing for the realism of the portrait, these scholars have viewed Basil as an elderly man, and dated the image to the last years of his reign.[14] Those now able to view the crisp, color reproductions of the illumination in any number of recent publications could no longer subscribe to such a view.[15] Thus, if realism is an issue in dating the portrait, and Cutler insisted it is not, we need not opt for a late date.

---

[12] I. Ševčenko, "The illuminators of the menologium of Basil II," *DOP* 16 (1962), 245–76 at 272, offers a transcription and "pedestrian translation." Cutler, "Psalter," 10, offers a modified translation, but only so far as ". . . crowning [the emperor]". There is no explicit mention of "enemies," which Ševčenko introduces in square parentheses, in the final couplet (οἱ μάρτυρες δὲ συμμαχοῦσιν ὡς φίλῳ, ῥίπτοντες τοὺς ποσὶ προκειμένους). Mathews, *Byzantium from Antiquity to the Renaissance*, 38, also supplies "enemies" in his translation: "fight beside him as with a friend, laying low the enemies prone at his feet." Ševčenko (p. 272) suggested that the poem does not fit the illumination as exactly as we might have expected. The emperor is handed not a sword, which is the usual English translation for *romfaia*, by Archangel Michael, but a lance, and the martyrs are more particularly the military saints. However, martyrs seems, to me, entirely appropriate for military saints. Moreover, while *romfaia* does refer most frequently to a sword, it can also mean spear. See T. G. Kolias, *Byzantinische Waffen. Ein Beitrag zur byzantinischen Waffenkunde von den Anfängen bis zur lateinischen Eroberung*, Byzantina Vindobonensia 17 (Vienna, 1988), 191, n. 38. The *Souda* (rho. 226) offers the description "τὸ μακρὸν ἀκόντιον, ἢ μάχαιρα," i.e. as a "long lance, or a sword [or knife]." See *Suidae Lexicon*, ed. A. Adler, 5 vols. (Leipzig, 1928–38), IV, 299.

[13] I. Ševčenko, "The illuminators of the menologium," 272, n. 91: "The two works show a close resemblance in dimensions . . . script and make-up. Considered as books, they could have been executed only a few years apart, or could even have been contemporaneous." Besides numerous editors of the Marcian collection, see: K. Wessel, "David," in *Reallexikon zur byzantinischen Kunst*, ed. K. Wessel (Stuttgart, 1966), I, 1146–61 at 1148, for a date c. 1000. Contra: S. Der Nersessian, "Remarks on the date of the menologion and the psalter written for Basil II," *Byzantion* 15 (1940–1), 104–25.

[14] For example, Der Nersessian, "Remarks," 115.

[15] Mathews, *Byzantium from Antiquity to the Renaissance*, 36, with the caption "Triumph of Basil II over the Bulgarians"; Evans and Wixom, *The glory of Byzantium*, 186, cropped, with the caption "Basil II Triumphs Over His Enemies."

More significant for dating the psalter may be the content of the illumination, the scene portrayed. Scholars have sought an historically attested episode, and have opted, quite naturally in view of Basil's enduring reputation as the Bulgar-slayer, for the ceremony marking his victory over the Bulgarians: the emperor appears in battledress, weapons in hand, surrounded by military saints, receiving the crown of victory and the *proskynesis* of his defeated enemies, the Bulgarians. However, as Cutler has demonstrated, this is not the case. The scene portrayed is not a particular episode, but a general image of Basil as Christian emperor and Roman general.[16] This is clear when one considers that the scene does not match accounts of Basil's victory celebrations of 1019 provided in extant sources. First, the principal captives led in the victory procession were Bulgarian women; the prostrate figures in the illumination are men, and probably not Bulgarians. Second, Basil is shown wearing the *stemma*, the crown which represents imperial rulership. This was not the crown worn during his triumphal entry into Constantinople. Several objects associated with imperial victory celebrations show emperors wearing or receiving a crested crown, which we know Basil also wore during his triumphal entry into Constantinople.[17]

According to our principal source, John Skylitzes, Basil's triumphal entry into Constantinople involved his leading Maria, the wife of the Bulgarian ruler John Vladislav, and the daughters of Samuel, all of whom had previously submitted to him.[18] This much is confirmed by a contemporary, albeit geographically distant writer, Yahya of Antioch, and in a later twelfth-century synoptic account by John Zonaras.[19] Therefore, while a number of Bulgarian male captives were without doubt paraded for the cheering crowd in Constantinople, the principal captives were the Tsarina Maria

---

[16] C. Jolivet-Lévy, "L'image du pouvoir dans l'art byzantin à l'époque de la dynastie macédonienne (867–1056)," *Byzantion* 57 (1987), 441–70 at 450. See also R. Cormack, *Writing in gold. Byzantine society and its icons* (London, 1985), 183, with a monochrome reproduction of the illumination, fig. 65. The caption begins: "The frontispiece portrait . . . is one of the most effective images in Byzantine art of the emperor as Christian ruler and soldier. The visual elements are explained in an accompanying poem."

[17] On crowns in general see K. Wessel, "Insignien," in *Reallexikon zur byzantinischen Kunst*, III, 370–498 at 373–97; M. McCormick, "Crowns," *ODB*, I, 554, who notes there were no hereditary Byzantine "crown jewels." Particular crowns do not appear to be handed down, but instead were buried with the emperor, or given to churches as votive offerings.

[18] Skylitzes, 364–5. An interpolation by Michael of Devol adds the information that the procession also included "the rest of the Bulgarians and the Archbishop of the Bulgarians," who was named David.

[19] *Ioannis Zonarae epitome historiarum*, eds. M. Pinder and T. Büttner-Wobst, 3 vols., CSHB (Bonn, 1841–97), III, 566–7; Yahya, PO II, [38–9], 406–7: "All the Bulgarian chieftains came to meet Basil, and brought with them the wife and children of the Bulgarian ruler Aaron." Yahya here confuses John Vladislav with his father, Aaron. See also *Yahyā al-Antakī, Cronache*, tr. Pirone, 284, §13:46–7.

and the daughters of Samuel. We would expect any representation of this victory celebration to include these women. However, those eight figures performing *proskynesis* before Basil in the psalter illumination are all men. Who are these eight men?

The prevailing identification has been Bulgarian chieftains, following a suggestion by J. Ivanov, and this would not contradict the texts here cited. However, it does not match them very closely. Ivanov maintained that the figures are wearing specifically Bulgarian ethnic costume, and drew a comparison with miniatures in the fourteenth-century illustrated Chronicle of Manasses.[20] However, as Cutler notes, this comparison is not valid. The prostrate figures do not wear the same "distinctive pointed fur hats and frogged jackets."[21] Nor, more significantly, do they resemble the Bulgarians in ethnic dress portrayed in Basil's *menologion*.[22] Arguments about their wearing earrings are also inconclusive since Bulgarians were not the only ethnic group to wear such jewelry. We know that earrings were popular with the Rus', and Leo the Deacon provides a fine description of Sviatoslav, a prince of the Kievan Rus', sporting one. He is shown wearing one in subsequent miniatures.[23] However, the prostrate figures are probably not Rus' either (nor members of Basil's famous "Varangian" Guard). As Cutler has argued, following Schramm, it is possible that these figures are Byzantine citizens.[24] More particularly, the scene "could conceivably represent the gratitude of Byzantine citizens liberated in the exchange of prisoners that accompanied the ten-year truce" with the Fatimid Caliphate in 1000–1.[25] This would not contradict the poem which does not call these figures enemies. However, the poem does imply quite clearly that these figures have been thrown down before Basil as a result of his divinely inspired victories, and that would lead one to believe that the prostrate figures represent a range of those brought to heel in the first decades of Basil's reign. This

---

[20] J. Ivanov, "Le costume des anciens Bulgares," in *L'art byzantin chez les Slaves, II: Les Balkans* (Paris, 1930), 325–33. See I. Dujčev, *Minijaturite na Manasjevata Letopis* (Sofia, 1962). These figures seem to fit Gregory Antiochos' description of the pointed felt hats sported by Bulgarians in the later twelfth century. See J. Darrouzès, "Deux lettres de Grégoire Antiochos écrites de Bulgarie vers 1173," I, *BSl* 23 (1963), 276–84; II, *BSl* 24 (1963), 65–86.

[21] Cutler, "Psalter," 10.

[22] *Il menologio di Basilio II (Cod. Vaticano Greco 1613)* (Turin, 1907), 345, for the scene depicting the martyrdom of Saints Manuel, George and Leontos by the Bulgarians.

[23] *Leonis Diaconi Caloensis historiae libri decem*, ed. C. B. Hase, CSHB (Bonn, 1828), 156–7. See I. Ševčenko, "Sviatoslav in Byzantine and Slavic miniatures," *Slavic Review* 24 (1965), 709–13.

[24] P. E. Schramm, "Das Herrscherbild in der Kunst der frühen Mittelalters," *Vorträge der Bibliothek Warburg*, ed. F. Saxl, III. Vorträge 1922–3 (Leipzig and Berlin, 1924), I, 145–224 at 171. The image is modeled on a well-known prototype, for which see Cutler, "Psalter," 11, who notes parallels with the cameo of Constantius now in the Hermitage.

[25] Cutler, "Psalter," 11.

Figure 6　A bronze *follis* of Theophilos, depicted wearing the *toupha* or *tiara*. Photo: Paul Stephenson.

included his own subjects, since Basil had fought and won a war against the Anatolian magnate families led by the Phokades and Skleroi. We should also remember that *proskynesis* was not an act performed only by defeated enemies – although it certainly was performed by them – but was also the formal act of adoration performed by the Roman emperor's own subjects since the age of the Severi.[26] It is a commonplace in Byzantine art, and therefore its representation here cannot be considered as evidence for Basil's triumph over the Bulgarians.[27]

A further indication that the scene does not specifically represent Basil's celebrations after victory over the Bulgarians is the absence of any representation of the *tiara* (τιάρα) or *toupha* (τοῦφα), the appropriate headgear at this time for an emperor celebrating a victory.[28] We can see a stunning representation of this crested crown on the Bamberger Gunthertuch, to which we will turn shortly. A common representation of the *toupha* can be seen, albeit highly stylized, on the bronze *follis* of Theophilos (829–47), issued shortly after his triumphal return from Kilikia in 831. Theophilos, Constantine VII Porphyrogennetos wrote, was crowned with a *tiara*, otherwise known as the *toupha* (the text states τιάραν, a *scholion* supplies τοῦφαν), in a pavilion erected outside the city walls, from which he rode out on a white horse to enter the city through the Golden Gate. Having

---

[26] For example, I. Spatharakis, "The proskynesis in Byzantine art. A study in connection with a nomisma of Andronicus II Palaeologue," in his *Studies in Byzantine manuscript illumination and iconography*, 193–224 at 196: "The relief on the base of the obelisk of emperor Theodosius I (379–395), in the Hippodrome in Constantinople, shows defeated barbarians in *proskynesis*." The relief dates from 391–2.

[27] *Pace* Spatharakis, "Proskynesis," 207–8, who follows Der Nersessian, and indicates that such an interpretation is based on "historical evidence" and the fact that Basil is shown with a gray beard. The text accompanies a dark gray reproduction of the psalter illumination (p. 209).

[28] See in general A. Kazhdan, "Toupha," *ODB*, III, 2100.

Figure 7   Renaissance drawing of the statue of Justinian which stood in the Augusteion, Constantinople. Seraglio manuscript, now in Budapest University Library, MS 35, fol. 144v. Reproduced from C. Mango, *Studies on Constantinople* (Aldershot, 1993).

Figure 8   Ivory Casket, Constantinople 10th or 11th century, depicting an imperial triumphal entry into Constantinople (lid) and metaphorical hunting scene (front panel). The hunter flexing his bow wears the *toupha* or *tiara*. Trésor de la Cathédrale de Troyes, Troyes, France. Reproduced from H. C. Evans and W. D. Wixom, eds., *The glory of Byzantium: art and culture in the middle Byzantine era, A.D. 843–1261* (New York, 1997).

entered the gate the emperor was presented by the eparch of the city with a further golden crown (χρυσοῦν στέφανον) studded with precious stones and pearls which he wore on his right arm.[29] An equally curt description of the *toupha* is offered by Constantine of Rhodes, who wrote in the middle of the tenth century of a "golden crown with a strange crest."[30] A fuller description is offered by the twelfth-century author John Tzetzes, who recounts "The *tiara* was a Persian headdress. Later, our emperors, in their victories, placed on their heads the *tiara*, or *toupha* (τύφας), such as the one worn by Justinian's equestrian statue on top of the column [in the

[29] For the triumphal entry see *Constantine Porphyrogenitus. Three military treatises on imperial military expeditions*, ed. and tr. J. F. Haldon, CFHB 28 (Vienna, 1990), 146–51. For the coins, see P. Grierson, *Catalogue of Byzantine coins in the Dumbarton Oaks collection, III: Leo III to Nicephorus III, 717–1081* (Washington, DC, 1973), I, 128, 129–30; pl. xiv–xvi. Cf. Hunger, "Reditus Imperatoris," 24–5. Also, see below at note 54.

[30] E. Legrand, "Description des oeuvres d'art et de l'Eglise des Saints Apôtres à Constantinople par Constantin le Rhodien," *REG* 9 (1896), 36–65 at 37. See now P. Speck, "Konstantinos von Rhodos. Zweck und Datum der Ekphrasis der sieben Wunder von Konstantinopel und der Apostelkirche," *Varia 3*, Poikila Byzantina 11 (Bonn, 1991), 249–61.

Augusteion]."[31] The first description of this statue was provided by Procopius, and it was still in the Augusteion in the eighth century, although the subject was then not so widely known.[32] This statue of Justinian is the subject of a Renaissance drawing discovered in the Seraglio Library in Istanbul in 1864, which was transferred to Budapest in 1877.[33] As C. Mango has pointed out, the drawing also corresponds to the verbose description, contained in an *ekphrasis* on the Augusteion, offered by Pachymeres in the late thirteenth century.[34] Justinian also sports the plumed helmet on both faces of a gold medallion discovered in Kappadokian Caesarea in 1751. It was stolen in 1831 from the Cabinet des Médailles of the Bibliothèque Nationale in Paris and subsequently destroyed, but a cast of it has been preserved in the British Museum.[35]

A mounted hunter wearing a crested helmet can be seen on the front panel of the ivory casket of emperors and hunters, housed in Troyes Cathedral.[36] This piece, which has been dated to both the mid-tenth and later eleventh centuries, bears closer examination since, on its lid, it boasts a rare illustration of an imperial triumph. Here two mounted emperors, probably representing senior and junior co-rulers, carry spears and wear *stemmata*. The senior emperor, on the right-hand side and facing forwards (the junior emperor, on the left, is in semi-profile), is offered a victor's crown by a

---

[31] *Ioannis Tzetzae historiae*, ed. P. Leone (Naples, 1968), 310; an English translation is provided by C. Mango, in a letter to the editor, *ArtB* 41 (1959), 351–6; repr. as "Justinian's equestrian statue," in his *Studies in Constantinople* (Aldershot, 1993) no. XI, with new pagination.

[32] Procopius, *Aed*, 1.2.1; *Procopius IV. De aedificiis libri IV*, ed. J. Haury (Leipzig, 1964), 15–16. For commentary see G. Prinzing, "Das Bild Justinians I," *Fontes Minores* 7, ed. D. Simon (Frankfurt am Main, 1986), 1–99; C. Mango, "The columns of Justinian and his successors," in *Studies in Constantinople*, no. X, 1–20; J. W. Barker, *Justinian and the later Roman empire* (Madison, WI, 1966), 290–2. For the eighth-century situation, see *Constantinople in the eighth century. Parasteseis Syntomai Chronikai*, eds. and tr. A. Cameron and J. Herrin (Leiden, 1984), 148–9, 262–3. The *toupha* is visible, its plume picked out in red, in a twelfth-century miniature of Constantinople (Cod. Vat. gr. 751, fol. 26r.) which depicts Justinian's column. See S. Papadaki-Oekland, "The representation of Justinian's column in a Byzantine miniature of the twelfth century," *BZ* 83 (1990), 63–71, esp. 68.

[33] However, as Mango notes, the form of the *toupha* may have changed somewhat during the reign of Theophilos, at least on the statue, after it fell down. It was restored and replaced by a bold steeplejack who scaled the 100-foot column.

[34] George Pachymeres, "Ekphrasis on the Augusteion," in L. Schopen, ed., *Nicephori Gregorae byzantina historia*, CSHB (Bonn, 1830), II, 1217–20 at 1219–20. An English translation is offered at Mango, "Justinian's equestrian statue," 3 [= Letter, 351]. A fuller version may be found at C. Mango, *The art of the Byzantine empire* (Englewood Cliffs, NJ, 1972), 112–13.

[35] W. Wroth, *Catalogue of imperial Byzantine coins in the British Museum*, I (London, 1908; repr. Chicago, 1966), 25; C. Morrisson, *Catalogue des monnaies byzantines de la Bibliothèque Nationale, I. 491–711* (Paris, 1970), 58, 69, pl. VIII (1); Barker, *Justinian*, 286–7, and illustration I. Less lavish plumage can be seen on a number of Justinian's coins.

[36] Evans and Wixom, eds., *The glory of Byzantium*, 204–5, for illustrations and literature.

woman emerging from the gate of the city. The woman, wearing a mural crown, is *tyche*, a personification of the city, Constantinople. The victor's crown appears to be a *stemma*. Thus it is the same type of crown offered to Basil II by Archangel Gabriel. However, the representation of the *toupha* on the front panel is suggestive, and it has been established that the hunt is a metaphorical representation of the imperial campaign which preceded the triumphal entry.[37]

The scene on the lid of the casket fits generally, although not in detail, with the description of the triumphal entry of 879 by Basil I and his son Constantine following victory in Tephrike and Germanikeia, written by Constantine VII Porphyrogennetos.[38] Like Theophilos, Basil I and Constantine entered the Golden Gate mounted on white horses. Basil appears not to have worn a *toupha*, but instead a "Kaisar's diadem" (διάδημα καισαρίκιν); Constantine wore a turban with a likeness on his forehead of a gold-embroidered crown.[39] Basil received a golden crown (στέφανον χρυσοῦν) from the eparch, as well as laurel wreaths.[40] Both emperors crossed the Forum "wearing crowns" (στεφέντες).[41]

---

[37] H. Maguire, "Imperial gardens and the rhetoric of renewal," in P. Magdalino, ed., *New Constantines. The rhythm of imperial renewal in Byzantium, 4th to 13th centuries* (Aldershot, 1994), 181–98 at 193–8; M. Restle, "Hofkunst und höfische Kunst Konstantinopels in der mittelbyzantinischen Zeit", in R. Laurer and H. G. Majer, eds., *Höfische Kultur in Südosteuropa. Bericht der Kolloquien der Südosteuropa-Kommission 1988 bis 1990* (Göttingen, 1994), 25–41 at 35–7.

[38] *Three military treatises*, ed. Haldon, 140–7: "The victorious return of the Christ-loving emperor Basil from campaign in the regions of Tephrike and Germanikeia." This would appear to support a date in the mid-tenth century for the casket. However, the casket lid may better be treated as a general, rather than a particular illustration of an imperial entry.

[39] *Three military treatises*, ed. Haldon, 142, line 752. A *scholion* explains that the tunic the emperor wore (not the Kaisar's diadem, as may appear from the sentence structure) was called "rose-cluster." During Theophilos' entry (148, line 838) "rose-cluster" (ῥοδόβοτρυν) is also used to describe the "gold-embroidered breastplate-style tunic."

[40] *Three military treatises*, ed. Haldon, 143, offers the translation: "[The eparch and the emperor's representative] presented to the emperor a golden crown, after the old custom, along with other crowns of laurel, as symbols of victory." It is clear, however, that the "old custom" does not refer solely to the presentation of a golden crown, but also to the laurel wreaths. See pp. 138–9 for the standardized account of a fifth- or sixth-century imperial entry, and particularly the entry by Justinian I (11 August 559) who was received without crowns.

[41] *Three military treatises*, ed. Haldon, 144, line 784. The description in the *Vita Basilii* of Basil I's celebrations in 879 refers to his coronation with the "crown of victory" (νίκης στεφάνῳ). See *Theophanes continuatus, Ioannes Caminiata, Symeon Magister, Georgius Monachus continuatus*, ed. I. Bekker, CSHB (Bonn, 1825), 271. Cf. *Genesios on the reigns of the emperors*, tr. A. Kaldellis, Byzantina Australiensia 11 (Canberra, 1998), 100, n. 450, where it is suggested that Basil I had particular reasons for wishing to be crowned once more. Several crowns may be worn during the course of a single ceremony, for which see Constantine Porphyrogenitus, *De Cerimoniis*, book 1, ch. 37, which records the use of white, red, green and blue *stemmata* for portions of particular processions to and from Hagia Sophia. *Constantini Porphyrogeniti De Cerimoniis Aulae Byzantinae*, ed. J. Reiske, CSHB, 2 vols. (Bonn, 1829), I, 187–91. M. McCormick, "Crowns," *ODB*, I, 554, suggests this means visible colored cloth (presumably silk) linings. See also McCormick, *Eternal victory*, 156–7.

The differences between Theophilos' and Basil I's triumphal entries are, therefore, quite marked with regard to use of headgear. If he had access to his grandfather's treatise on expeditions, and the composition of the only surviving manuscript (Cod. Lip. Rep. I 17) in the imperial scriptorium between 963 and 969 under the supervision of Basil the *parakoimomenos* strongly suggests that he did, Basil II appears to have followed Theophilos' example.[42] In fact, he is more likely to have had in mind the example of John I Tzimiskes, who, as we shall shortly see, had in 971 celebrated a victory over the Bulgarians with a triumphal entry involving a *toupha*.

So, we have here evidence that the same headgear, the *toupha*, was adopted from a Persian model and worn by East Roman emperors in triumphal celebrations from at least the time of Justinian to the time of Tzetzes, although it was probably not in continuous use. Moreover, a prototype was there for all to see throughout the period on the equestrian statue of Justinian in the Augusteion. According to both Skylitzes and Zonaras, Basil did indeed wear a "crested golden crown" during his triumphal entry into Constantinople through the Golden Gate.[43] Yet, in Basil II's psalter illumination, Basil does not wear, nor is he offered, the *toupha*. Indeed, we should remember that the associated poem specifically states that his *stemma* is the symbol of rulership, and the spear he is handed by Archangel Michael represents victories.[44]

Relating the portrait and poem to other features of the psalter, it is clear that Basil's qualities as a ruler, if not his particular exploits, are to be compared with those of King David. The portrait illumination (fol. IIIr) is juxtaposed with a composite illustration of David's actions in six panels (fol. 4v). Thus the scenes of David killing the bear and lion may be intended to remind Basil of his own victory over "barbarians" who are often compared in panegyrical literature to wild beasts. (One is reminded of the hunt scene of the Troyes Casket.) However, Basil is also reminded of his own humility, as David prays for forgiveness for his adultery. Basil was unmarried and notoriously celibate.[45] The David scenes, therefore, represent general virtues appropriate to a ruler, and need not be considered

---

[42] On the date of composition of the Leipzig Codex, which alone contains the longer treatise of expeditions (C), see *Three military treatises*, ed. Haldon, 37, 53, 54–61.

[43] Skylitzes, 364, lines 89–365, line 90: "χρυσῷ στεφάνῳ λόφον ἐφύπερθεν ἔχοντι"; Zonaras, 566, lines 15–16: "τιάρᾳ ταινιωθεὶς ὀρθίᾳ (ἣν τοῦφαν ...)".

[44] Jolivet-Lévy, "L'image du pouvoir," 450.

[45] Although Basil was as notoriously profligate in his youth, so the David scenes may allude back to this period. If so, they need not allude back so far if produced c. 1000. But this is to argue both sides. For one explanation for Basil's celibacy see Arbagi, M., "The celibacy of Basil II," *ByzSt* 2 (1975), 41–5.

as illustrative of particular episodes in Basil's reign.[46] That is also the case with the portrait illumination. While it cannot be doubted that this image represents Basil as a warrior emperor, and the associated poem credits the martyrs with bringing him victories, it is a general portrait which cannot be associated with any certainty to a specific episode, and therefore cannot be interpreted as illustrating the celebrations to mark Basil's victory over the Bulgarians.[47]

The Gunthertuch, a Byzantine silk now housed in the treasury of Bamberg Cathedral, was discovered, during restoration work on 22 December 1830, in the grave of Gunther, Bishop of Bamberg (1057–65).[48] Bishop Gunther had acquired the silk in Constantinople during the great pilgrimage of 1064–5, on which he died (23 July 1065). He may have worn it during his trek through Palestine, where he attracted the attention of robbers because of his ostentatious display of wealth.[49] The silk shows an emperor wearing the *stemma* and carrying the *labarum*, mounted on a white horse. He is flanked by two women wearing walled crowns: these are clearly *tychai* who personify cities. The *tychai* have bare feet, since they, and the citizens they represent, are the emperor's *douloi*. They wear ankle-length

---

[46] H. Maguire, "Images of the court," in Evans and Wixom, eds., *The glory of Byzantium*, 182–91 at 188; N. P. Ševčenko, "Illuminating the liturgy: illustrated service books in Byzantium," in L. Safran, ed., *Heaven on earth. Art and the Church in Byzantium* (University Park, PA, 1998), 186–228 at 201, 203–4. For further comments on the model provided by David, see Jolivet-Lévy, "L'image du pouvoir," 460–2; Wessel, "David" (see n. 13), and "Kaiserbild," *Reallexikon zur byzantinischen Kunst*, III, 722–853 at 758–60.

[47] Jolivet-Lévy, "L'image du pouvoir," 469: "Qu'il s'agisse de portraits officiels ou d'iconographie ty-pologique, l'image du pouvoir reste dans l'ensemble conventionelle et «universelle», dans la mesure où elle ne se réfère que rarement à des circonstances historiques particulières ... Ce n'est que plus tard, à partir du XIIe siècle, que commence à se manifester un certain intérêt pour la représentation d'événements historiques précis." *Pace* Spatharakis, "Three portraits of the early Comnenian pe-riod,"18, who maintains that "Any military successes [the emperor] might score would be the result of divine help and on such occasions he is again shown receiving the victor's diadem from Christ or another representative of God." The two examples he cites (above at n. 10) are the aforementioned portrait of Basil I and the psalter portrait considered here. Both, as we have seen, can be shown not to relate to a particular victory. On the ubiquity of the "symbolic coronation of the [Macedonian] em-peror by Christ or a delegated figure (Virgin, angel or saint)," see Jolivet-Lévy, "L'image du pouvoir," 445–52. On coronation by an angel, see Wessel, "Kaiserbild," 751–2. On twelfth-century imperial portraits illustrating specific episodes, see P. Magdalino and R. Nelson, "The emperor in Byzan-tine art of the twelfth century," *ByzF* 8 (1982), 123–83, esp. 158–9, 169–77. However, Magdalino and Nelson emphasize continuity as well as innovation, and, while noting Cutler's intervention, appear to accept Grabar's conclusions on the psalter portrait (p. 158), and also the Gunthertuch (p. 155).

[48] S. Müller-Christensen, *Das Guntertuch im Bamberger Domschatz* (Bamberg, 1984), 6. See also S. Müller-Christensen, "Beobachtungen zum Bamberger Gunthertuch," *Münchner Jahrbuch der bildenden Kunst*, n.f. 17 (1966), 9–16.

[49] J. Riley-Smith, *The first crusaders, 1095–1131* (Cambridge, 1997), 39.

transparent gowns, over which are worn opaque colored tunics in blue (left) and green (right). The colors of their tunics are all that distinguish the *tychai*, who are mirror images of each other, except for the tokens they offer the emperor: she on the right offers what appears to be a *stemma* (this part of the silk is badly damaged), and she on the left a crested crown, a *tiara* or *toupha*.[50] The classic interpretation of the silk, its production and meaning, like that of Basil's psalter illumination, was provided by A. Grabar, who maintained that it, like the illumination, should be associated with Basil II's celebrations following his victory in Bulgaria.[51] Until recently this attribution seemed certain.[52] However, in 1993 G. Prinzing advanced a compelling alternative: he associated the production of the Gunthertuch with the victory celebrations held to mark John Tzimiskes' victory over the Rus' and Bulgarians in 971.[53]

Upon his re-entry into the city, the emperor Tzimiskes enjoyed splendid triumphal victory celebrations. Leo the Deacon and Skylitzes provide interlocking, if contradictory, accounts of the celebrations, and provide the crux of Prinzing's argument.[54] According to Leo, Tzimiskes rode a white horse behind a wagon containing an icon of the Virgin and the Bulgarian imperial regalia, in particular two crowns. Behind the emperor rode Boris, the deposed Bulgarian tsar.[55] Upon reaching the Forum of Constantine, the emperor was acclaimed before Boris was symbolically divested of his imperial regalia.[56] Then the procession moved on to Hagia Sophia where

[50] Far fuller and better descriptions of the Gunthertuch are provided by Grabar and Prinzing, cited below. See also the excellent photos in R. Baumstark, ed., *Rom und Byzanz. Schatzkammerstücke aus bayerischen Sammlungen* (Munich, 1998), 206–10.

[51] A. Grabar, "La soie byzantine de l'évêque Gunther à la cathédrale de Bamberg," *L'art de la fin de l'antiquité et du Moyen Age* (Paris, 1968), I, 213–27; repr. with new pagination from *Münchner Jahrbuch der bildenden Kunst*, n.f. 8 (1956). Grabar (p. 227) considered Basil's use of the *toupha* to be unique.

[52] See, for example, Jolivet-Lévy, "L'image du pouvoir," 456. The identification of Basil was contested by H. Wentzel, "Das byzantinische Erbe der ottonischen Kaiser. Hypothesen über den Brautschatz der Theophano," *Aachener Kunstblätter des Museumsvereins* 43 (1972), 11–96.

[53] G. Prinzing, "Das Bamberger Gunthertuch in neuer Sicht," *BSl* 54 (1993), 218–31.

[54] Leo the Deacon, 158–9; Skylitzes, 310; Hunger, "Reditus Imperatoris," 29. A short poem by John Geometres may also have marked this occasion: PG 106, 922–3: "On the imperial crowns on the arm of the emperor John: Your right hand, my Christ, has routed the enemy. Your right hand [Emperor John] is crowned by Christ, all offer you thanks for your victories." See above (n. 29) for the practice of crowning the right arm.

[55] The scene is depicted in the Madrid Skylitzes, fol. 172v (a). See S. Cirac Estopañan, *Skyllitzes Matritensis, I. Reproducciones et minituras* (Barcelona and Madrid, 1965), 174, 374, fig. 450; O. Grabar and M. Manoussacas, *L'illustration du manuscrit de Skylitzès de la Bibliothèque Nationale de Madrid* (Venice, 1979), plate 34 and fig. 221. Notably, no image of Basil's triumphal entry is included: folios 186v to 195, where it would have been, are not illustrated.

[56] Skylitzes, 310; Leo the Deacon, 158, omits this episode and appears to imply that the highly symbolic divestiture took place in the palace. This seems less likely. For further comment see McCormick, *Eternal victory*, 174.

Boris' imperial crown was given to God, and the former tsar was given the Byzantine rank of *magistros*.[57] Thus, his authority and the symbols of it were absorbed within the imperial hierarchy, and the independent realm of Bulgaria was absorbed into the Byzantine *oikoumene*. Although several details in Leo the Deacon's account are ignored or contradicted by Skylitzes, three points are certain. First, John Tzimiskes rode a white horse during the procession. Second, the Bulgarian imperial regalia played a central role in the triumphal ceremony, and this contained two crowns. Third, both authors explicitly state that the second crown was a *tiara*, which as we have already seen is identical with the *toupha*. The Gunthertuch shows a triumphant emperor sitting astride a white horse being handed two crowns: one (mostly lost) a *stemma*, the other a *tiara* or *toupha*.

A further subject of considerable importance is the identity of the two *tychai*, that is the identity of the cities they personify, who are shown handing the emperor the two crowns. Schramm, and afterwards Déer, saw the *tychai* as personifying the Old and New Romes.[58] Grabar argued for the personification of Constantinople and Athens, where Basil II celebrated his two triumphs; a solution which need no longer detain us.[59] Prinzing suggested that both *tychai* represent only Constantinople, and more particularly the two political factions, the Blues and the Greens, who would have acclaimed the victorious emperor, Tzimiskes, upon his entry into the city.[60] It is indeed striking that the two *tychai* are identical, and wear similar robes, one blue and the other green. Still, Prinzing invites further comment, and it strikes me that we can find an additional solution to the identification of the two *tychai* in the accounts of Tzimiskes' Bulgarian campaigns offered by Leo the Deacon and Skylitzes. The figures may represent the two principal Bulgarian strongholds, Preslav and Dristra, the capture of which ensured Tzimiskes' victory over the Rus' and annexation of Bulgaria. Preslav was the capital of the Bulgarian realm, where dwelt the Bulgarian tsar. However, the fate of Bulgaria lay with Dristra, where the Rus' under Sviatoslav had established control, and Tzimiskes therefore laid a siege. Leo the Deacon and Skylitzes provide detailed accounts of the fight for Dristra, which show remarkable similarities.[61] It seems that both authors have drawn from a

---

[57] Prinzing, "Bamberger Gunthertuch," 230, has suggested that the silk itself may have been hung in Hagia Sophia at this time, and was still there when Bishop Gunther visited in 1064–5.

[58] Schramm, "Das Herrscherbild," 159–61; J. Déer, *Die heilige Krone Ungarns* (Vienna, 1966), 59.

[59] Grabar, "La soie byzantine de l'évêque Gunther," 227.

[60] Prinzing, "Bamberger Gunthertuch," 228–9. For the role played by the demes in the triumphal entries by Theophilos and Basil I, see *Three military treatises*, ed. Haldon, 142–5, 148–9, 279–80. Cf. McCormick, *Eternal victory*, 204–5.

[61] S. McGrath "The battles of Dorostolon (971): rhetoric and reality," in *Peace and war in Byzantium. Essays in honor of George T. Dennis, S. J.*, eds. T. S. Miller and J. Nesbitt (Washington, DC, 1995), 152–64, provides an intelligent commentary on the two passages.

common source, perhaps an official account of the episode which was produced for Tzimiskes on his triumphant return to Constantinople. Leo, writing shortly after the events he describes, places greater emphasis on Tzimiskes' abilities as a general, recounting how he rallied his troops after the heroic death of a certain Anemas, and personally led a renewed assault on the Rus'.[62] Skylitzes omits the emperor's final charge, but emulates Leo in recounting how suddenly a wind storm, divinely inspired, heralded the appearance of St. Theodore the Stratelate mounted on a white steed. This *deus ex machina* signals the defeat of the Rus', and brings an end to the narrative for both Leo and Skylitzes. The appearance of the martyr, and consequent victory, confirmed the legitimacy of Tzimiskes' protracted campaign in Bulgaria, and was seen to absolve him for his role in the murder of his predecessor, the emperor Nikephoros Phokas. God was on Tzimiskes' side.

To mark his victory Tzimiskes revived the Roman practice of renaming cities: Preslav was renamed Ioannoupolis, after the emperor himself. Lead seals discovered during excavations in Preslav prove that the city thus renamed was placed under the command of Katakalon *protospatharios* and *strategos*.[63] Furthermore, a second city was renamed Theodoroupolis, and we have the seal of a certain Sisinios who was appointed as *strategos*.[64] The identification of Theodoroupolis has been debated, but given the location of the miracle it seems likely that we can trust Leo the Deacon, who states plainly that it was Dristra.[65] The act of renaming cities confirms that Tzimiskes had determined to use his victory to maximum political advantage in Constantinople. His victory in Bulgaria, and in particular the divine intervention, confirmed his legitimacy. It is possible that the *tychai* in the silk, produced to mark this victory, also personified the two principal cities captured and renamed during the victorious campaign: Preslav-Ioannoupolis, and Dristra-Theodoroupolis. This is merely possible, but it is now all but certain that the Gunthertuch was produced to mark Tzimiskes', and not Basil II's, triumphal entry into Constantinople following victory in Bulgaria.

---

[62] Leo the Deacon, 153–4; McGrath, "The battles of Dorostolon," 161–2.
[63] I. Iordanov, *Pechatite ot strategiiata v Preslav (971–1088)* (Sofia, 1993), 134–5.
[64] Iordanov, *Pechatite*, 124–5.
[65] Leo the Deacon, 158; I. Hutter, "Theodorupolis," in *ΑΕΤΟΣ. Studies in honour of Cyril Mango*, ed. I. Ševčenko et al. (Stuttgart and Leipzig, 1998), 181–90.

5

Basil the younger, porphyrogennetos

If Basil were known generally as the Bulgar-slayer after his victory in Bulgaria we might expect him to have been called this by contemporary writers. He was not, as Du Cange was aware in 1680.[1] In Basil's psalter portrait, as we have seen, he is styled ὁ νέος, literally "the young" but used relatively as "the later," "the second," or "the younger," to distinguish him from his grandfather's grandfather, Basil I. In this context Basil II might also be called πορφυρογέννητος, "born in the purple" chamber of the imperial palace, and therefore to a reigning emperor, which Basil I was not. Thus, in the dedicatory epigram of his *menologion*, Basil is "Sun of the purple, reared in the purple robes."[2] *Neos* and *porphyrogennetos* were Basil II's preferred epithets, and were used in his official documents. In the titular rubrics of two extant pieces of legislation, novels, issued in 988 and 996, Basil is styled both *neos* and *porphyrogennetos*. That is, in variant readings of the rubrics preserved in manuscripts of both novels, Basil is called either *neos* or *porphyrogennetos*, or, in one instance, both. It is possible that the novel dated to 988 is a forgery from the reign of Isaak I Komnenos (1057–9), and in that event it is of additional interest that the forger did not yet call the emperor *Voulgaroktonos*.[3]

Very little literature has survived from Basil's reign, and even less makes mention of the emperor. This may fairly be attributed to Basil's lack of interest in hearing himself praised, and an unwillingness to encourage or

---

[1] C. Du Cange, *Historia Byzantina duplici commentario illustrata*, 2 vols. [in one]: I, *Familias ac stemmata imperatorum Constantinopolitanorum* (Paris, 1680), 144, cites only Niketas Choniates' use of the cognomen, which as we will see below was the earliest.

[2] I. Ševčenko, "The illuminators of the menologium of Basil II," *DOP* 16 (1962), 272.

[3] N. Svoronos, ed., *Les nouvelles des empereurs macédoniens concernant la terre et les stratiotes* (Athens, 1994), 185–217, esp. 188, 199. English translations, although not of all variants of the rubrics, are provided by E. McGeer, *The land legislation of the Macedonian emperors* (Toronto, 2000), 109–32. G. Schlumberger, *L'épopée byzantine à la fin du dixième siècle, I. Jean Tzimiscès; les jeunes années de Basile II, le tueur de Bulgares (969–989)* (Paris, 1896), 727–8, offers a French translation of the novel of 988, which is taken to be genuine.

to sponsor court oratory.[4] Two eye-witnesses to Basil's early campaigns against the Bulgarians of course did not yet call Basil *Voulgaroktonos*. Leo the Deacon, who wrote of the ill-fated Balkan campaign of 986 in which he participated, and also is attributed with an *enkomion* in praise of Basil, called the emperor simply *autokrator*.[5] Leo's contemporary, the court poet John Kyriotes, known as Geometres, wrote both of defeats and of victories for the Romans against the Bulgarians, but treated Basil as a pale imitation of his hero, Nikephoros Phokas. Geometres had been banished from court in 985–6, as a follower of Basil the *parakoimomenos*, so we can understand his hostility. His sentiments were shared by John of Melitene, also a supporter of the Phokades. Both wished to summon Phokas from his grave to remedy the troubles in the western half of the empire.[6]

We may better search for the Bulgar-slayer in extant work of literature produced in the century and a half after 1025. The *Life of St. Nikon*, a text written c. 1050 in southern Greece, alludes to the emperor's activities as a general in a Balkan arena, but on no occasion does it refer to Basil as the Bulgar-slayer.[7] Nor is he called this in the *Life of St. Achilleios*, nor in the *Life of St. Mary the Younger*, where he appears as the *porphyrogennetos*.[8] Indeed, Basil is rarely mentioned at all in contemporary works of hagiography. For example, he is not mentioned in the *Life of St. Luke the Stylite*, who lived and died near Constantinople during Basil's reign, and had earlier fought against the Bulgarians.[9] The situation, as one would expect, is different in historiography, but still Basil is nowhere called Bulgar-slayer.

---

[4] M. Lauxtermann, "Byzantine poetry and the paradox of Basil II's reign," in P. Magdalino, ed., *Byzantium in the year 1000* (Leiden, 2003), 199–216 at 207, 216.

[5] *Leonis Diaconi Caloensis historiae libri decem*, ed. C. B. Hase, CSHB (Bonn, 1828), 171–3; I. Sykoutres, "Leontos tou diaconou anekdoton enkomion eis Vasileion ton II," *EEBS* 10 (1933), 425–34 at 426. This is one of only two known poems which praise Basil. The second encomium, by John Sikeliotes, also dates from his early years and is lost. For the deafening silence, which is attributed to Basil's lack of interest in hearing himself praised, see Lauxtermann, "Byzantine poetry and the paradox of Basil II's reign," 199–216, esp. 214–16.

[6] PG 106, 919–20, 934. See also K. Argoe, "John Kyriotes Geometres, a tenth century Byzantine writer," Ph.D. thesis, University of Wisconsin (Madison, 1938), 81–3, 87, 89.

[7] *The life of St. Nikon*, ed. and tr. D. F. Sullivan (Brookline, 1987), 2–7. For further comments on the date of composition, see R. Jenkins and C. Mango, "A synodicon of Antioch and Lacedaemonia," *DOP* 15 (1961), 225–42 at 240, who suggest c. 1050, and certainly before 1057. None of the strident criticisms leveled at Sullivan's edition by J. O. Rosenqvist, "The text of the Life of St. Nikon 'Metanoeite' reconsidered," in *ΛΕΙΜΩΝ. Studies presented to Lennart Rydén on his sixty-fifth birthday*, ed. J. O. Rosenqvist (Uppsala, 1996), 93–111, directly concerns passages dealing with Basil and Samuel.

[8] "Life of St. Mary the Younger," tr. A. Laiou, in *Holy women of Byzantium*, ed. A.-M. Talbot (Washington, DC, 1996), 239–89 at 255. Laiou suggests that this *vita* was composed towards the middle of the eleventh century.

[9] *Vie de Saint Luc le Stylite (879–979)*, ed. F. Vanderstuyf, Patrologia Orientalis 11 (Paris, 1915), 145–299; H. Delehaye, *Les saints stylites*, Studia hagiographica 14 (Paris, 1923), lxxxvi–cv, 195–237.

Michael Psellos' account of Basil's reign was composed within thirty years of the emperor's death. While military matters do not feature in Psellos' account – he fails entirely to mention Basil's Bulgarian campaigns, and notes only in passing that Basil had conquered Bulgaria during an account of a rebellion there in 1040[10] – he would surely have called Basil by the name most familiar to his contemporaries. Where Psellos needs to distinguish Basil II from other Basils, whether in his *Chronographia* or his many orations, he does not use the cognomen *Voulgaroktonos*, but instead makes reference to Basil's lineage or birth, for example calling him the son of Romanos II, or *porphyrogennetos*.[11] Historians with a more traditional interest in military matters also fail to associate Basil's Bulgarian wars with the use of the cognomen *Voulgaroktonos*. Nikephoros Bryennios and Michael Attaleiates, like Psellos, both refer to Basil as *porphyrogennetos*, as does Anna Komnene writing in the middle of the twelfth century.[12] John Tzetzes, a poet and courtier during the reign of Manuel I Komnenos (1143–80), reminded his contemporaries of the days when "From the Pindos mountains and the area of Larissa, and from Dyrrachion they [the Bulgarians] once held sway almost as far as Constantinople, until the reign of the mighty emperor Basil, who completely subjugated them and made them subservient to the power of the Romans." But Basil was not called the "Slayer of the Bulgars" by John Tzetzes, nor by the twelfth-century historian John Zonaras, who portrays Basil as something of a tyrant with no respect for established law. Finally the verse chronicler Constantine Manasses fails to call Basil the Bulgar-slayer.[13]

Those familiar with two fairly obscure, ostensibly eleventh-century synoptic histories may believe that Basil was swiftly called Bulgar-slayer, since the epithet *Voulgaroktonos* can be found in the published editions of these two texts produced in the late nineteenth century. The two works are the *Chronicon Bruxellense*, and the text known as *Georgius Monachus*

---

[10] *Michel Psellos Chronographie, ou histoire d'un siècle de Byzance (976–1077)*, ed. E. Renauld, 2 vols. (Paris, 1926–8), I, 76.

[11] Despite this, Basil appears as *Voulgaroktonos* in the index, but not the text, of *Michaelis Pselli scripta minora*, eds. E. Kurtz and F. Drexl, 2 vols. (Milan, 1936), I, 160, 485. Cf. *Michel Psellos Chronographie*, II, 115, 130; *Michaeli Pselli poemata*, ed. L. G. Westerink (Stuttgart and Leipzig, 1992), 176; *Michaeli Pselli orationes panegyricae*, ed. G. T. Dennis (Stuttgart and Leipzig, 1994), 21.

[12] *Nicéphore Bryennios histoire*, ed. and tr. P. Gautier, CFHB 9 (Brussels, 1979), 97; *Michaelis Attaliotae historia*, ed. I. Bekker, CSHB (Bonn, 1853), 229; *Annae Comnenae Alexias*, eds. D. Reinsch and A. Kambylis, CFHB 40/1 (Berlin and New York, 2001), 162; *Anne Comnène, Alexiade*, ed. B. Leib, 3 vols. (Paris, 1937–45), II, 33.

[13] *Ioannis Tzetzae historiae*, ed. P. M. Leone (Naples, 1968), 185; *Ioannis Zonarae epitome historiarum*, eds. M. Pinder and T. Büttner-Wobst, 3 vols., CSHB (Bonn, 1841–97), III, 561–4; *Constantini Manasses breviarum chronicum*, ed. O. Lampsidis, CFHB 36 (Athens, 1996), 317–20.

continuatus, or the continuation of the Chronicle of George the Monk, also known as George Hamartolos. The *Chronicon Bruxellense* is preserved in a single manuscript (Cod. Bruxellensis 11376, fol. 155r–165r), which the latest palaeographical research dates to the last years of the thirteenth century.[14] This chronicle comprises three sections composed separately and according to different principles, but transcribed in a single hand. The first part is merely a list of Roman emperors from Gaius Julius Caesar to Constantius Chlorus, the father of Constantine I.[15] The second part comprises an annotated list of emperors who ruled in Constantinople, from Constantine I to the end of the Amorion dynasty in 867. This longest section of the text draws on a number of known sources within the problematic oeuvre of the "Logothete's" chronicle.[16] The third section is a brief list of the Macedonian emperors to Romanos III (d. 1034), including Basil II, to whom it refers as Βασίλειος ὁ νέος ὁ Βουλγαροκτόνος πορφυρογέννητος καὶ τροπαιοῦχος. The full entry runs thus:

Basil the younger, the Bulgar-slayer born in the purple chamber, the victorious, a lover of war and wealth, achieved many triumphs and victories against the Bulgarian people and against many others, reigned together with his brother Constantine for fifty years.[17]

It has been assumed that this chronicle was compiled, and the third part composed in the eleventh century.[18] Why else would it end in 1034? However, the third part of the text may not have been transcribed in full, and later entries may have been omitted. In the same manuscript we find an incomplete version of the synoptic history of Patriarch Nikephoros (fol. 165v–170r), and a version of the synoptic history by Constantine Manasses which is separated from its continuation (fol. 1–155r; fol. 180v–182v).[19] If the third part of the text was transcribed in full, and if it can be dated to the eleventh century – neither being certain – the epithet *Voulgaroktonos*

---

[14] A. Külzer, "Studium zum Chronicon Bruxellense," *Byzantion* 61 (1991), 413–47 at 418. The author of the published edition, F. Cumont, *Anecdota Bruxellensia,* I: *Chroniques byzantines du manuscrit 11376* (Gand, 1894), had suggested a date early in the thirteenth century.

[15] Cumont, *Anecdota Bruxellensia,* 16–18; Külzer, "Studium zum Chronicon Bruxellense," 421. At least the first section of the list of emperors should be compared with those lists which accompanied the *Peri ton taphon ton Vasileon,* examined below.

[16] Cumont, *Anecdota Bruxellensia,* 18–33; Külzer, "Studium zum Chronicon Bruxellense," 422–4.

[17] Cumont, *Anecdota Bruxellensia,* 34; cf. *Fontes Graeci historiae Bulgaricae,* VI, eds. G. Cankova-Petkova, I. Dujčev, L. Jončev, V. Tăpkova-Zaimova and P. Tivčev [= Fontes Historiae Bulgaricae, XI] (Sofia, 1965), 73–6 at 76.

[18] G. Moravcsik, *Byzantinoturcica,* 2 vols., 2nd ed. (Berlin, 1958), I, 233; K. Krumbacher, *Geschichte des byzantinischen Litteratur von Justinian bis zum Ende des oströmischen Reiches (527–1453),* 2 vols. (Munich, 1897), I, 396.

[19] Cumont, *Anecdota Bruxellensia,* 10–12, 36–8.

is almost certainly an interpolation by the late-thirteenth-century scribe. It sits awkwardly between ὁ νέος and πορφυρογέννητος, the pair of epithets which, as we have seen, were generally applied to Basil during his reign and immediately afterwards. The whole entry, indeed whole third part of the chronicle, may have been composed at the time the Brussels manuscript was produced, shortly before 1300, or at any time in the preceding two and a half centuries. Certainly, the inclusion of a second general triumphal epithet, *tropaiouchos*, would suit a later dating, as would the concentration on Basil's Bulgarian victories to the exclusion of all else. We will return to these two themes in the following chapter. For now, however, all we can say with certainty is that, since the *Chronicon Bruxellense* exists in just one version, the text as it stands today was composed before 1300.[20]

The text known as *Georgius Monachus Continuatus* is preserved in four versions in four manuscripts, the earliest of which (Cod. Laurentianus gr. LXX) dates from the eleventh century. This version, however, ends with the death of Romanos I Lekapenos (944), and does not mention Basil at all. The second manuscript (Cod. Mosquensis synod gr. 406 (264/CCLI)), dating from the later twelfth century continues the history to the death of John II Komnenos in 1143. This is the manuscript on which the only current edition, by E. Muralt, is based.[21] Muralt's edition, rapidly incorporated into J. P. Migne's PG, has been described as "a totally chaotic conglomerate which...gives readings from different sources."[22] That is, it incorporates variant readings from two far later manuscripts: the third manuscript (Cod. Marc. gr. 608), of the fifteenth century, which refers to Basil and Constantine as "the brothers born in the purple chamber," but makes no mention of Bulgar-slaying; and the fourth and latest manuscript, of the sixteenth century (Cod. Par. gr. 1708), which described Basil as *Voulgaroktonos*. This is the line which Muralt chose to present as the

---

[20] Külzer, "Studium zum Chronicon Bruxellense," 425: "Da nun das *Chronicon Bruxellense* von einer Hand geschrieben ist, bleibt aber diese Möglichkeit nur für die Vorläge unseres Chronisten bestehen; ob er selbst den Text bis auf Romanos III. fortführte oder aber das Geschichtwerk schon fertig vorgefunden hat, das wird sich mit Sicherheit nie ermitteln lassen."

[21] *Georgii Monachi, dicti Hamartoli chronicon ab orbe condito usque ad annum p. Chr. n. 842 et diversis scriptoribus usque ad a. 1143 continuatum*, ed. E. de Muralto (St. Petersburg, 1859); reproduced in PG 110, col. 41–1261. Excerpts pertaining to Bulgaria are reproduced in the Bulgarian source collection *Fontes Graeci historiae Bulgaricae*, VI, 152–7. This led S. Antoljak, *Srednovekovna Makedonija*, 3 vols. (Skopje, 1985), I, 251; idem., *Samuel and his state* (Skopje, 1985), III, 191, to claim that Basil was called "Bulgaroctonus" in the eleventh century.

[22] S. Wahlgreen, "Symeon the Logothete: some philological remarks," *Byzantion* 71 (2001), 251–62 at 252.

correct reading in his edition, but it is clearly no more than a late interpolation, in keeping with the nature of this and associated texts.[23]

Basil II's Bulgarian campaigns received their fullest coverage during the reign of Alexios I Komnenos (1081–1118), in John Skylitzes' *Synopsis historion*, written certainly after 1079 and probably before 1096. We have used this account extensively in foregoing chapters, and favored it over other interpretations where these are extant. We have also considered Skylitzes' account of the battle of Kleidion, fought in 1014, in some detail and pointed out several possible influences, conscious or unconscious.[24] Furthermore, we should not ignore the possibility that Skylitzes had his own agenda when writing on the Balkans. At the time Skylitzes was composing, Alexios I was engaged in a protracted series of campaigns in the northern Balkans. Alexios confronted both the Normans, who had invaded areas of modern northern Greece and Albania, and the Pechenegs, fierce steppe nomads who had crossed the Danube into modern Romania and Bulgaria. It has recently been suggested that Skylitzes wished to promote aristocratic support for Alexios' Balkan campaigns. Indeed, if Skylitzes wrote his account in order to inspire powerful clans to rally to Alexios' cause, we might better understand the chronicler's copious references to aristocrats – for example his praising the general Nikephoros Xiphias far more highly than Basil himself for the victory at Kleidion – and his use of family names whenever possible. Basil's generals were the ancestors of Alexios' nobles, and the latter might thereby be inspired to emulate the prolonged efforts of their forebears.[25] This was perhaps the first stage in a process which linked the Komnenoi with Basil, a process which saw Basil's reputation revived and revised through the twelfth century. At no stage does Skylitzes call Basil *Voulgaroktonos.*

[23] Wahlgreen, "Symeon the Logothete," 261: ". . . these texts tend to grow, and a lot of things turn up in [later] MSS that we do not find earlier."

[24] Above at pp. 2–6, 26.

[25] It is also clear that many aristocrats might otherwise have felt disinclined to campaign at length in western lands when their estates in the east had been overrun, or were threatened by the Seljuk Turks. See C. J. Holmes, "Basil II and the government of empire (976–1025)," D.Phil. dissertation, University of Oxford (Oxford, 1999), 102–5. Holmes builds on research which has identified in Skylitzes' account of this period traces of secular biographies of Nikephoros Phokas, Eustathios Daphnomeles and Katakalon Kekaumenos: C. Roueché, "Byzantine writers and readers: storytelling in the eleventh century," in R. Beaton, ed., *The Greek novel A.D. 1–1985* (London, 1988), 123–33, 127–8; J. Shepard, "A suspected source of Scylitzes' *Synopsis Historion*: the great Catacalon Cecaumenus," *BMGS* 16 (1992), 171–81. On family names in Skylitzes one may also consult with profit: S. Fatalas-Papadopoulos McGrath, "A study of the social structure of Byzantine aristocracy as seen through Ioannes Skylitzes' *Synopsis Historion*," Ph.D. thesis, Catholic University of America (Washington, DC, 1996), 33–66, and 89–230, which presents a prosopography of the Byzantine aristocracy drawn from Skylitzes.

Besides Skylitzes, Kekaumenos is the only eleventh-century source to refer to Basil's blinding of Bulgarians after the battle of Kleidion. In doing so, he refers not to the Bulgar-slayer, but "the *porphyrogennetos*, Lord Basil the emperor," as he does on almost every occasion he mentions Basil.[26] Kekaumenos, who probably lived in the region where Basil had confronted Samuel and his successors, clearly thought highly of the warrior emperor. This was also true of writers at the opposite end of the empire, composing in languages other than Greek. A brief account of Basil's activities in Bulgaria was composed within a few years of the events described, but from a considerable distance, by Yahya of Antioch, who regards Basil as a staunch general, but not as a slayer. Yahya suggests that Basil's conquest of Bulgaria was not a protracted war of attrition against a centralized Slavic state, but rather a series of negotiated settlements which secured the loyalty of regional and municipal potentates, Slavs and others, and extended Byzantine authority in a piecemeal fashion across the northern Balkans. Thereafter, Bulgaria was to be governed through existing local power structures overseen by Byzantine *strategoi* with broad jurisdictions.[27]

Similar sentiments can be observed in Armenian sources. Asołik, also known as Stephen of Taron, writing at the start of the eleventh century, provides fascinating insights into Basil's actions to both east and west. He was also acquainted with the actions of Samuel and one of his brothers, to whom he attributes Armenian origins, and whom he calls *Komsajagk'n*, "the sons of the Koms." This compound noun incorporates a transliteration of the Greek κόμης and a literal translation of πῶλος (*jag*) linked by the conjoining vocal "*a*", and ends with the plural suffix "*k*" and the article "*n*." While the Kometopouloi are thus identified by their recently acquired name, the emperor Basil sports no such explicatory epithet.[28] Between 1072 and 1079, the Armenian historian, Aristakes of Lastivert, remembered Basil as "mighty among rulers and always victorious in battle, who had

---

[26] *Cecaumeni Strategicon*, eds. B. Wassiliewsky and P. Jernstedt (St. Petersburg, 1896), 18, 29, 33, 65, 66, 96, 98; *Sovety i rasskazy Kekavmena. Sochinenie vizantiiskogo polkovodtsa XI veka*, ed. G. G. Litavrin (Moscow, 1972), 152, 174, 180–2, 250, 252, 282, 284. On one occasion, Basil is called simply "the blessed." See Kekaumenos, eds. Wassiliewsky and Jernstedt, 96; ed. Litavrin, 280.

[27] *Histoire de Yahya-Ibn-Saïd d'Antioche*, fasc. 2, eds. and tr. I. Kratchkovsky and A. Vasiliev, Patrologia Orientalis 23/2 (Paris, 1932); *Histoire de Yahyā ibn Saʿīd d'Antioche*, fasc. 3, ed. I. Kratchkovsky, tr. F. Micheau and G. Tropeau, Patrologia Orientalis 47/4, no. 212 (Turnhout, 1997); *Yahyā al-Antakī, Cronache dell'Egitto fāṭimide e dell'impero bizantino 937–1033*, tr. B. Pirone (Milan, 1997). References to Basil are usefully presented with copious commentary by V. R. Rozen, *Imperator Vasilij Bolgarobojca. Izvlečenija iz Letopisi Jaxi Antioxijskago* (St. Petersburg 1908; repr. London 1972).

[28] *Des Stephanos von Taron armenische Geschichte*, tr. H. Gelzer and A. Burckhardt (Leipzig, 1907), 185–6; W. Seibt, "Untersuchungen zur Vor- und Frühgeschichte der 'bulgarischen' Kometopulen," *Handes Amsorya. Zeitschrift für armenische Philologie* 89 (1975), 65–98 at 82–3.

trampled underfoot many lands."[29] Both Asołik and Aristakes consider Basil a successful general, but neither calls him Bulgar-slayer.

Finally, we may consider non-Greek sources composed in the Balkans, or further west. First, the *Chronicle of the Priest of Duklja* (*LPD*), which was probably written in Bar in the late twelfth century, but survives only in later Slavic and Latin versions. Here, Basil is called neither "Bolgaroboitsa," nor "Bulgaroctonus," despite his dealings with Bulgarians being covered in some detail.[30] Second, Basil and his wars with the Bulgarians are mentioned in the chronicle of Ademar of Chabannes (d. 1034), written in western France.[31] Here we learn of events which took place shortly after the death of Hugh Capet in 996.

In these same days, the Bulgarians rebelled and gravely ravaged Greek lands (*Greciam*), so the emperor Basil became exceedingly angered by them and swore by a vow to God that he would become a monk if he might subject the Bulgarian people to the Greeks. And after striving against them for 15 years with his army, he was victorious in two great battles. In the end, after the kings of the Bulgarians, Samuel and Aaron, had been killed, not in open battle but by Greek cunning (*astucia*), he took possession of all their land and destroyed the strongest cities and castles, and everywhere established garrisons of Greeks against them, and captured the greater part of the Bulgarian people. And just as he had vowed, he adopted the habit after the Greek fashion, and abstained from intercourse and meat for the rest of his life, although externally he appeared to remain surrounded by imperial protocol. Then he subdued Iberia, which had been in rebellion for seven years, so that everything there was done according to his wishes.

Ademar appears to offer a reason for Basil's failure to marry, although we must perhaps discount his revelation that Basil had sworn to become a monk if he should defeat the Bulgarians for want of corroboration in sources closer to the events described. This note attests to the importance attached in France, at least, to the emperor's Balkan wars, which were of greater interest than those in Iberia. At no point, however, does Ademar call Basil the Bulgar-slayer.

As will be apparent from the foregoing analysis, historiography dating from the period after Basil II's death is far from copious. The opposite can be

---

[29] *Aristakēs Lastiverc 'i's History*, tr. R. Bedrosian (New York, 1985), 31.

[30] *Letopis Popa Dukljanina*, ed. F. Šišić, Posebno Isdanje Srpske kr. akademije, knj. 67 (Belgrade and Zagreb, 1928).

[31] *Ademari Cabannensis opera omnia*, I, eds. P. Bourgain, R. Landes and G. Pon, Corpus Christianorum 129 (Turnhout, 1999), 154–5, 285–6. See also, for earlier commentary, M. Arbagi, "The celibacy of Basil II," *ByzSt* 2 (1975), 41–5; R. L. Wolff, "How the news was brought from Byzantium to Angoulême; or, the pursuit of the hare in an ox cart," *BMGS* 4 (1978), 139–89, esp. 143–4.

said of theological literature, in particular religious polemic, and those familiar with such texts may object to the notion that Basil was not immediately called Bulgar-slayer.[32] Works devoted to the developing tensions between Constantinople and Rome were increasingly common after 1054, and within this literature one finds allusions to a tradition that there was a schism during the patriarchate of Sergios II (999–1019), in the reign of Basil II. The first text to record the supposed Sergian schism is attributed to Niketas of Nicaea, *chartophylax*, the archivist of Hagia Sophia. The text, widely available in the edition produced by A. Mai, and reproduced by Migne (who added the date 1055), states that Sergios II was patriarch *epi tou Voulgaroktonou*, which is translated into Latin as "qui sub bulgaroctono" with the explicatory addition "(Basil II)."[33] J. Darrouzès has identified the author of this text as Niketas *tis Koronitzas* (or *tis Koronidos*, son of Koronitza or Koronis, his mother), who is referred to as *protosynkellos* and *chartophylax* in a patriarchal act of 1051/2.[34] He noted further that Niketas Stethatos, biographer of St. Symeon the New Theologian, exchanged several letters with this Niketas, whom he always addressed as *chartophylax* and *synkellos*, *tis Koronidos*.[35] Two eleventh-century lead seals have survived, one of Niketas [*proto*] *synkellos* and a second of Niketas *chartophylax*, both of which may have been struck by Niketas *tis Koronidos*.[36] However, several other men named Niketas held the office of *chartophylax* between 1050 and 1150, and, therefore, any one may conceivably have struck the second seal, and also have been the author of our text.

A second Niketas, archdeacon and *chartophylax*, was mentioned in a patriarchal act of 1076/7.[37] In 1081 this Niketas was promoted to the office of

---

[32] H.-G. Beck, *Kirche und theologische Literatur im byzantinischen Reich* (Munich, 1959), 609–28; Krumbacher, *Geschichte des byzantinischen Litteratur*, I, 79–82; A. Michel, *Humbert und Kerullarios*, 2 vols. (Paderborn, 1924–30), I, 20–3.

[33] A. Mai, ed., *Novae Patrum bibliothecae*, 10 vols. (Rome, 1853–1905), VI/ii, 446–8, 448; PG 120, 712–19, 717D: "But under Sergios, who was patriarch under the Bulgar-slayer, it is said that there arose a schism, for what reason I do not know, but the dispute was apparently over some sees." Cf. Krumbacher, *Geschichte des byzantinischen Litteratur*, I, 81, n. 7, for other editions of the text; and F. Dvornik, *The Photian Schism, history and legend* (Cambridge, 1948), 394, for a partial English translation.

[34] V. Grumel, *Les regestes des actes du patriarcat de Constantinople, I. Les actes des patriarches, II–III: Les regestes de 715 à 1206*, 2nd ed., ed. J. Darrouzès (Paris, 1989), no. 858; J. Darrouzès, ed., *Documents inédits d'ecclésiologie byzantine* (Paris, 1966), 26, n. 5; J. Darrouzès, *Recherches sur les Offikia de l'église byzantine* (Paris, 1970), 66, n. 2, 184, n. 4.

[35] *Nicétas Stéthatos, opuscules et lettres*, ed. J. Darrouzès (Paris, 1961), 15–17, 228–91. Stethatos also wrote to a Niketas, *didaskalos* and deacon of Hagia Sophia, whom Darrouzès has identified as the nephew of the *chartophylax*.

[36] V. Laurent, *Le corpus de sceaux de l'empire byzantin, V. L'église* (Paris, 1965), 74–5, no. 93 (*chartophylax*); 150–1, no. 220 (*protosynkellos*).

[37] Grumel, *Regestes*, ed. Darrouzès, no. 907; Laurent, *Sceaux*, 75, attributes the seal to this Niketas.

megas oikonomos, missing the two intervening positions of *megas sakellarios* and *megas skeuophylax,* and so cannot have been the Niketas *chartophylax* who was the recipient of a letter sent by Archbishop Theophylaktos from Ohrid. The letter was sent, and the third Niketas must therefore have been *chartophylax,* between 1091 and 1094, or between 1106 and 1111.[38] Either of these two men may have been the Niketas *chartophylax* who became Metropolitan of Nicaea after the incumbent, Eustratios, was convicted of heresy in 1117.[39] B. Leib, and after him A. Michel and H.-G. Beck, identified Niketas, Metropolitan of Nicaea, as the author of our text, and thus dated it to c. 1100.[40] This would rule out a fourth potential author, the theologian Niketas "of Maroneia," who held the office of *chartophylax* after 1121/2, before his promotion to Metropolitan of Thessalonika in 1132/3, and wrote six dialogues between a Greek and a Latin on the procession of the Holy Spirit which were sympathetic to the Latin stance on the *Filioque.*[41]

The text itself, which presents a brief outline on the history of schisms between Constantinople and Rome, reads like a series of notes taken from the patriarchal archives. This may have been requested by the emperor or patriarch, and the *chartophylax,* as patriarchal archivist, would have been the obvious person to conduct the research. Such a realization does not clarify the matter of date or authorship, since every patriarch or emperor between 1050 and 1150 would have been interested in the subject matter. Nevertheless, we should remember that Alexios I Komnenos made several approaches to the pope, after 1089, on the subject of Church union, and it seems likely that he would want to establish when and why the pope's name was removed from the diptychs.

It is impossible, therefore, to be certain who composed the text, and in what circumstances. However, the essential point for the present study is that the text had enduring interest, and its brevity and clipped style

---

[38] *Théophylacte d'Achrida, II, lettres,* ed. P. Gautier, CFHB 16/2 (Thessaloniki, 1986), 93–4, 438–9, no. 83. Gautier suggests a scribal error, and that this was not, in fact, sent to Niketas, but to Nikephoros *chartophylax,* recipient of four other letters from Theophylaktos. However, see now M. Mullett, *Theophylact of Ochrid. Reading the letters of a Byzantine archbishop,* Birmingham Byzantine and Ottoman Monographs 2 (Birmingham, 1997), 326, 356. Darrouzès, in *Nicétas Stéthatos,* 20, n. 3, also states that a third Niketas held the office of *chartophylax* after 1090, but provides no further information.

[39] Grumel, *Regestes,* ed. Darrouzès, nos. 1002–3.

[40] Beck, *Kirche und theologische Literatur,* 619; Michel, *Humbert und Kerullarios,* I, 20–3. These both seem to rely on B. Leib, *Deux inédits byzantins sur les azymes au début du XIIe siècle,* Orientalia Christiana 9 (Paris, 1924), 17–18, 53. However, Leib's attribution was based on a second text written by Niketas of Nicaea, on azymes. Others are less certain that both texts were written by the same author. See, for example, S. Runciman, *The Eastern Schism. A study of the papacy and the eastern Churches during the XIth and XIIth centuries* (Oxford, 1955), 33.

[41] *Pace* Runciman, *Eastern Schism,* 33. Cf. Beck, *Kirche und theologische Literatur,* 621–2.

encouraged later additions and revisions. The text has survived in four recensions, the earliest of which (Cod. Vat. gr. 1150, fol. 109B seq.) dates from the late fourteenth or early fifteenth century, and makes no mention of the Bulgar-slayer.[42] A later version of the text (Cod. Monac. gr. 256, fol. 442 seq.), of the fifteenth century, is similar, but contains a marginal note (fol. 444a) which provides additional information, in a second hand, on events during the patriarchate of Sergios *epi tou Voulgaroktonou*.[43] The text published by Mai and Migne is the latest version which contains elements added long after it was first composed, including the reference to the actions of Patriarch Sergios II *epi tou Voulgaroktonou*.[44] The most obvious addition is the last paragraph which is devoted to Patriarch Michael Keroullarios. Notably, in this paragraph those who observe the Roman rite, who are called *Romaioi* throughout the rest of the text, are referred to as Latins (*Latinoi*).[45]

Darrouzès has suggested that the additions to the last part of this text were introduced by somebody familiar with later texts on the origins of the schism, and indeed in one such text we find a similar reference to the actions of Sergios in the reign of "Lord Basil the Bulgar-slayer (*kyrou Vasileiou tou Voulgaroktonou*)."[46] This second text was edited by Hergenröther, who grouped it with two further short texts from quite different manuscripts under the general heading *opuscula de origine schismatis*.[47] In a separate work Hergenröther attributed the text to Nicholas, theologian and bishop of Methone (d. 1160–6), but it has since been established that none of the three *opuscula* were Nicholas' work, but date from the thirteenth and fourteenth centuries.[48] Therefore, we can state, with due caution, that references to Basil II as *Voulgaroktonos* in texts concerned with the schism,

[42] J. Hergenröther, *Photius, Patriarch von Constantinopel sein Leben, seine Schriften und das griechische Schisma*, 3 vols. (Regensberg, 1867–9), III, 869–75, esp. 873–4, n. 127, which is Hergenröther's transcription of the relevant paragraph from the three recensions of the text he consulted. Michel, *Humbert und Kerullarios*, I, 26–7, refers to a fourth recension in the Synodal Library which was unknown to Hergenröther, which is almost identical to the first Vatican text.

[43] Michel, *Humbert und Kerullarios*, I, 20.

[44] Hergenröther, *Photius, Patriarch von Constantinopel*, III, 248, 870–1; Michel, *Humbert und Kerullarios*, I, 30.

[45] Mai, *Novae Patrium bibliothecae*, VI/ii, 448; PG 120, 719B.

[46] Grumel, *Regestes*, ed. Darrouzès, 330.

[47] J. Hergenröther, ed., *Monumenta Graeca ad Photium ejusque historiam pertinentia* (Regensberg, 1869; repr. 1969), 171–81, from Cod. Marc. gr. 575, fol. 380 seq., and Cod. Mon. gr. 28, fol. 290 seq.

[48] Hergenröther, *Photius, Patriarch von Constantinopel*, III, 728, n. 110, judged to be incorrect in Grumel, *Regestes*, ed. Darrouzès, 329. For an overview of religious polemic of the thirteenth and fourteenth centuries, see Beck, *Kirche und theologische Literatur*, 663–89; Krumbacher, *Geschichte des byzantinischen Literatur*, 93–5, 113–15. Tia Kolbaba has indicated to me that the work in question almost certainly was composed after 1274. The author refers to "some people" who claim that Photios started the schism when he wrote against the Franks in Bulgaria.

and by implication more generally in theological literature, cannot be dated before c. 1200. Indeed, our noted examples all date from after the Second Council of Lyons in 1274.

A final type of text, neither theological nor historiographical in nature, appears to mention the Bulgar-slayer in an eleventh-century context. In the so-called *Peri ton taphon ton Vasileon,* a list of the tombs of emperors, the tomb of Constantine VIII (1025–8) is the last to be located within the Mausoleum of Constantine at the Church of the Holy Apostles in Constantinople. It is identified as that of "Constantine *porphyrogennetos,* the brother of (Basil) the *Voulgaroktonos,* the sons of Romanos [II] the so-called good little child."[49] The text represents a development and continuation of a list originally produced in the middle of the tenth century, which is included in Constantine VII Porphyrogennetos' *De Cerimoniis.*[50] It occurs in at least two slightly different versions, neither of which replicates exactly the text of the *De Cerimoniis,* and which are sufficiently distinct from each other to be considered separate redactions. The editor of these two published "Lists of Tombs," G. Downey, labeled them "Anonymous List C," and "Anonymous List R."[51]

The fact that both published redactions of the list end with mention of the tomb of Constantine VIII would lead one to believe that a continuation for the list in the *De Cerimoniis* was compiled soon after that emperor's death in 1028. Moreover, there would appear to be further support for supposing the existence of an eleventh-century original. Downey, working from earlier published versions of both texts by C. Du Cange and A. Banduri, and from photocopied extracts obtained from the Paris manuscripts, did not realize that both "Lists of Tombs" were associated with the rich and varied text known as the *Patria Konstantinopoleos,* and more particularly with one version of that text known to be produced during the reign of

---

[49] G. Downey, "The tombs of the Byzantine emperors at the Church of the Holy Apostles in Constantinople," *JHS* 79 (1959), 27–51 at 37, and 40 (slightly different). Earlier versions of both texts were published by A. Banduri, *Imperium Orientale sive antiquitates Constantinopolitanae,* 2 vols. (Paris, 1711), I [part 3, book 6], 121–4; Du Cange, *Historia Byzantina duplici commentario illustrata:* II, *Constantinopolis Christiana,* book 4, 109–10. Banduri's edition was reprinted with some of the notes at PG 157, 725–40. The description is quite distinct from that provided by Nicholas Mesarites in 1198–1203, discussed below at pp. 92–4.

[50] *Constantini Porphyrogeniti De Cerimoniis Aulae Byzantinae,* ed. J. Reiske, CSHB, 2 vols. (Bonn, 1829), 642–6; reproduced by Downey, "Tombs of the Byzantine emperors," 30–2.

[51] The letters refer to the manuscripts, which are respectively: Bibliothèque Nationale, Colbert 3607 = Fonds grec 1788 (15th c.), fols. 69v–71v; Bibliothèque Nationale, Cod. Reg. 3058, 4 = Fonds grec 1783 (dated A.D. 1440), fols. 71–3. H. Omont, *Inventaire sommaire des manuscrits grecs de la Bibliothèque Nationale,* 4 vols. (Paris, 1888), II, 142, 143–4; H. Omont, *Les manuscrits grecs datés des XVe et XVIe siècles de la Bibliothèque Nationale et des autres bibliothèques de France* (Paris, 1892), 11.

Alexios I Komnenos (1081–1118), which is referred to as the Topographical Recension.[52] However, the Topographical Recension of the *Patria* is itself preserved in two recensions, which its editor, T. Preger, labeled M and C (not to be confused with Downey's "Anonymous List C").[53] Recension M has been dated by the scribe's hand to 1085–95.[54] This version does not contain the "List of Tombs." Recension C of the *Patria*, while retaining references to Alexios I, exists only in five far later manuscripts, being the two Paris manuscripts we have already noted (Downey's C = Preger's D; Downey's R = Preger's E), and three additional fifteenth-century manuscripts. Each of these three manuscripts also incorporates an unpublished version of the "List of Tombs."[55] In the words of A. Maricq: "[The List of Tombs] features in all the complete manuscripts of that recension [C of the *Patria*], and in those alone."[56] However, a further text is always included between the *Patria* and the "List of Tombs," and this provides far better dating clues than the varied and growing *Patria*.

Downey, while unaware of the *Patria* connection, observed that "further evidence of the origins of the lists... may be furnished by the association, with both the list in the [*De Cerimoniis*] and anonymous list C, of lists of the Roman emperors. In the present text of the [*De Cerimoniis*] this list of emperors is missing, but an entry in the index (μβ′, ed. Bonn) shows that

---

[52] P. Grierson, "The tombs and obits of the Byzantine emperors (337–1042)," *DOP* 16 (1962), 3–60 at 8, asserted, therefore, that "Though both manuscripts are of the fifteenth century, the versions themselves date from the eleventh." The *Patria* connection was noted by A. Maricq, "Notes philologiques, 4: Les sarcophages impériaux de Constantinople," *Byzantion* 22 (1952), 370–2 at 370–1. Downey may have been led astray by the order in which the material is presented in the published edition by Banduri, which presents the text of the *Patria*, but then interpolates additional texts between that and the list of tombs. For manuscripts of the *Patria* see T. Preger, *Beiträge zur Textgeschichte der* Πάτρια Κωνσταντινουπόλεως (Munich, 1895), 20–5; A. Berger, *Untersuchungen zu den Patria Konstantinupoleos*, Poikila Byzantina 8 (Bonn, 1988), 86–92. Preger did not include the list of tombs in his edition of the *Patria*, since they did not form part of the original version. However, when we now think of the *Patria*, "we should think of a growing body of material in which much overlap and variation is possible, and in which fidelity to an original text is far from being the prime concern." A. Cameron and J. Herrin, eds., *Constantinople in the eighth century. Parastaseis Syntomoi Chronikai* (Leiden, 1984), 5.

[53] Preger, *Beiträge zur Textgeschichte*, 22–4.   [54] Berger, *Untersuchungen zu den Patria*, 88.

[55] Preger, *Beiträge zur Textgeschichte*, 24, labels this version F, with the fourteenth/fifteenth-century manuscript Cod. Vat. Palatinus gr. 328 being the earliest example. Cod. Vat. Palatinus gr. 302 is a sixteenth-century copy of this. The descriptions of the Palatine manuscripts can be seen in H. Stevenson, *Codices manuscripti Palatini graeci Bibliothecae Vaticanae* (Rome, 1885), 170–1, 190–2: "Catalogus Impp. a Iulio Caesare ad Constantinum Chlorum. Catalogus Impp. Christianorum CPolis, a Constantino Magno ad Michaelum Comnenum Palaeologum... Sequuntur nonnulla de S. Sophia ubi in primis rescensentur λάρνακες, seu urnae, quibus principum Augustorumque corpora conduntur."

[56] Maricq, "Les sarcophages," 371, lists five versions of recension C: the two Paris mss., the two Vatican mss. and one further ms., Seragliensis 6 (dated 1474).

preceding the catalogue of tombs there was a list of emperors who reigned at Constantinople beginning with Constantine the Great."[57] "Anonymous List C" is preceded by a list of Roman emperors, written in the same hand, which commences with Julius Caesar and continues to Michael VIII Palaiologos (1261–82). Therefore, one would be inclined to date "Anonymous List C" to after 1282. Berger came to the same conclusion for the associated version of the *Patria*, noting that in "manuscript E of recension C," mention is made of Andronikos II Palaiologos (1282–1328).[58] So, at least this version of the list should not be considered an eleventh-century production.

Although Downey does not mention it, according to Banduri's description of the manuscript (BN Cod. Reg. 3058.4), an annotated list of emperors also accompanies "Anonymous List R." That is, a "brief chronicle of emperors" is placed immediately before "Anonymous List R," which, as with "Anonymous List C," runs from Julius Caesar to Michael VIII.[59] A third unpublished version of the "List of Tombs," in Cod. Vat. Palatinus gr. 328, is also preceded by a list of emperors, from Julius Caesar to Michael Palaiologos. We may state with some confidence, therefore, that all versions of the extended "List of Tombs" date from, at the earliest, the last years of the thirteenth century. If an eleventh-century original existed, we do not know it.[60]

The "Lists of Tombs," like the synoptic histories and treatises mentioning the Sergian schism, may well have their origins in the mid-eleventh century. But in the forms in which they are preserved they should be regarded as products of a later date, with interpolations from the thirteenth

---

[57] Downey, "Tombs of the Byzantine emperors," 29.

[58] Berger, *Untersuchungen zu den Patria*, 90.

[59] Banduri, *Imperium Orientale*, I, vi: "Deinde habetur [Codice Regio num. 3058.4] Catalogus Imperatorum Romanorum a Julio Caesare ad Michaelam Palaeologum. Catalogus sepulcrorum Imperialium, quae in aede SS. Apostolorum, & in variis Monasteriis erant." Omont, *Inventaire sommaire*, II, 142, describes this as an "anonymi breve chronicon a Julio Caseare ad Michaelam Comnenum [sic]." It occupies fols. 67v–69, and as such is shorter even than the list of emperors in C (fols. 67v–71).

[60] I have been unable to consult the manuscripts discussed here. Therefore, I cannot confirm, but only express a suspicion, that Basil will have been described as *Voulgaroktonos* in the lists of emperors which precede each "List of Tombs." Indeed, these lists of emperors may well resemble the *Chronicon Bruxellense*, discussed above. Closer inspection of these lists, and comparison with the *Chronicon Bruxellense* may well yield fascinating results. However, such lists of emperors were extremely common, as Grierson, "Tombs and obits," 12–13, pointed out. For one further such list of emperors with exact regnal dates, see P. Schreiner, ed., *Die byzantinischen Kleinchroniken*, CFHB 12/1 (Vienna, 1975), 156–62, being Chronicle 15, a list of emperors from Constantine I to Alexios I culled from a late-fifteenth-century manuscript to be found in Florence: Bibl. Laur., plut. 13, fol. 165v–166v. Basil is here called "the son of Romanos."

century and later. By the time the extant versions were written down, in fifteenth-century manuscripts, it was quite standard to add the epithet "Bulgar-slayer" to the name Basil, to distinguish him from other Basils, particularly his grandfather's grandfather. In the eleventh century, the epithets "the younger" and "born in the purple" served this same function. In the next chapter we will determine when, and why Basil *o neos*, *porphyrogennetos* became the *Voulgaroktonos*.

6

The origins of a legend

For more than a century after his death Basil was not known as the Bulgar-slayer. There are two reasons for this. The first is the way Bulgaria and Bulgarians were perceived and portrayed by the Byzantines after the annexation of 1018. The second is the way Byzantine emperors were perceived and portrayed after Basil. The two are closely related, but may be treated in turn.

Basil blinded Bulgarians, certainly more than he slew, for acts he considered treacherous. But he also rewarded their leaders with court titles and stipends, and married Bulgarians to Romans. It was his desire to eliminate bad blood between Bulgarians and Romans by establishing new bloodlines, and thus to eliminate the threats that independent Bulgarian potentates and warlords posed to his empire. It was not his desire to eliminate Bulgarians, who would prove to be productive, tax-paying subjects. After 1018, the Romans did not need a slayer of Bulgarians, since slayers slay barbarians. As Christian subjects of the Byzantine emperor living under Roman law, the Bulgarians were not barbarians. Indeed, their passage from barbarism had begun a century before Basil's birth, with the conversion of Khan Boris (852–89).

The Byzantine attitude to Bulgaria after its annexation can best be seen in the works of Theophylaktos Hephaistos, archbishop of Ohrid in the late eleventh century. In his *History of the fifteen martyrs of Tiberioupolis*, we learn that, following conversion: "What was previously not a people but a barbarian race (*ethnos*) became and was called a people (*laos*) of God... the Bulgarian people have become, as it is written, a royal priesthood, a holy nation, a peculiar people."[1] Theophylaktos stresses the Pauline nature of the mission by using a Pauline quotation. He is more explicit in his

---

[1] *Historia martyrii XV martyrum*, PG 126, 152–221 at 200–1. For a translation of this passage and further commentary see D. Obolensky, *Six Byzantine portraits* (Oxford, 1988), 71–7. See now also M. Mullett, *Theophylact of Ochrid. Reading the letters of a Byzantine archbishop*, Birmingham Byzantine and Ottoman Monographs 2 (Birmingham, 1997), 235–9.

Life of St. Clement, a disciple of Saints Cyril and Methodios who had preached Christianity in ninth-century Bulgaria and translated works from Greek using the new Slavonic script. Here we find a people called into being and given a recognized identity through conversion by Clement, "a new Paul to the new Corinthians, the Bulgarians."[2] Thus, Theophylaktos demonstrates a grudging respect for distinct Bulgarian institutions in the Cyrillo-Methodian tradition, including the Slavonic language.[3]

Theophylaktos was involved frequently in the minutiae of civil administration in the western Balkans, and had regular dealings with military and civilian officials throughout the region. Through his letters we can detect how far Byzantine civilian and fiscal institutions had developed by 1100 in lands which had been subject to Samuel. Indeed, Theophylaktos himself was emblematic of change, being the Greek-speaking metropolitan of an autocephalous, but no longer independent Bulgarian Church. Among Theophylaktos' earliest letters is one to the *doux* of Dyrrachion, John Doukas, requesting that a village near Pelagonia (Bitola) be returned to his jurisdiction.[4] After 1092 Theophylaktos despatched at least eight letters to a new *doux* of Dyrrachion, John Komnenos, making a series of quite specific requests concerning: the taxation of monks in the Vardar valley; taxes imposed on the bishopric of Devol; the conscription of infantrymen from the region of Ohrid; recognition of a particular village (*chorion*) owned by the church of Ohrid but not recorded in its charter (*praktikon*).[5] On two occasions Theophylaktos makes particular mention of the wicked *kastrophylakes*, guardians of *kastra*, who were in receipt of a peculiar military levy on land, the *kastroktisia*.[6] Theophylaktos' *bête noir* was the tax-collector (*praktor*) Iasites who was based at the *praitorion* in Ohrid,[7] and his letters make it plain that the *doux* of Dyrrachion had the authority to issue written instructions (*pittakia*) to empower a local official (*ek prosopou*) to overrule the *praktor*. Thus, the *ek prosopou* was to intervene

---

[2] *Monumenta ad SS Cyrilli et Methodii successorum vitas resque gestas pertinentia*, ed. N. L. Tunickij (London, 1972), 66–140 at 126. D. Obolensky, "Theophylaktos of Ohrid and the authorship of the Vita Clementis," in *Byzantium. A tribute to Andreas N. Stratos*, 2 vols. (Athens, 1986), II, 601–18, convincingly argued for Theophylaktos' authorship; cf: Mullett, *Theophylact of Ochrid*, 235–9.

[3] Although he notoriously parodied Slavonic terms and place names, Theophylaktos knew and used them: Mullett, *Theophylact of Ochrid*, 272–3.

[4] *Théophylacte d'Achrida, II, lettres*, ed. and tr. P. Gautier, CFHB 16/2 (Thessaloniki, 1986), 186–9; Mullett, *Theophylact of Ochrid*, 360, nr. 38.

[5] *Théophylacte, lettres*, 166–9, 194–5; 202–5; 208–11; 214–17.   [6] *Théophylacte, lettres*, 237, 324.

[7] *Théophylacte, lettres*, 162–5, 168, 460, 486, 568; Mullett, *Theophylact of Ochrid*, 130, 369; Obolensky, *Six Byzantine portraits*, 53–4.

if Iasites' functionaries (*mesazontes*) abusively detained monks to perform personal services.[8]

Certainly, Ohrid was not Constantinople, and Theophylaktos complained that "having lived for years in the land of the Bulgarians, the bumpkin lifestyle is my daily companion."[9] The phrase he uses is adapted from Euripides' *Orestes* (485) and is used more literally a century later by Michael Choniates to describe his "becoming a barbarian by living a long time in Athens."[10] The Athenians may have appeared as provincial and parochial to Archbishop Michael as Theophylaktos' Bulgarian flock did to him. Yet Theophylaktos associated closely with his charges, and was inclined to write that he was now "a Constantinopolitan, and, strange to tell, also a Bulgarian."[11] Perhaps he considered himself the most refined resident of a second, lesser *oikoumene* with an autonomous but inferior church with its own liturgy and hierarchy. In a letter to the *kaisar* Nikephoros Melissenos, Theophylaktos even coins the phrase "*barbaros oikoumene*" to refer to Bulgaria, and this appears to sum up his attitude of ambivalence and grudging recognition.[12] Such a region, a Christian land subject to Roman law, and taxation, had no need of a slayer.

A second reason for Basil not to have been known as a slayer in the eleventh century is that this would run contrary to prevailing norms for describing emperors. This is not to suggest that "-ktonoi," and other slayers, did not appear in Byzantine literature before the eleventh century, for indeed they did in some numbers.[13] The use of "-ktonos" is well established in classical and Patristic writings.[14] As just one example of many, Plutarch (*Moralia*, 349C) praised such past rulers as Themistokles the "Persianslayer" (*Persoktonos*) and Miltiades the "Mede-slayer" (*Midophonos*).[15] The fourth century A.D. is rich in preserved texts, and therefore also rich in

---

[8] *Théophylacte, lettres*, 167–9, 194.

[9] *Théophylacte, lettres*, 243.17; Mullett, *Theophylact of Ochrid*, 276; Obolensky, *Six Byzantine portraits*, 58.

[10] *Michail Akominatou tou Choniatou ta sozomena*, ed. S. Lambros, 2 vols. (Athens, 1879–80), II, 44.

[11] *Théophylacte, lettres*, 141, lines 58–60; Mullett, *Theophylact of Ochrid*, 274.

[12] *Théophylacte, lettres*, 171; Mullett, *Theophylact of Ochrid*, 274–5, 298.

[13] C. D. Buck and W. Petersen, *A reverse index of Greek nouns and adjectives* (Chicago, 1944), 282–3, lists 102 compound adjectives with the nasal termination "-ktonos" (and 71 more with "-phonos"). A search of the TLG database using "κτόνο", to allow for various cases, turned up 815 references in the period A.D. 1–1500, of which 668 date before 700. However, later "hits" are limited by the absence, as yet, of rhetorical and panegyrical texts from the database. Search conducted 29 January 2002 at Dumbarton Oaks.

[14] J. B. Bauer, ed., *A reverse index of Patristic Greek* (Graz, 1983), 122, is incomplete. It omits several epithets, including the fairly common ἀδελφοκτόνος and παιδοκτόνος.

[15] *Plutarchi Moralia*, ed. and tr. F. C. Babbitt et al., 15 vols. (Cambridge, MA, 1927–69), IV, 514.

references to "-ktonoi." John Chrysostomos alone uses variations on this nasal termination on ninety-nine separate occasions.[16] Eusebius, in his *Life of Constantine*, refers to his subject as the Tyrant-slayer (*tyrannoktonos*), in honor of his victories over Maxentius and Licinius, although Constantine did not use the epithet of himself, preferring merely Victor.[17] Such epithets were less popular in the fifth century, but still used in the sixth and seventh centuries. For example, according to the *Greek anthology* (XVI, 62, 63), two inscriptions on a statue of Justinian I set up in the Hippodrome of Constantinople by Eustathios (Prefect of the City) and Julian (Praetorian Prefect of the East), described the emperor as "Slayer of the Medes" (*Midoktonos, Midophonos*).[18] However, classicizing epithets referring to the slaying of particular peoples were most uncommon. Thus, in his *Herakleias* (II, 187–8) George of Pisidia uses only the general epithets *brotoktonos* and *patroktonos*, "slayer of mortal man" and "father-slayer."[19] In the tenth century, Theodore the Deacon, writing of Nikephoros Phokas' capture of Crete in 961, exceptionally used the particular epithet *Kritoktonos*. Alluding in but a few lines to Homer, Herodotos and Aeschylos, he wrote that a "ten-thousand-man throng of barbarians rushed from the gates like a cloud of the South Wind... encouraged to sally forth by the formulated plan devised as a Cretan-slayer." Significantly, the plan, but not the general, was a slayer of Cretans, meaning in this instance those Arabs who occupied the island and "suffered the punishment due to their faith."[20]

Following the lavish praise heaped on the military achievements of Nikephoros Phokas and John Tzimiskes by such authors as Leo the Deacon and John Geometres, "the warrior-emperor vanishes from the eulogies of the mid-eleventh century. There re-emerges instead the traditional image of the pious ruler adorned by the four imperial virtues celebrated in Byzantine rhetoric."[21] These virtues were justice, philanthropy, piety and intelligence, which may be elaborated upon to include such traits as reverence to one's

---

[16] TLG search cited.

[17] Eusebius, *Vita Constantini*, I, 12; *Eusebius, Werke, I.1. Über das Leben des Kaisers Konstantin*, ed. F. Winkelmann, 2nd ed. (Berlin, 1992), 21; *Eusebius, Life of Constantine*, tr. Averil Cameron and S. G. Hall (Oxford, 1999), 73.

[18] *Anthologia Graeca*, ed. H. Beckby, 4 vols., 2nd ed. (Munich, 1965), IV, 334; C. Mango, *The art of the Byzantine empire, 312–1453* (Englewood Cliffs, NJ, 1972), 117–18, provides an English translation of the inscriptions and identifies the donors.

[19] *Georgio di Pisidia poemi*, ed. and tr. A. Pertusi (Ettal, 1959), 259.

[20] *Theodosius Diaconus de Creta capta*, ed. H. Criscuolo (Leipzig, 1979), 19: "πεπλασμένην πάγην ἐτεχνάζοντο τὴν Κρητοκτόνον."

[21] A. Kazhdan, "The aristocracy and the imperial ideal," in M. Angold, ed., *The Byzantine aristocracy IX to XIII centuries* (Oxford, 1984), 43–57 at 48. Basil, as we have seen, did not encourage such literary praise. Cf. M. Lauxtermann, "Byzantine poetry and the paradox of Basil II's reign," in P. Magdalino, ed., *Byzantium in the year 1000* (Leiden, 2002), 199–216.

parents, generosity to the poor and chastity. Thus, Michael IV (1034–41) was praised by Christopher of Mytilene for his almsgiving, and Constantine IX Monomachos (1042–55) for his generosity, piety and intelligence.[22] John Mauropous praised Monomachos not for his abilities as a general, but as a peacemaker, following the invasion of the empire by Pechenegs in 1047.[23] And when shortly afterwards a rebellion took place under the command of Leo Tornikios, in a letter to the emperor Mauropous advised not vengeance and blinding of the traitors, as perhaps would have pleased Basil II, but appealed for leniency in the following manner:

God, the defender of your salvation and of your kingdom, who has put all the rebels under your feet, who has now granted you a bloodless victory over them, he demands no other recompense from you for this alliance than your gentleness alone and your magnanimity towards the guilty... For to strike back against those who have struck us and to return the evil to those who started it may perhaps seem pleasant but it is actually inglorious... but to control through long suffering your justifiable wrath against those who have seriously wronged you and to use philosophy to force this passionate and faint-hearted and contemptuous nature of ours to become an impassible and divine one, this is a rare act among the sons of men and more rare especially among emperors, whose power and freedom from liability allows them to inflict punishment with an insatiable appetite upon those who have offended them or even worse upon those suspected without reason.[24]

Mauropous' pupil, Michael Psellos, similarly wrote in praise of the emperor who did not take the field when the shuddering Scythians were driven back across the frontier at the Danube.[25] Yet in a letter, rather than an oration, Psellos criticized imperial inadequacies which had allowed the frontier defenses to fail. Since "this barrier is broken down, all those opposite rush into our lands like the flood of a river when a dyke is breached. Now Romanity and barbarity are not kept distinct, they are intermingled and live together. For this reason the barbarians are at war with us, some at the Euphrates, others on the Danube."[26]

---

[22] *Die Gedichte des Christophoros Mitylenaios*, ed. E. Kurtz (Leipzig, 1903), 11–12, 32–3; Kazhdan, "The aristocracy and the imperial ideal," 48–9.

[23] *Ioannis Euchaitorum metropolitae quae in cod. Vat. gr. 676 supersunt*, eds. J. Bollig and P. de Lagarde (Göttingen, 1882), 142–7; J. Lefort, "Rhétorique et politique: trois discours de Jean Mauropous en 1047," *TM* 6 (1976), 265–303; Kazhdan, "The aristocracy and the imperial ideal," 49.

[24] *The letters of John Mauropous metropolitan of Euchaita*, ed. and tr. A. Karpozilos, CFHB 34 (Thessaloniki, 1990), 104–7, ep. 26. For Mauropous' description of the revolt see *Ioannis Euchaitorum*, eds., Bollig and de Lagarde, 178–95; Lefort, "Rhétorique et politique," 268–70.

[25] *Michaeli Pselli orationes panegyricae*, ed. G. T. Dennis (Stuttgart and Leipzig, 1994), 116; *Michaeli Pselli poemata*, ed. L. Westerink (Stuttgart and Leipzig, 1994), 257.

[26] *Michaelis Pselli scripta minora*, ed. E. Kurtz and F. Drexl, 2 vols. (Milan, 1936–41), II, 239.

If there was a growing divide between the perception and public portrayal of imperial virtues towards the end of the eleventh century, during the twelfth century civilian virtues were increasingly subsumed beneath a tide of martial imagery. We may detect the first traces of a revival of Basil II's reputation in writings dating to the reigns of Alexios I Komnenos (1081–1118) and his son John II (1118–43), who both personally commanded Byzantine armies in the northern Balkans. Moreover, the origins of the Komnenian ascent to power were associated with the promotion of their dynasty by Basil. Several authors writing under, or about, Alexios draw attention to the promotion of his great-grandfather, the *patrikios* Manuel Komnenos Erotikos. Anna Komnene in particular, claims he was named *strategos autokrator* of the East during Basil's struggles with Bardas Skleros. Manuel's brother, Nikephoros Komnenos, held the rank of *protospatharios* and the command of Vaspurakan.[27] Most significantly, according to Anna's husband Nikephoros Bryennios, Manuel's sons were entrusted to the care of Basil II, who "appointed instructors and teachers for them."

Some he told to shape the boys' character, others he told to teach them the arts of war: how to arm themselves properly and use their shields to defend themselves against the strokes of their opponents; to handle a lance and to ride a horse with skill; to shoot an arrow right at the mark; and, to put it concisely, to study the tactical treatises so that they would know how to deploy a phalanx and array the files, how to prepare a camp correctly and set up a palisaded encampment, and the many other things the tactical treatises teach. The Stoudios monastery was assigned as their place of residence, for two reasons: to acquire virtue by imitating the finest men, and so that they were able to leave the City easily to go hunting or take part in military exercises.[28]

It is unsurprising, therefore, that for Isaak I Komnenos, who ascended the imperial throne in 1057, Basil was the archetypal warrior emperor. Isaak is said often to have quoted Basil, not least his jokes, and sought to project a similar martial image for himself.[29] The most enduring evidence for this can be found on Isaak's gold coins where, breaking with imperial tradition, he chose to portray himself holding not the *labarum*,

[27] *Annae Comnenae Alexias*, eds. D. Reinsch and A. Kambylis, CFHB 40/1 (Berlin and New York, 2001), 324; *Anne Comnène, Alexiade*, ed. B. Leib, 3 vols. (Paris, 1937–45), III, 9–10. Cf. Skylitzes, 323, 355.

[28] *Nicéphore Bryennios histoire*, ed. and tr. P. Gautier, CFHB 9 (Brussels, 1979), 75–7. The translation is provided by E. McGeer, *Sowing the dragon's teeth. Byzantine warfare in the tenth century*, DOS 23 (Washington, DC, 1995), 192–3.

[29] *Michel Psellos Chronographie, ou histoire d'un siècle de Byzance (967–1077)*, ed. E. Renauld, 2 vols. (1926–8), II, 130. On Isaak's appreciation of Basil's humor, see L. Garland, "Basil II as humorist," *Byzantion* 69 (1999), 321–43.

the Byzantine imperial scepter, but a drawn sword. Isaak's empress was also a legacy of Basil's Bulgarian wars: Isaak had been betrothed by the emperor to Catherine, the daughter of the defeated Bulgarian ruler John Vladislav. Isaak's brother, John, rose to command the imperial armies as *domestikos ton scholon*. His early training stood him in good stead, and his five sons all followed military careers. One, Alexios, drew on his military reputation and connections to launch a successful coup in 1081.

Initially, following Alexios' usurpation, the *porphyrogennetos* Constantine Doukas remained heir to the imperial throne, and was encouraged to look to his own military prowess. Theophylaktos of Ohrid warned him not to think "the purple-edged golden imperial robes will prevail over the servants of Ares, men whose appearance is as fierce as lions if they do not see you in a bronze cuirass applying yourself to war." But Theophylaktos did not advocate aggressive military action, merely vigilant guard and careful preparation.

In matters of war [the emperor] concerns himself with everything, examining all and helping everyone. Above all he should not put himself in danger thoughtlessly, nor die like a simple soldier, but must reason like a general who has won many victories. In times of peace he must prepare himself for war and train himself on every occasion in all forms of war, without neglecting a single one, participating in exercises with all his troops, and taking veterans and experienced warriors as his instructors and observers at his drills.[30]

Such good advice should also have been directed against the Komnenoi since, shortly after a decisive victory over the Pechenegs in 1091, Alexios promoted his own son John over Constantine. Thereafter, military prowess was paramount. Whereas Constantine IX was praised by Christopher of Mytilene for having distributed rivers of gold and titles, quite different fluvial imagery was employed to praise the emperors of the twelfth century, who dispensed only floods of sweat and rivers of barbarian blood.[31] Not all observers were convinced there was value in this shift in emphasis, nor the policies it masked. John Zonaras wrote a notorious criticism of Alexios I's policy, noting that "the qualities proper to an emperor are care for justice, provision for his subjects and the preservation of the old customs of the

---

[30] *Théophylacte d'Achrida, I, discours, traités, poésies*, ed. and tr. P. Gautier, CFHB 16/1 (Thessaloniki, 1980), 207.
[31] *Christophoros Mitylenaios*, ed. Kurtz, 33; Kazhdan, "The aristocracy and the imperial ideal," 48–51; G. Dennis, "Imperial panegyric: rhetoric and reality," in H. Maguire, ed., *Byzantine court culture from 829 to 1204* (Washington, DC, 1997), 131–40 at 135.

state."[32] However, the image-makers at the Komnenian court, and those who aspired to imperial access, lavished praise on the warrior emperors, and triumphal epithets became a staple of court panegyric.

Panegyrical literature flourished in the courts of the Komnenian emperors and the lesser courts of their extended family. Moreover, after a period in abeyance, John II revived the imperial triumphal entry and procession, following a revised route through the city. On such occasions, orators competed with each other to praise the emperor most lavishly, often employing triumphal epithets. Thus Theodore Prodromos addressed John as Περσόλεθρε Σκυθοδαλματοκτόνε, "ruin of the Persians, and slayer of the Scytho-dalmatians." Elsewhere John was Περσοκτόνος, "slayer of the Persians," or Περσολέτα and Σκυθολοιγέ, "ruin of the Persians and Scythians," being the Pechenegs and Seljuk Turks.[33] Theodore Prodromos also wrote in praise of John's son Manuel Komnenos, marking triumphal celebrations of 1149.[34] Further orations were delivered on this occasion by the so-called "Manganeios" Prodromos, who went on to praise Manuel lavishly for numerous subsequent campaigns.[35]

Manuel Komnenos celebrated his victories even more splendidly than his father, and his deeds were compared by hyperbolic panegyrists to those of great leaders and warriors of myth and history. Manuel used his victories to promote his claims to be sole and universal Roman emperor, and to the same effect revived the practice of using additional personal names derived from the names of conquered peoples (*cognomina devictarum gentium*).[36] In the *intitulatio* to his conciliar edict of 1166 (fig. Figure 9), which followed soon after a series of victorious campaigns in the northern Balkans, Manuel called himself, amongst other cognomens, "*Dalmatikos, Ouggrikos, Bosthnikos, Chrovatikos . . . Voulgarikos, Servlikos.*"[37]

---

[32] *Ioannis Zonarae epitome historiarum*, eds. M. Pinder and T. Büttner-Wobst, 3 vols., CSHB (Bonn, 1841–97), III, 766; P. Magdalino, "Aspects of twelfth-century Byzantine Kaiserkritik," *Speculum* 58 (1983), 326–46 at 330.

[33] *Theodoros Prodromos, historische Gedichte*, ed. W. Hörandner (Vienna, 1974), poem XVI, 276–85 at 277, line 7; poem XVIII, 302–8 at 305, line 83; poem X, 248–51 at 251, line 22; poem II, 185–90 at 186, line 46.

[34] *Theodoros Prodromos*, ed. Hörandner, poem 30, 348–62.

[35] The poems of Manganeios Prodromos, which will be published with an English translation by Elizabeth and Michael Jeffreys, are, judging from the few I have examined, replete with similar imagery. See poems 1, 2, 27 (addressing Manuel's campaigns against the Serbs and Hungarians, delivered, probably, between December 1150 and April 1151), and 7, 31 (probably delivered in 1155).

[36] P. Magdalino, *The empire of Manuel I Komnenos, 1143–1180* (Cambridge, 1993), 419–22, 434–54; M. McCormick, *Eternal victory. Triumphal rulership in Late Antiquity, Byzantium and the early medieval West* (Cambridge and Paris, 1986), 21–2, 112–15, 277–8.

[37] C. Mango, "The conciliar edict of 1166," *DOP* 17 (1963), 317–30, 324; Magdalino, *Empire of Manuel Komnenos*, 88, 287–8, 461–2.

We find a series of triumphal epithets which link the Komnenoi with Basil, slayers all, in a poem associated with a series of portraits, now lost. A late thirteenth- or early fourteenth-century manuscript (Cod. Marc. gr. 524) preserves a poem (fol. 46r) which relates to the construction by Manuel of a new hall to serve as a refectory for the monastery of St. Mokios, in the western part of Constantinople. It begins as follows:[38]

On the hall newly built by the emperor the Lord Manuel, to serve as a refectory for the monks, wherein was represented beside himself, his grandfather, the emperor Lord Alexios, and his father the emperor Lord John, as well as the Bulgar-slayer Lord Basil.

If buildings were naturally endowed with a voice then surely the monastery of Mokios...would have said that it had been fashioned by imperial hands. Indeed the four emperors represented here remind viewers that Emperor Basil, who transformed the honed sword of the Bulgarians into the plow in his unblemished reign, first made it into a habitation of monks, and that Alexios Komnenos the Persian-slayer (περσοκτόνος) instituted for them a communal life and furnished them most abundantly with every necessity; that his son the purple-born John, the ruin of the Scythians and Persians (Σκυθοπερσόλεθρος) ceaselessly poured out benefactions in countless ways; and their descendant, Manuel the purple-bloom emperor, at whose very name trembles the Paion, the Italian, the Dalmatian, the Persian, the Scythian, and by whose rule the four corners of the earth are enriched; he increases these donations many times more.

As the poem relates, the monastery owed much to the four emperors portrayed on the walls of the hall: Manuel and John Komnenos, who were great benefactors, Alexios who made the monastery coenobitic, and Basil who first turned the fourth-century church of St. Mokios into a monastery. The principal point of significance, however, in understanding how the emperors were portrayed is the martial nature of the imagery, and the fact that they are described with triumphal epithets. Manuel Komnenos is lauded for his triumphs over Hungarians, Italians, Serbs, Turks and Cumans, allowing us to date the poem to the second half of his reign. Indeed, the list of epithets closely resembles those used in the *intitulatio* of Manuel's conciliar edict of 1166. This then would provide us with a tentative *terminus post quem* for the poem.[39] Manuel's father, John Komnenos, once

---

[38] S. Lambros, "O Markianos kodiks 524," *Neos Ellin.* 8/2 (1911), 123–92 at 127–8; partial translation by Mango, *Art of the Byzantine empire*, 226–7, who omits all the martial imagery save *Persoktonos*.

[39] Mango, "The conciliar edict," 324. The Mokios portraits were clearly an imperial commission, in contrast to others which were commissioned by subjects. As Kinnamos records, this was "the custom among men placed in authority": *Ioannis Cinnami epitome rerum ab Ioanne et Alexio Comnenis gestarum*, ed. A. Meinecke, CSHB (Bonn, 1836), 266. See P. Magdalino and R. Nelson, "The emperor in Byzantine art of the twelfth century," *ByzF* 8 (1982), 123–83 at 135–7, for a translation of

again enjoys the compound distinction of being the ruin of both Scythians and Persians, the Pechenegs and Turks. Perhaps most significantly, Alexios Komnenos is called *Persoktonos*, recalling his wars with the Seljuk Turks, and echoing the epithet used by Theodore Prodromos for John Komnenos. Notably, Basil's victory over the Bulgarians is mentioned in a far less martial manner: the poet uses the biblical allusion to the beating of swords into plowshares. Basil is not called *Voulgaroktonos* in the body of the poem, but this epithet does appear in the introductory *lemma* (which I have translated in italics). The *lemma* was added to explain the original location and context of the poem when it was copied into this, or an earlier manuscript. It probably dates, therefore, from the thirteenth century.

This, and other extant poems noted, are the tip of a panegyrical iceberg, which demonstrates that the emperor as slayer of various barbarians had become a touchstone in the militaristic atmosphere at the courts of the Komnenoi. However, since the Bulgarians were throughout this period under Byzantine rule, they, unlike the Pechenegs, Cumans and Seljuk Turks, required no slayer. This changed in 1185, when Bulgarians once again became enemies and, therefore, were characterized once again as barbarians.

In 1185–6 a rebellion by Vlachs and Bulgarians in the lands between the Balkan mountains and the lower Danube led to the foundation of what is now called the "Second Bulgarian Empire." According to George Akropolites, writing in the later thirteenth century, Kalojan also known as Ioanitsa, the ruler of the Vlachs and Bulgarians after 1196, began to call himself *Romaioktonos*, "the Roman-slayer," because he had heard that in the past the Roman emperor Basil had taken the name *Voulgaroktonos* to mark his victories over the Bulgarians.[40] For Kalojan to invoke, and invert, the reputation of the Bulgar-slayer suggests that the Byzantines were alluding to Basil's exploits in the context of the renewed struggles in the northern Balkans. This is confirmed by the historian Niketas Choniates, who records that the emperor Isaak II Angelos (1185–95) failed in his attempts to crush the Vlachs and Bulgarians because he paid no heed to the Bulgar-slayer. After his first encounter with his enemies, Isaak returned swiftly to his capital to celebrate a premature victory. This earned him the opprobrium of the *krites* Leo Monasteriotes who accused the emperor of offending the soul of Basil "the Bulgar-slayer" by violating his *typikon* and his dispositions concerning the monastery at Sosthenion. This is the monastery

a complementary poem in Cod. Marc. 524, fol. 34r–v. This describes a series of portraits, of Alexios, John and Manuel, with a similar array of barbarians portrayed as Manuel's subjects, but no Basil.

[40] *Georgii Acropolitae opera*, ed. A. Heisenberg, 2 vols. (Leipzig, 1903), I, 23.16–19; 18.19–20.

Figure 9   The conciliar edict issued in 1166 by Manuel I Komnenos, where the emperor enjoys numerous triumphal epithets, including "*Dalmatikos, Ouggrikos, Bosthnikos, Chrovatiko[s]*." This plaster cast copy of the marble original hangs today in the outer narthex of Hagia Sophia. Reproduced from C. Mango, "The conciliar edict of 1166," *DOP* 17 (1963), 317–30.

of the Archangel Michael whose church Isaak had embellished. So, when the Vlachs returned across the Danube, bringing with them Cuman allies, they found the plains "swept clean and emptied of Byzantine troops... [Therefore] they were not content merely to preserve their own possessions and to assume control over Mysia, but also were compelled to wreak havoc against Byzantine lands and unite the political power of the Mysians and Bulgarians into one polity as of old."[41]

Why should an author writing of the events of 1185–6 choose to compare Isaak with Basil, and more particularly why should he, apparently for the first time, call Basil *Voulgaroktonos*? The simplest answer seems to be because Isaak himself was seeking to make the comparison. That is, Isaak appears to have wished to rework the image of Basil to bolster his own campaigns of "reconquest" in the northern Balkans. Among Isaak's first acts as emperor was to strike a deal with the Hungarian King Béla III (1172–96) whereby he married Béla's daughter, and recovered as her dowry the region of Niš-Braničevo.[42] In an oration to mark the wedding Niketas Choniates addressed Isaak as *barbaroktonos*.[43]

Niketas Choniates, our principal source for this crucial period, provides us with perhaps the first extant use of *Voulgaroktonos*. However, a second example, which is exactly contemporary, is provided by Nicholas Mesarites in his *Description of the Church of the Holy Apostles*. This *ekphrasis* was composed between 1198 and 1203. The date is provided by an allusion within the text to the kinship between the incumbent Patriarch John X Kamateros (1198–1203) and his niece, who was at that time Empress Euphrosyne, the wife of Alexios III Angelos (1195–1203).[44] Concluding a section describing the tombs contained in the Mausoleum of Constantine at the Holy Apostles, Mesarites notes that "The tomb in the inner part of the church contains Constantine, born to the purple, the brother of the great emperor

---

[41] *Nicetae Choniatae historiae*, ed. J.-L. van Dieten, CFHB 11/1 (Berlin, 1975), 373–4, 442. J. van Dieten, the editor, notes (at pp. lvi, xciii) that this section belongs to the b(revior) version of the text. Therefore, it was first written c. 1195–1203, and must be considered one of the first two extant uses of the term *Voulgaroktonos*.

[42] *Nicetae Choniatae historiae*, 368.

[43] *Fontes Byzantini historiae Hungariae aevo ducum et regum ex stirpe Árpád descendentium*, ed. G. Moravcsik (Budapest, 1984), 262–4 at 262. The significance of the use of *barbaroktonos*, and its relation to Kalojan's subsequent claim to be *Romaioktonos*, was noted by G. Prinzing, *Die Bedeutung Bulgariens und Serbiens in den Jahren 1204–1219 in Zusammenhang mit der Entstehung und Entwicklung der byzantinischen Teilstaaten nach der Einnahme Konstantinopels infolge der 4. Kreuzzuges*, Miscellanea Byzantina Monacensia 12 (Munich, 1972), 58–9, 74 n. 62.

[44] G. Downey, "Nikolaos Mesarites: description of the Church of the Holy Apostles at Constantinople," *Transactions of the American Philosophical Society*, N.S. 47, part 6 (1957), 855–924 at 859.

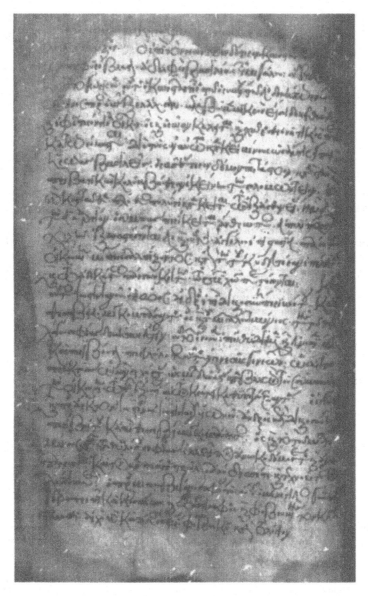

Figure 10   A page from the thirteenth-century manuscript of Nikolas Mesarites'
Description of the Church of the Holy Apostles, which contains one of the two first uses of
the epithet Bulgar-slayer (at the end of line 3, running on to the beginning of line 4). Cod.
Ambrosianus gr. 352, fol. 11v. Photo: Dumbarton Oaks Research Library, Washington,
DC.

who is known as Bulgar-slayer."[45] The manuscript in which this text has been preserved dates from the thirteenth century.[46] However, it is likely to have been copied from Mesarites' original and, unlike in the *peri ton taphon ton Vasileon* discussed in a previous chapter, the use of *Voulgaroktonos* with the qualifying phrase "who is known as" appears not to be a later interpolation, but original and authentic. The fact that Basil's name is not mentioned, but merely his epithet, suggests that the use of the latter was at the time of composition so common as to render use of the former optional, thus placing the Bulgar-slayer on a par with his wise great-grandfather, also lacking his Christian name Leo in Mesarites' text.[47]

Therefore, we have two discrete uses of the epithet in two quite distinct contexts, but both dating to within a very few years of 1200. In 1204, Constantinople itself fell to the forces of the Fourth Crusade, leading to the establishment of the Latin empire of Constantinople. Byzantine authors dwelt at length on past glories as they sought reasons for the cataclysm. The fullest and best account was penned by Niketas Choniates, who, as we have seen, recorded an unfavorable comparison between Isaak II Angelos and Basil the Bulgar-slayer. Niketas' brother, Michael Choniates, who was then archbishop of Athens, sought similarly to compare a contemporary ruler to Basil, but in his case it was in order to embolden the ruler of Nikaea, Theodore I Laskaris, to recover the capital. Thus, in a letter to Laskaris, Michael compared his addressee to past rulers of Constantinople, and declared him to have been matched only by Herakleios and Basil *Voulgaroktonos*. "For they alone fought wars for so long and, enslaving the greatest of peoples, remained undefeated."[48]

The historical context for the evocation of Basil as Bulgar-slayer is fairly clear, as Byzantine authority was challenged first by Bulgarians and Vlachs at the northern frontier, and then by Latins in the very heart of the empire.

---

45 Downey, "Nikolaos Mesarites: description of the Church of the Holy Apostles," 892, 915: ὁ ἐπὶ τὸν νεὼν τὸν ἐνδότερον Κωνσταντῖνον φέρει τὸν πορφυρόβλαστον, ἀδελφὸν βασιλέως τοῦ μεγάλου, οὗ Βουλγαροκτόνος τὸ γνώρισμα. Cf. A. Heisenberg, *Grabeskirche und Apostelkirche. Zwei Basiliken Konstantins. Untersuchungen zur Kunst und Literatur des ausgehenden Altertums, II: Die Apostelkirche in Konstantinopel* (Leipzig, 1908), 84–5.

46 Downey, "Nikolaos Mesarites: description of the Church of the Holy Apostles," 860–1, explains that "At some time the manuscript which we possess was dismembered and its sheets were bound up, in some disorder, with other writings of Mesarites." Therefore, the text is contained in folios of two separately numbered documents: Cod. Ambrosianus gr. 350, and Cod. Ambrosianus gr. 352. The latter (called B by Heisenberg, *Apostelkirche in Konstantinopel*, 9) contains the reference to *Voulgaroktonos* at fol. 11v. See fig. 10.

47 Downey, "Nikolaos Mesarites: description of the Church of the Holy Apostles," 915; Heisenberg, *Apostelkirche in Konstantinopel*, 83.

48 *Michaelis Choniatae epistulae*, ed. F. Kolovou, CFHB 41 (Berlin and New York, 2001), 285, ep. 179, lines 27–30; *Michail Akominatou tou Choniatou*, ed. Lambros, II, 354.

Theodore Laskaris, despite Michael Choniates' encouragement, failed to recover Constantinople, and it fell to Michael VIII Palaiologos (1261–82) to recover the empire's capital. On that occasion the Bulgar-slayer returned in person. According to the chronicler George Pachymeres, in 1260 the Byzantine forces under Michael Palaiologos advanced to the walls of Constantinople and placed the Latin occupants under siege. A small body of Byzantine troops approached the ruins of the Hebdomon Palace, and there, inside the Church of St. John the Evangelist, they found upright in a corner a corpse with a shepherd's flute in its mouth. An inscription on the sarcophagus next to it allowed the men to identify the body as that of Basil *Voulgaroktonos*. Hearing this Palaiologos had the body transported to his base at Galata, and placed in his tent next to his bed. Shortly afterwards Basil's remains were transferred to the monastery of the Savior at Selymbria, and the empire was restored.[49] The inscription which identified Basil was presumably his now familiar epitaph. It is interesting to note that the earliest of the four manuscripts which record the epitaph (Cod. Ambros. gr. 801. fol. 2v) dates from the late thirteenth or early fourteenth century, and therefore is contemporaneous with Pachymeres' account. All four manuscripts supply a heading to explain that the original inscription was a "verse epitaph on the tomb of the emperor lord Basil *Voulgaroktonos*," but the epithet *Voulgaroktonos* is not used in the epitaph itself. Therefore, the identification of the corpse by the epithet must have been the surmise of the troops, who would now have been familiar with the term Bulgar-slayer.[50]

Clearly, by 1261 the legend of Basil the Bulgar-slayer was well established. The story was retold on a number of occasions to inspire Byzantines confronted with the various hostile peoples – Normans and Pechenegs, Bulgarians and Vlachs, Latins and Turks – who had established control first in the peripheries, and then the capital of the empire. By the beginning of the fourteenth century it was believed that Basil had always been called *Voulgaroktonos*, and the verse chronicler Ephraim states explicitly that this was as a result of his blinding of Bulgars.[51] Nikephoros Gregoras repeated the new orthodoxy that "after many battles Basil the Bulgar-slayer finally defeated and enslaved" the Bulgarians.[52] Basil also appears in the six miracles of St. Eugenios, attributed to John Lazaropoulos, metropolitan of

---

[49] *Georges Pachymérès. Relations historiques*, ed. A. Failler, tr. V. Laurent, 5 vols., CFHB 24 (Paris, 1984–2000), I, 174–7.

[50] S. G. Mercati, "Sull'epitafio di Basilio II Bulgaroctonos," in his *Collectanea Byzantina*, 2 vols. (Bari, 1970), II, 226–31 at 230–1. See above p. 49.

[51] *Ephraem Aenii historia chronica*, ed. O. Lampsides, CFHB 27 (Athens, 1990), 109.

[52] *Nicephori Gregorae Byzantina historia*, eds. B. Niebuhr and L. Schopen, 3 vols., CSHB (Bonn, 1829–55), I, 27.

Trebizond (1365–8). It has been suggested that Lazaropoulos made extensive use of a lost eleventh-century historical source, probably one also used by Skylitzes and Zonaras. If this is true, we can be sure that only Lazaropoulos, and not his source, called Basil *Voulgaroktonos*.[53]

---

[53] N. M. Panagiotakes, "Fragments of a lost eleventh century Byzantine historical work," in *ΦΙΛΕΛΛΗΝ. Studies in honour of Robert Browning*, ed. C. N. Constantinides et al. (Venice, 1996), 321–57 at 354 (c. 18).

7

Basile après Byzance

The encounters between laymen and clerics from the Latin West and their counterparts in the East in the Komnenian period, and more particularly the successes enjoyed by the westerners, not least their capture of Constantinople in 1204, gave Byzantine writers and intellectuals reason to reconsider their identity and mission. Those whom we call Byzantines referred to themselves most often as Romans and Christians. After 1204, these same people witnessed their capital and empire subjected to Christians who recognized the primacy of Rome, which characteristic did not make them "Roman" in Byzantine eyes. However, what constituted "Roman" was now subject to discussion in the East, as it had not been since the restoration of the western empire in the year 800. The fact that westerners referred to the Byzantine ruler as the *imperator Grecorum*, "emperor of the Greeks," did not encourage East Romans to consider themselves Greeks before 1150, despite the fact that Greek had been the empire's principal language of literature and administration for six centuries. However, in the years between the Second and Fourth Crusades, the Byzantines chose to rearticulate the defining characteristics of their culture and society in order to contrast these with western Latin traits. Byzantine writers began to write of themselves not only as Romans, but also as Greeks (Ἕλληνες). "Their Hellenism is the beginning of a steady trickle which continues throughout late Byzantine literature and terminates with a loud gurgle in the fifteenth century, notably in Gemistos Plethon's famous programme for the creation of a Hellenic nation based on the Peloponnese."[1] This tendency was no doubt accelerated by the fact that, in the aftermath of the Fourth Crusade,

---

[1] P. Magdalino, "Hellenism and nationalism in Byzantium," in his *Tradition and transformation in medieval Byzantium* (Aldershot, 1991) no. XIV, 1–29 at 10; repr. with same pagination, in J. Burke and S. Gauntlett, eds., *Neohellenism*, Australian National University: Humanities Research Monograph 5 (Melbourne, 1992). See also M. Angold, "Byzantine 'nationalism' and the Nicaean Empire," *BMGS* 1 (1975), 49–70; S. Xydis, "Medieval origins of modern Greek nationalism," *Balkan Studies* 9 (1968), 1–20.

much imperial territory which had been occupied by non-Greek speakers was lost forever. After 1204, therefore, what had been a multiethnic empire, where subjects speaking numerous languages had contributed to the development of cultural and intellectual life, became a series of small states governed by groups of inter-married Greek-speaking families. For the last two centuries of its existence, as never before, Byzantium was essentially Greek.

In 1453, the last emperor, a member of the Palaiologos family, died as Constantinople fell to the Ottomans, and thus began the so-called *Tourkokratia*, the period of Turkish rule. An awareness of a common Greek past certainly existed in the first centuries of the *Tourkokratia*. However, the Byzantine centuries were not regarded then, as they came to be in the nineteenth century, as a "golden age" of freedom and heroes, and historical stories were not used to construct a sense of community among Greek speakers under Ottoman rule. Literature in Greek followed strictly in the tradition of pre-1453 Byzantine literature, being largely theological, but including also contemporary chronicles, collections of letters, laudatory poetry and school textbooks.[2] We may contrast this with the prevailing interests in Slavic literature and historiography, which dwelt quite specifically on pre-Ottoman glories, and failures. The story of the battle of Kosovo Polje is perhaps the finest example, for, it has been argued, this remained a central motif through the period of Ottoman domination.[3]

One element of the Byzantine tradition that attracted especial attention among all literate Greeks throughout the *Tourkokratia* was messianic and prophetic literature. In perhaps the first instance in an extant source that Basil is called *Voulgaroktonos*, he is cast in the role of prophet. The historian Niketas Choniates records that Basil's "soul was aggrieved" because the emperor Isaak II Angelos (1185–95) had failed to take account of Basil's *typikon*, or foundation document, for the monastery at Sosthenion. Whereupon, Isaak accused Basil of having "belched forth empty lies and vain prophecies

[2] C. Mango, "The Phanariots and the Byzantine tradition," in R. Clogg, ed., *The struggle for Greek independence. Essays to mark the 150th anniversary of the Greek War of Independence* (London, 1973), 41–66 at 50. Mango's view may be contrasted with that held by his predecessor in Oxford's Bywater and Sotheby Chair of Medieval and Modern Greek Language and Literature: C. A. Trypanis, "Greek literature since the fall of Constantinople in 1453," in C. Jelavich and B. Jelavich, eds., *The Balkans in transition. Essays on the development of Balkan life and politics since the eighteenth century* (Berkeley, 1963), 227–57. For a less rosy, but generally positive view see the essays in J. Yiannis, ed., *The Byzantine tradition after the fall of Constantinople* (Charlottesville and Oxford, 1991).

[3] M. Braun, *Die Schlacht auf dem Amselfelde in geschichtlicher und epischer Überlieferung* (Leipzig, 1937). For more recent Serbian interpretations see S. Terzić, ed., *Kosovska bitka u istoriografiju* (Belgrade, 1990).

as from the bay-eating throat and tripod," referring thus to the Pythian oracle at Delphi.[4]

As far as I am aware, oracles, false or otherwise, attributed to Basil did not retain widespread popularity, and his memory was not much invoked during the *Tourkokratia*.[5] Nevertheless, it is worth considering briefly a parallel, the so-called *Oracles of Leo the Wise*.[6] These oracles took the form of sixteen iambic poems illustrated with a symbolical picture which foretold the fate of several emperors and their capital city, Constantinople. They were widely known as early as the middle of the twelfth century, when they were interpreted somewhat inconsistently to explain aspects of the reigns of the Komnenian emperors. By the end of the thirteenth century the form of the illustrated oracles was fixed, and a group of longer poems in popular Greek had been added, reflecting their continued popularity and vitality. However, it was in the two centuries after the fall of Constantinople that the number of manuscript copies produced was, in C. Mango's words, "truly staggering."[7] After 1453 the Leonine oracles were taken to foretell the deliverance of the City from Turkish domination. Thus, according to the sixteenth-century *Chronicon maius* of Pseudo-Phrantzes: "The most wise Leo, emperor of the Romans, himself made a prediction and found that the powerful race of the Agarenes [Turks] was to abide for a thrice-numbered circle, that is three hundred years." Pseudo-Phrantzes clearly identified Leo the Wise as the Byzantine emperor Leo VI (886–912). However, as Mango has convincingly demonstrated, the emperor Leo VI, although known in his own time as *sophos*, the wise, was not associated with the oracles until centuries after his death. It is likely that Leo the Wise was previously identified as Leo the Mathematician, one of the prominent figures in the Byzantine intellectual revival of the middle of the ninth century, a generation before Leo VI came to power. Therefore, through a misunderstanding, and the subsequent wide circulation and evolution of a group of oracles, a rather unspectacular Byzantine emperor became the prophet of Greek emancipation.[8] A similar fate was to befall Leo VI's

---

[4] *Nicetae Choniatae historiae*, ed. J.-L. van Dieten, CFHB 11/1 (Berlin and New York, 1975), 373–4.

[5] N. Iorga, *Byzance après Byzance* (Bucharest, 1935; repr. 1971), 167, refers to a certain Lupu, the prince of Moldavia, who in April 1634 took the name Basil, after the emperor Basil "The Lawmaker." This was surely Basil I, but in the index he is identified as "Basile II (empereur de Byzance)." It is unclear whether this mistake should be attributed to Lupu, Iorga or Iorga's indexer (Liliane Iorga-Pippidi).

[6] C. Mango, "The legend of Leo the Wise," *ZRVI* 6 (1960), 59–93, 78; repr. in his *Byzantium and its image* (London, 1984), no. XVI.

[7] Mango, "Leo the Wise," 78.

[8] Mango, "Leo the Wise," 90–2. See now S. Tougher, "The wisdom of Leo the Wise," in P. Magdalino, ed., *New Constantines: the rhythm of imperial renewal in Byzantium, 4th to 13th centuries* (Aldershot, 1994), 171–9, for a defence of Leo's wisdom.

great-great-grandson, Basil II, whom Pseudo-Phrantzes referred to quite naturally as the Bulgar-slayer.

It is now widely realized that Byzantine history began to play a significant role in Greek life and thought in the context of the struggle for emancipation from Ottoman rule.[9] That is not to say that a Byzantine tradition did not endure through the period of Ottoman domination, but we must draw a distinction between the Byzantinism of the *Tourkokratia*, and the vision of Byzantium which emerged in the independent Greek state.[10] Moreover, for the century before 1821 the classical past prevailed over the Byzantine period for those seeking a model past for the new Greece.[11] The Byzantine centuries were considered dark by the leading, if not all, Greek intellectuals of the Enlightenment. The most famous detractor was Adamantios Korais, for whom "Byzantium stood for obscurantism, monkishness, opression, inertia."[12] Korais championed instead the ideal of classical Greece, and the example of revolutionary France. He was present in Paris in 1789, and believed that modern Greeks, in order to emulate their ancient forebears, could do no better than imitate the French.

Korais' contemporary Rigas Velestinlis also took the French Revolution as his inspiration. His publications included a projected constitution, modeled on the French constitutions of 1793 and 1795, for a new state called the *Elliniki Dimokratia*, or Hellenic Republic. It was to be a unitary, not a federal, state which embraced the whole Balkan peninsula and Asia Minor.

---

[9] Byzantium came to play a role in Ottoman Turkish thought only after 1870, probably as a reaction to Greek claims. See M. Ursinus, "From Süleyman Pasha to Mehmet Fuat Köprülü: Roman and Byzantine history in late Ottoman historiography," *BMGS* 12 (1988), 305–14.

[10] C. Mango, "Byzantinism and Romantic Hellenism," *Journal of the Warburg and Courtauld Institutes* 28 (1965), 29–43; repr. in his *Byzantium and its image*, no. I. This was Mango's inaugural lecture in the Koraes Chair, King's College, London. S. Vryonis, Jr., "Recent scholarship on continuity and discontinuity of culture: classical Greeks, Byzantines and modern Greeks," in S. Vryonis, Jr., ed., *Byzantina kai metabyzantina, I: The "past" in medieval and modern Greek culture* (Malibu, 1978), 237–56, challenges Mango's interpretation, and questions his limited conception of "culture." However, the fallacy of seeking continuity in Greek, or any Balkan nation's cultural history, is made plain by P. Kitromilides, " 'Imagined communities' and the origins of the national question in the Balkans," *European History Quarterly* 19/ii (1989), 149–92; repr. in his *Enlightenment, nationalism, orthodoxy. Studies in the culture and political thought of south-eastern Europe* (Aldershot, 1994), no. XI.

[11] A. Politis, "From Christian Roman emperors to the glorious Greek ancestors," in D. Ricks and P. Magdalino, eds., *Byzantium and the modern Greek identity* (Aldershot, 1998), 1–14.

[12] Mango, "Byzantinism and Romantic Hellenism," 37. Paschalis Kitromilides warned against relying too heavily on Korais, and drew attention to various, positive conceptions of Byzantium in the writings of Greek Enlightenment thinkers, in an unpublished paper presented at Dumbarton Oaks, 24 April 2002. A fuller exposition of such positive conceptions was presented by Despina Christodoulou, in a paper entitled "Refusing the past: the contest for Byzantium as Hellenic history," given at the University of Wisconsin-Madison, on 12 December 2002.

Sovereignty was to reside in the people, who were to comprise all the state's inhabitants without distinction of language or religion. However, the official language was to be Greek. In R. Clogg's words: "Essentially, what Rigas seems to have envisaged was a kind of restored Byzantine Empire with republican in the place of monarchical institutions, ruled, as in Byzantium, by an elite that was Greek by culture if not necessarily by race."[13] Clearly, there were substantial problems with Rigas' vision of a Greek nation state as a restored Byzantine empire, not least the facts that the Byzantine system was monarchical and anti-national.[14] To serve as a model, therefore, Byzantium had to be redefined so that it might fit within, and not contradict, the national and nationalist framework of nineteenth-century Greece.[15] The greatest provocation to the discussion of medieval Greece, and of medieval Hellenism, however, was the thesis of J. P. Fallmerayer, which posited that modern Greeks were not descended from the ancients. The Greeks, Fallmerayer maintained, had been eliminated by massive influxes of Slavs and Albanians, such that any notion of continuity was a fiction. Fallmerayer's hypothesis rested largely on his reading of Evagrius, a church historian of the later sixth century. Fallmerayer's statements were extremely bold and provocative considering how meager was his basis for making them. For example, and notoriously, he claimed that "not a single drop of real pure Hellenic blood flows in the veins of the Christian population of modern Greece." By "pure Hellenic blood" he meant that which had flowed in the veins of Pericles and Alcibiades, or indeed Sophocles and Plato.[16]

---

[13] R. Clogg, "Aspects of the movement for Greek independence," in his *The struggle for Greek independence*, 1–40 at 28. Cf. D. A. Zakythinos, *The making of modern Greece from Byzantium to independence* (Oxford, 1976), 157–67 at 163: "Clearly the principle governing Rhigas's state is to be a racial and religious tolerance which will lead to such a degree of joint solidarity that 'the Bulgar must feel himself roused when the Greek suffers and the Greek in his turn must feel for the Bulgar'." The same for the Albanian and the Vlach, the text continues: A. Daskalakis, ed., *To politeuma tou Riga Velestinli. Proton syntagma Ellinikis Dimokratias kai eleutheras diaviossios ton Valkanikon laon* (Athens, 1976), 85. For all his alleged "Byzantinism," glancing at Rigas' famous map one notices a complete absence of references to Byzantium, symbols of the medieval empire, and medieval place names.

[14] *Pace* the convincing arguments advanced by Magdalino, "Hellenism and nationalism," 1–29.

[15] Kitromilides, "Imagined communities," 177–86; R. Clogg, "The Byzantine legacy in the modern Greek world: the *megali idea*," in L. Clucas, ed., *The Byzantine legacy in Eastern Europe* (Boulder, 1988), 253–81; repr. in R. Clogg, *Anatolica: studies in the Greek East in the 18th and 19th centuries* (Aldershot, 1996), no. IV; A. Liakos, "The construction of national time: the making of the modern Greek historical imagination," *Mediterranean Historical Review* 16 (2001), 27–42.

[16] J. P. Fallmerayer, *Geschichte der Halbinsel Morea während des Mittelalters*, 2 vols. (Stuttgart, 1830–6), I, iii–xiv. See authoritatively G. Veloudis, "Jakob Philipp Fallmerayer und die Entstehung des neugriechischen Historismus," *SüdostF* 29 (1970), 43–90. See also G. Bel, "Classical Greece, Byzantium and the struggle for Greek national identity," in *Polyphonia Byzantina. Studies in honour of William J. Aerts* (Groningen, 1993), 325–37, which places necessary emphasis on Fallmerayer.

In the middle years of the nineteenth century Fallmerayer's challenge was accepted, and Byzantium was embraced by scholars of philology, linguistics and folklore as the missing link which proved the continuity of Hellenism.[17] Byzantine texts were compiled, edited and published, and Byzantine themes were a commonplace in contemporary literature. Much recent work has explored this Byzantine renascence. Most importantly for our purposes, the history of the Byzantine empire was embraced as a subject worthy of study, and redefined as the history of medieval Greece, the link between the classical past and the national present. In 1834, a new capital city, Athens, was chosen over the previous, provisional capital, Nauplion. Athens was itself considered provisional by many, including the then minister of the interior, Ioanis Kolettis, for whom Constantinople was the only possible permanent capital. Still, strenuous efforts were made to establish Athens as a worthy European capital city, and one which reflected the unique status and heritage of the Greek people. Even before 1834 elaborate plans for Athens were drawn up, which oriented the political, intellectual and cultural institutions around the historical heart of the ancient city, the Akropolis. Classical visions prevailed: the Royal Palace, designed by Karl Friedrich von Schinkel, was to stand on the Akropolis; where Byzantine buildings obscured ancient ruins they were removed.[18] Gradually, however, and not without a fierce struggle, attitudes shifted, and a Byzantine flavor was incorporated into the new cityscape.[19] The cathedral, it was determined

[17] This is true both in Greece and elsewhere. For example, in Athens, between November 1993 and May 1994, a series of lectures, now a published series of pamphlets, addressed "Byzantine reality and neohellenic interpretations" (*Vyzantini pragmatikotita kai neoellinikes ermineies*). Elsewhere, see for example: P. Agapitos, "Byzantine literature and Greek philologists in the nineteenth century," *Classica et Medievalia* 43 (1992), 231–60; M. Alexiou, "Writing against silence: antithesis and ekphrasis in the prose fiction of Georgios Vizyenos," *DOP* 47 (1993) 263–86, which were both initially presented at a colloquium entitled "The familiar stranger: Byzantium in modern Greece," held at Dumbarton Oaks in May 1991. Similar themes were explored at a colloquium held at King's College, London, in May 1996, published as Ricks and Magdalino, eds., *Byzantium and the modern Greek identity*. A useful compendium of nineteenth-century Greek opinions, quotations and references is provided by F. Dimitrakopoulos, *Vyzantio kai neoelliniki dianoisi sta mesa tou dekatou enatou aionos* (Athens, 1996).

[18] G. Huxley, "Aspects of modern Greek historiography of Byzantium," in Ricks and Magdalino, eds., *Byzantium and the modern Greek identity*, 15–25 at 16. According to his journal, George Finlay condemned such selective "preservation," and considered the Greek government's "negotiations with the town of Athens about excavating half the city [a] very silly project." He did so in something of an official capacity, for he had been appointed, in 1834, as "commissioner extraordinary to assist the nomarch of Athens in preparing the plans for the town." See W. Miller, "The Finlay papers," *EHR* 39 (1924), 386–98 at 389; W. Miller, "The journals of Finlay and Jarvis," *EHR* 41 (1926), 514–25 at 516.

[19] An exhibition at Athens' Byzantine and Christian Museum, 29 March–31 October 2002, illuminated the struggle to establish a role for preserved or conserved Byzantine artifacts in the new capital. This still left no room for Frankish or Turkish "accretions," which were summarily removed. For foreign

in 1846, should be constructed in a "Helleno-Byzantine" style. King Otto made this the subject of an architectural competition, and favored the designs of one Demetrios Zezos, who had previously won Otto's support for his vision for the Church of the Life-giving fountain, *Zoodochos Pege*. The Helleno-Byzantine style had still properly to be invented. According to one commentator, Zezos' designs for the cathedral epitomized this new/medieval/ancient order of architecture, since it "followed the Byzantine style, borrowing also from ancient architectural details," and might truly be compared to Hagia Sophia.[20] One can still make this comparison, and observe the absence of any architectural association.

This architectural discussion took place in the context of a wider debate over the relative rights of Greeks living within (*autochthons*) and outside (*heterochthons*) the borders of the new kingdom.[21] In response, a new doctrine had been formulated which was to govern Greece's foreign policy objectives for the remainder of the nineteenth century. The Great Idea (*Megali Idea*), expounded first and famously in 1844 by Kolettis, now prime minister, was to make all Greeks *autochthons* by extending the borders of the kingdom by force of arms. Although Kolettis did not mention Byzantium, a link was established between the medieval empire and the Great Idea within the prevailing political culture of "Romantic Hellenism."[22] The greatest exponent of Greek historical continuity was Konstantinos Paparrigopoulos (1815–91), author of a monumental *History of the Greek nation*. Paparrigopoulos' task was to chart the passage of "the Greek nation" (*to ellinikon ethnos*) from origins to emancipation, through the Byzantine era which he rechristened the age of the Hellenic Empire of Constantinople. The "golden age" of that empire was the period 867–1025, when the frontiers

commentary on this "purification," first published in the *International Review* in 1878, see E. A. Freeman, "First impressions of Athens," in his *Historical essays*, 3rd series (London, 1892), 289–90, "We can quite understand the feeling with which the founders of the regenerate Athens wished to wipe out all traces of Turkish rule, to make the regenerate city look as though the Turk had never been there. But such a feeling is not a wholesome one." *Ibid.*, 302, "The ducal tower on the Akropolis stood out boldly as a living teacher of the unity of history. But to the pedant who is happy to grope among the details of two or three arbitrarily chosen centuries, the unity of history has no meaning. He deems that the facts of past time can be wiped out by wiping out its material monuments. At the bidding of such men the ducal tower . . . has been levelled."

[20] E. Bastéa, *The creation of modern Athens: planning the myth* (Cambridge, 2000), 161–5.

[21] Kitromilides, "Imagined communities," 165; Clogg, "The Byzantine legacy in the modern Greek world: the *megali idea*," 253–81.

[22] P. Kitromilides, "On the intellectual content of Greek nationalism: Paparrigopoulos, Byzantium and the Great Idea," in Ricks and Magdalino, eds., *Byzantium and the modern Greek identity*, 25–33 at 28. See also M. Nystazopoulou-Pelekidou, "Oi vizantines istorikes spoudes stin Ellada. Apo ton Spyridona Zambelio ston Dionysio Zakythino," *Symmeikta. Ethniko Idryma Ereunon, Kentro Vyzantinon Ereunon* 9, 2 vols. (1994), II, 153–76 at 164–6.

of Greece reached their greatest extent and Greek cultural hegemony was established throughout southeastern Europe and Anatolia. Initially a mere sketch intended for school-children, Paparrigopoulos' vision expanded to five volumes for the second definitive edition (1885–7), of which three volumes were devoted to Byzantine history.[23] Even before this, it had appeared in a French translation, in the preface to which Paparrigopoulos set out his reasons for writing for an international readership. Many readers would be familiar with works "on the Greek people... published all the time, of lesser or greater merit, in England, Germany and in France."

The unity of Hellenic civilization has sometimes been denied, sometimes strongly affirmed... But few are those who have admitted that the Greek race never ceased to make a mark on history... The purpose of this work is to re-establish the neglected unity of Hellenic civilization, to give to its principal phases their true meaning, to make heard the voice of Greece in the historical trial where she has been judged *in absentia*.[24]

Paparrigopoulos gave solid historical foundations to contemporary Greek political ambitions, both abroad and at home. In his history, Basil I, the founder of the Macedonian dynasty was held to have established a line which reached its climax with his great-great-great-grandson, Basil II. This second Basil fought the Bulgarians to a standstill, earning himself the name *Voulgaroktonos*, and celebrated his victory first in Athens and then in Constantinople, which Kolettis had identified as the two poles of Hellenism. The fourth of five large format volumes, in its second revised edition of 1925, featured as its frontispiece a redrawn monochrome lithograph of Basil II's famous psalter portrait with the heading "Basil II the Bulgar-slayer receiving the obeisance of the rulers of the Bulgarians." No mention is made of the fact that the portrait is a reproduction (see fig. Figure 11).[25] Paparrigopoulos did not write in isolation. His contemporary Spyridon Zambelios (1815–81) published a collection of *Byzantine studies* in 1857, which bore the subtitle "On the sources of modern Greek nationality from the eighth to the tenth century after Christ." Zambelios argued that "the [appropriate] limits of

[23] K. Paparrigopoulos, *Istoria tou ellinikou ethnous [i proti morfi: 1853]*, ed. K. Th. Dimaras (Athens, 1970); *Istoria tou ellinikou ethnous*, 5 vols. (Athens 1860–74; 2nd ed. 1885–7). I have used the revised edition, with additions by P. Karolides (Athens, 1925). Paparrigopoulos was not the first writer to seek to incorporate the Byzantine millennium into a narrative of Greek history. He was, however, by far the most successful.

[24] C. Paparrigopoulo[s], *Histoire de la civilisation hellénique* (Paris, 1878), vii–ix.

[25] Paparrigopoulos, *Istoria tou ellinikou ethnous*, IV, 168–210 and unnumbered frontispiece. A smaller format version, produced later, featured not this black and white sketch, but instead the same color reproduction which now hangs in the National Historical Museum in Athens, for which see plate 3.

ΒΑΣΙΛΕΙΟΣ Ο Β΄ Ο ΒΟΥΛΓΑΡΟΚΤΟΝΟΣ
ΠΡΟΣΚΥΝΟΥΜΕΝΟΣ ΥΠΟ ΤΩΝ ΒΟΥΛΓΑΡΩΝ ΑΡΧΟΝΤΩΝ
(Εἰκὼν ἐκ Ψαλτηρίου τοῦ Βασιλείου Β΄ εὑρισκομένου ἐν τῇ Μαρκιανῇ Βιβλιοθήκῃ)

Figure 11   K. Paparrigopoulos, *Istoria tou ellinikou ethnous*, ed. P. Karolides, revised ed. (Athens, 1925), IV, frontispiece, being a reproduction of Basil II's psalter illumination with inappropriate title.

the Neohellenic Fatherland" (*ta oria tis Neoellinikis patridos*) were set by the greatest of emperors of the "Greco-Romans" (*Graikoromaioi*), Nikephoros Phokas and John Tzimiskes. Byzantium drew, he believed, on three distinct traditions: classical Greek language and literature; Christianity; and Roman law and institutions. He took issue, like Paparrigopoulos, with earlier foreign writers, especially Gibbon and Montesquieu, who had derided the medieval Greek empire.[26] His study did not continue into the eleventh century, and drew no attention to the achievements of Basil II.

A sympathetic "foreign" view was presented to an English-speaking audience by George Finlay, who wrote the following in the first of two volumes in his *History of Greece* devoted to the history of the Byzantine empire.[27]

Basil was the only emperor who for several ages honoured Athens with a visit. Many magnificent structures in the town, and the temples of the Acropolis, had then hardly suffered any rude touches from the hand of time. If the original splendour of the external paintings and gilding which once adorned the Parthenon of Pericles had faded, the mural paintings of saints, martyrs, emperors, and empresses, that covered the interior of the cella, gave a new interest to the church of the Virgin, into which it had been transformed. The mind of Basil, though insensible to Hellenic literature, was deeply sensible of religious impressions, and the glorious combination of beauty in art and nature that he saw in the Acropolis touched his stern soul. He testified his feelings by splendid gifts to the city, and rich dedications at the shrine of the Virgin in the Parthenon. From Greece the emperor returned to Constantinople, where he indulged himself in the pomp of a triumph, making his entry into his capital by the Golden Gate, and listening with satisfaction to the cries of the populace, who applauded his cruelty by saluting him with the title "The Slayer of the Bulgarians."

Finlay, who lived and wrote in Athens after 1827, believed that Basil's reign was "the culminating point of Byzantine greatness."[28] However, he astutely noted that Basil's "barbarous title [*Voulgaroktonos*] is not mentioned by the writers nearest his own time."[29] Finlay offered the further pertinent

[26] S. Zambelios, *Vyzantinai meletai. Peri pigon neoellinikis ethnotitos apo 8 achri 10 ekatonaetiridos m. X.* (Athens, 1857). Huxley, "Aspects of modern Greek historiography," 17–19; Agapitos, "Byzantine literature and Greek philologists," 238–9; Nystazopoulou-Pelekidou, "Oi Vizantines istorikes spoudes," 162–4, provide insightful comments.

[27] G. Finlay, *A history of Greece from its conquest by the Romans to the present time, B.C. 146 to A.D. 1864*, 2nd ed., ed. H. F. Tozer, 7 vols. (Oxford, 1877). Volume two, the first on the Byzantine empire, was posthumously reissued as G. Finlay, *History of the Byzantine empire from DCCXVI to MLVII* (London, 1906). This title is slightly misleading since, according to J. M. Hussey, "George Finlay in perspective – a centenary reappraisal," *Annual of the British School at Athens* 70 (1975), 135–44 at 140: "to assess [Finlay] fairly, particularly on the Byzantine period, it must be remembered that he was writing about what he calls 'the fortunes of the Greek nation.' This led him to omit much that would now be included in any 'Byzantine' history."

[28] Finlay, *History of Greece*, II, 368.   [29] Finlay, *History of Greece*, II, 383, n. 2.

observation, that the "Byzantine empire had never had less of a national character than at the present period, when its military glory reached the highest pitch." However, by this he meant that no "national population," meaning Greek settlers, was introduced into the lands despoiled by Basil's campaigns against the "national energy... of the united Bulgarians and Sclavonians."[30]

William Miller, the British philhellene, traveler and writer, elaborated on Finlay's account, noting that Basil "proceeded to Athens, which no Byzantine emperor had visited since the days of Constans II." This was appropriate because the whole "Balkan peninsula was once again under Greek domination. In the Church of the Virgin on the Akropolis, the very centre and shrine of the old Hellenic life in bygone days, the victorious emperor offered up thanks to Almighty God." Miller also proposed that Basil's special feeling for Athens, which saw him donate spoils of war to, and commission frescoes for, the Church of the Virgin, was emulated by others. This, he explained, was the reason for the abundance of churches in Athens built or restored in the early eleventh century.[31] E. A. Freeman, an historian best known for his multivolume treatment of the Norman conquest of England, expounded similarly on "the forms of Patriarchs and saints [who] looked down on the rites of that day when the slayer of the Bulgarians came to pay homage in the Parthenon, which had passed from Athene to Panagia."[32]

If Finlay, Miller and Freeman were correct, and Basil thought more fondly of Athens than other cities, we can identify a rather different sentiment in the verse of his contemporary, John Geometres, who expressed a gloating sense of satisfaction that Athens had declined so in comparison to Constantinople.[33] Moreover, it is now clear that the eleventh-century spurt of church building is a common phenomenon, the consequence of the increasing wealth of the empire as a whole, and of provincial magnates in particular, at this time. For example, at Kastoria, in the heart of the region where Basil campaigned, there are still more surviving churches of the eleventh and twelfth centuries, which are testament to the increased wealth of the local aristocracy.

Ferdinand Gregorovius wrote more extensively on medieval Athens even than Finlay, although like Miller and Freeman he came to Athens via Rome. Born in East Prussia, Gregorovius spent his earlier years as a teacher and, from 1848, as the editor of a newspaper, the *Neue Königsberger Zeitung*.

[30] Finlay, *History of Greece*, II, 383.
[31] W. Miller, *Essays in the Latin Orient* (Cambridge, 1921), 47–8.
[32] Freeman, "First impressions of Athens," 300–1.
[33] John Geometres, PG 106, 950–1; noted by Magdalino, "Hellenism and nationalism," 13, n. 71.

In 1852 he journeyed to Italy, and returned almost annually thereafter, keeping detailed journals published in five volumes between 1856 and 1877. In addition, he completed an eight-volume *History of the city of Rome in the Middle Ages*. In the last decade of his life, Gregorovius' attention shifted to Greece, where he traveled in 1880 and 1882, and subsequently began work on a companion volume to this Roman history, a *History of the city of Athens in the Middle Ages*.[34] Gregorovius' conception of medieval Athens was clearly influenced by contemporary attempts to place that city at the heart of a medieval Hellenic empire. Thus, he wrote of the wars between Samuel and Basil II: "Never was the threat to Greece greater than now, where the violent Tsar [Samuel] had in mind the annexation of this province to his empire." Moreover, like Paparrigopoulos and others of his western European counterparts, Gregorovius regarded Basil II's Balkan campaigns as the conclusion of a project begun by his great-great-great-grandfather. Thus, "What the founder of the Macedonian dynasty, Basil I had begun, [namely] the reconquest of the Slavic lands of the Balkans, the victorious Basil II completed, an outstanding commander and leader who restored the Greek empire, so long feeble, to its former extent."[35] But the march to Athens did not reflect Basil's profound Hellenism, Gregorovius noted, since "it was hardly a thirst for antiquarian knowledge that led the terrible Bulgar-slayer thither...but rather it was the knowledge that through the extinction of the Bulgarian realm the victory of Greece over the Slavs had been decided."[36]

If not for the reasons Gregorovius advanced, Basil's journey to Athens was indeed remarkable, and inspired a remarkable, imaginative re-creation by Kostis Palamas. His *I flogera tou Vasilia* (*The king's flute*), which was dedicated on 1 August 1909, presents Basil's journey as an expression of his profound Hellenism.[37] Palamas also draws on the episode of 1260, recorded by the chronicler George Pachymeres, when Byzantine forces under Michael Palaiologos, found, inside the Church of St. John the Evangelist in the ruins of the Hebdomon Palace, an inscribed sarcophagus which identified a nearby corpse as belonging to Basil *Voulgaroktonos*. In his mouth was a

---

[34] F. Gregorovius, *Geschichte der Stadt Athen im Mittelalter von der Zeit Justinians bis zur türkischen Eroberung*, 2 vols. (Stuttgart, 1889). Gregorovius noted that he founded his work on the slightly earlier studies of C. Hopf (1832–73).

[35] Gregorovius, *Geschichte der Stadt Athen*, I, 160–1.

[36] Gregorovius, *Geschichte der Stadt Athen*, I, 162. Gregorovius' comments are clearly to be understood in the context of discussions over Fallmerayer's thesis. So much is clear from the insightful overview of contemporary scholarship he presents in his foreword.

[37] K. Palamas, *The king's flute*, tr. T. P. Stefaniades and G. C. Katsimbalis, The Kostes Palamas Institute 4 (Athens, 1982).

shepherd's flute.[38] Palamas' work drew the attention and appreciation of the great French Byzantinist Charles Diehl, who contributed a preface to the French translation of *The king's flute* in 1934. Diehl wrote of Palamas, "It would be difficult, I think, to know the history of Byzantium better than the great Greek poet, or to have a better feeling for its grandeur and beauty."[39] It has since been suggested that Palamas transformed and subverted Byzantium to make it conform to a Hellenism centered on Athens, and that this poem reveals many of the tensions inherent in integrating disparate aspects of the Greek past into a continuum.[40]

Byzantine scholarship had continued apace in Greece between Paparrigopoulos and Palamas, with perhaps the greatest achievements belonging to the editors of medieval Greek documents. Rallis and Potlis published six volumes on ecclesiastical canons; Konstantinos Sathas completed seven volumes of his *Medieval library*; and Ioannis Zepos produced a monumental legal compilation, the *Vasilika*.[41] Spyridon Lambros (1851–1919) was at the forefront of those scholars seeking to place Athens at the center of the Byzantine past.[42] His edition of the works of Michael Choniates was inspired, in part, by the fact that Michael had been archbishop in Athens, and its publication was supported by a subvention from Athens City Council. Lambros also produced a three-volume translation of Gregorovius' history of the city (Athens, 1904–6).[43] A final figure of note, both before and after 1900, is Pavlos Karolides, who re-edited Paparrigopoulos' history and added a continuation. He also wrote his own history of Byzantium in Turkish,

[38] *Georges Pachymérès. Relations historiques*, ed. A. Failler, tr. V. Laurent, CFHB 24, 5 vols. (Paris, 1984–2000), I, 174–7. K. Mitsakis, "Byzantium in modern Greek historical fiction," in *Byzantinische Stoffe und Motive in der europäischen Literatur des 19. und 20. Jahrhunderts*, ed. E. Konstantinou, Philhellenische Studien 6 (Frankfurt am Main, 1998), 239–51 at 244, suggests that Palamas first encountered this episode in a Greek novel published in 1883: I. Pervanoglou, *Michail o Palaiologos. Istorikon diigma* (Leipzig, 1883), 110. However, Palamas states explicitly that the idea for the poem sprang from his reading of Kedrenos (containing Skylitzes) and Pachymeres: K. Palamas, *Apanta*, 16 vols. (Athens, 1962–9), V, 31–2; X, 539.

[39] Palamas, *The king's flute*, 14.

[40] A. Hirst, "Two cheers for Byzantium: equivocal attitudes in the poetry of Palamas and Cafavy," in D. Ricks and P. Magdalino, eds., *Byzantium and the modern Greek identity*, 105–17. Cf. P. Agapitos, "Byzantium in the poetry of Kostis Palamas and C. P. Cafavy," *Kampos* 2 (1994), 1–20.

[41] G. Rallis and M. Potlis, eds., *Syntagma ton theion kai hieron kanonon ton te hagion kai paneuphimon apostolon*, 6 vols. (Athens, 1852–9); K. Sathas, *Mesaioniki vivliothiki*, 7 vols. (Athens, Paris and Venice, 1872–94); I. Zepos, *Vasilika kata tin en Leipsia ekdosin tou G.E. Heimbach kai to sympliroma tou Z. Lingenthal*, 5 vols. (Athens, 1896–1900).

[42] A brief biography is provided in the memorial volume *Eis mnimin Spyridonos Lambrou*, ed. G. Charitakis (Athens, 1935), γ'-ιδ'. See also Nystazopoulou-Pelekidou, "Oi vizantines istorikes spoudes," 167–9.

[43] *Michail Akominatou tou Choniatou ta sozomena*, ed. S. Lambros, 2 vols. (Athens, 1879–80); Agapitos, "Byzantine literature and Greek philologists," 242–4. See also the earlier study S. Lambros, *Ai Athinai peri ta teli tou dodekatou aionos* (Athens, 1878).

a language in which he was fluent. Karolides was born in Kappadokia, studied in Istanbul and Smyrna before stints in Germany and France, and served for four years in the Turkish parliament as a representative for Aydin (1908–12).[44]

There were after 1821, and particularly after 1844, major advances in Greek scholarship devoted to the Byzantine empire. A consensus was reached on the importance of the Macedonian period, which reached its apogee under Basil II. The Byzantine empire was, for these scholars, the medieval Hellenic empire, whose cultural influence was extended largely as a consequence of military successes. The victories of Basil II, the greatest warrior emperor of the age, symbolized the triumph of medieval Greek civilization over the Slavs, being the restoration of correct order, *taxis*, ending the centuries of *ataxia* which had followed the installation of Slavs and Bulgars in the empire's Balkan lands. Such sentiments suited Greek national aspirations in the later nineteenth century. However, the principal studies of the reign of Basil II, when this project was deemed to be completed, were undertaken by two scholars working not in Greece, but in St. Petersburg and Paris: Baron Viktor Romanovich Rozen and Gustave Schlumberger.

Rozen, born at Revel in Estonia in 1849, studied in St. Petersburg and Leipzig. He spent most of his career in St. Petersburg, where he was a member of the academy, and researched and taught oriental languages, literature and history. In 1878 he published, with A. Kurnik, a work on the ninth-century Arabic author al-Bakrî, with additional details from further authors who provided information on the early history of the Slavs and Russians. As a further stage in this research project he traveled, in 1879, to the Bibliothèque Nationale in Paris, seeking additional unpublished manuscript sources. There he discovered and identified the first, incomplete section of a work by the Christian Arabic author Yahya of Antioch, which provided, as we have often seen in this book, unique information on Byzantium in the tenth and early eleventh centuries. Rozen sought in vain for a continuation, before returning to St. Petersburg, where his attention was drawn to a Beirut manuscript in the private library of "M. Porphyrius" (F. Uspenskii). This, primarily a version of Eutychios' history, contained at the end an earlier and more complete version of Yahya's chronicle. Rozen determined to produce a complete edition of Yahya's works, but was prevented from doing so by other duties. Therefore, he produced instead a massively annotated series of translated excerpts relating

---

[44] Huxley, "Aspects of modern Greek historiography," 19–20.

to the reign of Basil II, "Bolgaroboitsa." Such a project, he determined, required little justification, for anything relating to Basil's reign would interest Russian historians.[45]

Rozen's work is still often cited, occasionally erroneously as a monographic study of Basil II, but rarely read. Its publication in Russian has made it inaccessible to many scholars, and the subsequent edition and translation into French of Yahya's work provided an accessible alternative. However, only 73 of Rozen's 398 pages of text were translated excerpts; the remainder were detailed notes which still repay attention.[46] According to M. Canard, in a preface to a reproduction of the work, only a few of Rozen's excerpts and fewer of his notes were used by Basil's first, and last, modern biographer, Gustave Schlumberger. In fact, Schlumberger refers frequently and explicitly to Rozen's publication, even citing a review by Uspenskii (Ouspensky).[47] He also cites with approval, and offers lengthy free translations of many secondary works, including those by Paparrigopoulos and Gregorovius, for example, in writing of Basil's entry into Athens in 1018.[48]

Schlumberger was born at Guebwiller, Alsace, in 1844, into a rich industrial family. He studied medicine in Paris, but his passion was history and its remains. A collector and publisher of Byzantine coins and lead seals, Schlumberger was already a member of the Académie des Inscriptions et Belles Lettres when he turned his attention to an historical study of Byzantium. Schlumberger's monograph on Basil II, the last biographic study of the emperor, was part of his broader study of Byzantium at the end of the tenth and beginning of the eleventh century, a period he considered a "golden age." So much would appear to be reflected in the title of his grand narrative, in three large illustrated volumes: *The Byzantine epic*. However, we learn from Schlumberger's *mémoires* that this title was imposed upon him by his publisher, Hachette, much to his regret, for it gave his readership the impression that his previous work on the emperor

[45] V. R. Rozen, *Imperator Vasilij Bolgarobojca. Izvlečenija iz Letopisi Jaxi Antioxijskago* (St. Petersburg, 1908; repr. London, 1972), vii. His allusion is, of course, to the baptism of the Kievan ruler Vladimir. The brief biography presented here draws on the introduction to the reprinted volume by M. Canard.

[46] As does Rozen's chronological survey of Basil's reign, cross-referenced to passages in Yahya: Rozen, *Imperator Vasilij Bolgarobojca*, 399–415.

[47] G. Schlumberger, *L'épopée byzantine à la fin du dixième siècle, I. Jean Tzimiscès; les jeunes années de Basile II, le tueur de Bulgares (969–989)* (Paris, 1896), iii, n. 2, 576, 603, 646, 650–1, 664, 670, 674–6, 678–5, 703, n. 3, 715 (Uspenskii review), 718–19; G. Schlumberger, *L'épopée byzantine à la fin du dixième siècle, II. Basile II le tueur des Bulgares* (Paris, 1900), iii, and passim, esp. 419, n. 1 (again on Uspenskii's review, which was the first publication "to signal the importance of Yahya's information on the new administration in Bulgaria").

[48] Schlumberger, *Basile II le tueur des Bulgares*, 400–5; Gregorovius, *Geschichte der Stadt Athen*, I, 162; Paparrigopoulos, *Istoria tou ellinikou ethnous*, IV, 202–4.

Nikephoros Phokas was not part of the series.[49] Thus, while Basil's reign is at the heart of the epic trilogy, which commenced with John Tzimiskes and ended with the last of the Macedonian dynasty, the sisters, Zoe and Theodora, it is a lesser part of the tetralogy. We cannot credit Schlumberger with a special attachment to the Bulgar-slayer, over and above his interest in the era of the Macedonian emperors, and indeed the publication of his great tome on Basil's later years passes without particular emphasis in the author's *mémoires*.[50] Moreover, while Schlumberger considered the Byzantine tetralogy his principal oeuvre, he later wrote a number of works on the crusades and crusaders: "studies on the formidable Renaud de Chatillon, the legendary crusader prince of Antioch, on the splendid campaigns of King Amaury of Jerusalem in Egypt in the twelfth century, and on the Catalan adventurers called 'Almugavares' in Asia Minor, Thrace and Greece at the start of the fourteenth century."[51] Schlumberger's epic trilogy was promptly translated into Greek (Athens, 1904–8), under a deal struck between the publishers Hachette and Bibliothèque Marasli which omitted his study of Nikephoros Phokas. The three-volume *Epopée*, with the Bulgar-slayer cast in the starring role, struck a popular note among Greek speakers who were at that time engaged in a struggle with Slavic speakers in exactly those regions where Basil II had fought the Bulgarians.

---

[49] G. Schlumberger, *Mes souvenirs 1844–1928*, 2 vols. (Paris, 1934), I, 264; G. Schlumberger, *Un empereur byzantin au dixième siècle, Nicéphore Phocas* (Paris, 1890).
[50] Schlumberger, *Souvenirs*, I, 91.   [51] Schlumberger, *Souvenirs*, II, 265.

8

Basil and the "Macedonian Question"

When, several weeks ago, the victorious king of Greece Constantine, arriving from Salonika, disembarked at Phaleros with great pomp and amidst indescribable popular enthusiasm, the correspondents of French newspapers noticed, among the frenetic acclamations and greetings, the strange epithet "*Voulgaroktonos*," that is to say "Slayer of the Bulgars." "Long live the liberator king! The victor king! The Bulgar-slayer!" cried the thousands of spectators at every opportunity, as the king passed among them visibly moved. They had rushed from Athens and all the cities of the Peloponnese and Attika to be present at this second modern resurrection of the Hellenic nation.[1]

Thus wrote Gustave Schlumberger in the French journal *Le Gaulois*, on 4 October 1913. He proceeded to explain the strange epithet, and why it should be employed by the Greeks of their new king, Constantine, victorious at the end of the Second Balkan War. He did not observe that this was no spontaneous outburst of Byzantine feeling, but an orchestrated acclamation, thus in true Byzantine style, of the king who claimed to be the successor to the last Roman emperor, Constantine XI. After the assassination of his father, posters (fig. Figure 12) were distributed of the new king wearing the uniform he had sported as crown prince and commander-in-chief of the Greek army, above the caption "The greatest of the Constantines, the Bulgar-slayer, [Constantine] XII."[2] The principal Greek prize in the Second Balkan War was a greater share of Macedonia, a territory they had disputed with Bulgarians, and also Serbs, for four decades. It appeared to be a favorable answer to the so-called "Macedonian Question." In the middle of the eighteenth century, following long years of war, the Ottoman empire was obliged to recognize western dominance in several theaters. Relations with the "Great Powers," being Austria-Hungary, France, Great Britain

---

[1] G. Schlumberger, "L'empereur Basile II à Athènes," *Le Gaulois*, 4 October 1913; repr. in G. Schlumberger, *Récits de Byzance et des Croisades*, 2 vols. (Paris, 1916–22), I, 50–8 at 50.
[2] I. Mazarakis-Ainian and E. Papaspyrou-Karadimitriou, *Valkanikoi polemoi 1912–1913. Elliniki laiki eikonografia*, 2nd ed. (Athens, 1999), 221, fig. 86.

Figure 12   A Greek poster of 1913 depicting the new king Constantine in his general's uniform. The caption reads "The greatest of the Constantines, the Bulgarslayer, [Constantine] XII." Historical and Ethnological Society of Greece.

and Russia, came to dominate Ottoman political life, just as the possible disintegration of the eastern empire became an urgent political concern among the "Great Powers." The "Eastern Question" had been a concern for more than a century before Macedonia came to the fore. The "Macedonian Question," as an element of the broader "Eastern Question," became an urgent consideration in 1870, following the unilateral declaration of an independent Bulgarian Church, the Exarchate.[3] Under the Ottoman *millet* system, separate nationalities did not exist within the empire, but religious affiliations were accorded recognition and rights. Thus, peoples who today live within separate nation states, including Albania, Bulgaria, the Republic of Macedonia, Serbia and Greece, were grouped according to their professed faith, and those who were Orthodox Christians were subject to the Greek-speaking Ecumenical Patriarch based in Istanbul. In 1833, the new sovereign Greek state declared the independence of a Greek Church from the Patriarchate, which was still subject to the Ottomans. Such autocephaly had been urged from the earliest days of the struggle for independence, for example by Korais, and was pursued subsequently by those nations who gained independence later: Romania in 1865; Bulgaria, as we have noted, in 1870; and Serbia in 1879, which exceptionally was conferred administrative independence by the synod of Constantinople before splitting.[4]

After 1870, therefore, regions occupied almost exclusively by Bulgarians were transferred from the Greek-speaking Patriarchate to the Exarchate. Elsewhere, however, the decision was to be made according to the wishes of a two-thirds majority, and those living in Macedonia were obliged to make a decision: to adhere to the Ecumenical Patriarchate, being the Greek-speaking Church, or join the Bulgarian-speaking Exarchate. A significant factor in this decision was pragmatism: joining the Exarchate alleviated the excessive burden of taxation imposed by the Ecumenical Patriarchate. A second, more significant factor was cultural, predicated on the notion that each Macedonian had an innate "national consciousness," to which we will turn shortly.

In 1878 Bulgaria won independence from the Ottoman empire. In the immediate aftermath of a Russian victory over the Turks, the preliminary

---

[3] An exarch is a prelate ranking between an archbishop and a patriarch. The modern literature on this subject is vast. Brief, accessible outlines are contained in R. Clogg, *A concise history of Greece* (Cambridge, 1992), 47–99; R. J. Crampton, *A concise history of Bulgaria* (Cambridge, 1997), 120–48.

[4] P. Kitromilides, "'Imagined communities' and the origins of the national question in the Balkans," *European History Quarterly* 19/ii (1989), 149–92 at 177–85; repr. in his *Enlightenment, nationalism, orthodoxy. Studies in the culture and political thought of south-eastern Europe* (Aldershot, 1994), no. XI. It should be noted, however, that independent Serbian and Bulgarian patriarchates had only finally been eliminated in 1766 and 1767 respectively.

Map 3   The Macedonian contested zone. Reproduced from B. Jelavich, *History of the Balkans, II. Twentieth century* (Cambridge University Press, 1983), p. 98.

Treaty of San Stefano was signed, which rewarded the new Bulgarian nation with substantial territories, including Macedonia. This was more than the western European powers were willing to allow, fearing the establishment of a Russian-controlled bloc in the Balkans. San Stefano was, therefore, set aside at the Congress of Berlin, and new borders established for Bulgaria and her neighbors. The largest single area lost to Bulgaria in 1878 was Macedonia.

From 1878, Greece and Bulgaria, and also Serbia, advanced competing claims to Macedonia, each seeking the support or sufferance of the "Great Powers." The competition inspired factionalism and insurrection within the region. In 1893 a body later known as the Internal Macedonian Revolutionary Organization (IMRO) was formed, whose objective was to achieve autonomy for the region through mass uprising. In 1894 an alternative vision was put forward by the so-called Supreme Committee, which favored incorporation of an autonomous Macedonia into Bulgaria. The proliferation of competing claims and visions for Macedonia led to an armed struggle, which culminated in the "Macedonian Struggle" of 1904–8.[5] Greek and Bulgarian guerrilla groups fought strenuously until the Young Turk coup of 1908 brought about a cease-fire. However, the Macedonian Question was not settled. In 1912 the Greeks, Serbs and Bulgarians allied successfully against the Ottomans in the First Balkan war, but the treaty of London (30 May 1913) which brought this to an end focused attention back on Macedonia (and on Albania, which was for the first time constituted as an independent state). According to the settlement Serbia and Greece received the largest parts of Macedonia; the Bulgarians demanded a larger share, to compensate for the loss of the southern Dobrudja (to Romania), and insisted that the issue be subjected to Russian arbitration. Serbian and Greek refusals led the Bulgarians to declare war on their recent allies (29 June 1913). However, the Second Balkan War was short-lived: the threat of Romanian mobilization forced the Bulgarians to sue for peace, and the treaties of Bucharest (10 August) and Constantinople (13 October) saw Bulgaria lose all but Pirin Macedonia and a portion of Thrace.

Efforts by all parties between 1870 and 1913 were directed to establishing the so-called "national consciousness" of the inhabitants of Macedonia, and it was not uncommon for families to be split, with one son fighting for, and "becoming" Greek, and another becoming by the same process Bulgarian.[6] However, many people felt neither Greek nor Bulgarian, nor even Serbian. This much may be gleaned from H. N. Brailsford's account of Macedonia, published in 1906:

---

[5] B. Gounaris, "Reassessing ninety years of Greek historiography on the 'Struggle for Macedonia 1904–1908'," *JMGS* 14 (1996), 235–51; repr. in P. Mackridge and E. Yannakakis, eds., *Ourselves and others. The development of Greek Macedonian identity since 1912* (Oxford, 1997).

[6] A modern perspective on this same phenomenon is explored in L. Danforth, "'How can a woman give birth to one Greek and one Macedonian?' The construction of national identity among immigrants to Australia from northern Greece," in J. Cowan, ed., *Macedonia: the politics of identity and difference* (London, 2000), 85–103.

One hundred years ago it would have been hard to find a central Macedonian who could have answered with any intelligence the question whether he were Servian or Bulgarian by race. The memory of the past had vanished utterly and nothing remained save a vague tradition among the peasants that their forefathers had once been free. I questioned some boys from a remote mountain village near Ohrida which had neither teacher nor resident priest, and where not a single inhabitant was able to read, in order to discover what amount of traditional knowledge they possessed. I took them up to the ruins of the Bulgarian Tsar's fortress which dominates the lake and the plain from the summit of an abrupt and curiously rounded hill. "Who built this place?" I asked them. The answer was significant: "The Free Men." "And who were they?" "Our grandfathers." "Yes, but were they Serbs or Bulgarians or Greeks or Turks?" "They weren't Turks, they were Christians." And this seemed to be about the measure of their knowledge.[7]

Politicians, writers and historians on all sides of the issue undertook to correct such ethnic and historical ignorance, initiating systematic cultural programs. Basil the Bulgar-slayer was to play a full and active role.

Greek treatments of Basil at this time were diverse and influential, and books were published with such titles as *Basil the Bulgar-slayer: an original historical novel* and *The warsongs of the Bulgar-slayer*.[8] Basil features occasionally, but tellingly in I. Dragoumis' *The blood of martyrs and heroes* (*Martyron kai eroon aima*). Here, the eleventh-century conflict is considered the immediate precursor of the current conflict, ongoing as Dragoumis wrote in 1907. It is noted, to disparage Samuel but nevertheless astutely, that Samuel and Basil did not engage in constant warfare. Instead, Samuel is characterized as an artful dodger, launching stinging raids and withdrawing before Basil's troops could arrive. Basil is cast as the "hunter of the Bulgarians (*o kynigos Voulgaron*), who killed and blinded whomever he discovered."[9] The period of Ottoman domination is regarded as an abomination, suppressing the natural, national urges of the Greeks and Bulgarians, who are enemies. For Dragoumis, the lessons of the past were there to be learned, and indeed one scene finds the principal characters observing and assisting Greek-speaking children to learn.

[7] H. N. Brailsford, *Macedonia: its races and their future* (London, 1906), 99. This passage is much cited, for example by M. Mazower, "Introduction to the study of Macedonia," *JMGS* 14 (1996), 229–35 at 231. If the issue of national consciousness appears absent from this account, one should recall that the same subjects questioned by Brailsford might on other occasions have suffered for providing a "wrong" answer, and an ambivalent answer such as this may have appeared simpler or safer.

[8] These, amongst others, are noted by V. Laourdas, *I Pinelopi Delta kai i Makedonia* (Thessaloniki, 1958), 35; repr. in his *Makedonika analekta* (Thessaloniki, 1980), 67–94. The eponymous novel was by A. N. Kyriakou (Athens, 1910). See also P. Mackridge, "Macedonia and Macedonians in *Sta mystika tou valtou* (1937) by P. S. Delta," *Dialogos* 7 (2000), 41–55 at 43.

[9] I. Dragoumis, *Martyron kai eroon aima* (Athens, 1907), 42. On Dragoumis see V. Laourdas, "O Ion Dragoumis kai i epochi tou," in his *Makedonika analekta*, 95–110.

They went to a school and into a history class on the empire of the Bulgar-slayer. One child was narrating how the emperor, after twenty years of war, had worn out Samuel and the Bulgarians; and how he had blinded 15,000 prisoners-of-war, leaving one of every hundred a single eye to guide them; and how, in the end, seeing such a tragedy, Samuel died from the evil deed.

Alexis then turned to the children and said: "The emperor, instead of blinding the men, a barbarous thing, should have killed them all. That would have been better than the torture of leaving the men blind but alive. Also, immediately there would have been 15,000 fewer Bulgarians: a useful thing."

The teacher smiled.[10]

The most enduring works of prose fiction are two novels for children by Dragoumis' lover, Penelope Delta. *For the homeland* (*Gia tin Patrida*) and *In the time of the Bulgar-slayer* (*Ton kairo tou Voulgaroktonou*) were published respectively in 1909 and 1911. Both are set during the reign of Basil II, and the action in both takes place in Macedonia. (However, Delta was careful to include a map in the second work showing that the Byzantine *thema* called Makedonia lay some distance to the northwest of Thessalonika.)

For the homeland begins late in 995, when Tsar Samuel confronts and defeats the garrison of Thessalonika, killing the Byzantine governor Gregory Taronites, and capturing the young Ashot and his friend Alexios Argyros. They are taken to Ohrid where Samuel's daughter Miroslava, described as Greek on her mother's side, falls in love with Ashot. After his defeat at the battle of Spercheios, Samuel submits to Basil and marries Miroslava to Ashot, who is appointed governor of Dyrrachion. However, shortly after Samuel reneges on his promises, and the young couple flee, with Alexios Argyros, to Constantinople. Before departing they have arranged with the *archon* Chryselios for Dyrrachion to rebel upon receiving word from the emperor. The remainder of the novel is taken up with the return journey by Alexios Argyros, and his young wife Thekla, to get word to Chryselios that Basil is committing a fleet to liberate Dyrrachion. On the way they meet a variety of Byzantine characters: a child monk called Gregory, his father Pankrates, a jail-keeper, and a boatman named Niketas, who all assist them. They are attacked by two Bulgarians, whom Alexios kills before he is captured by a patrol. Alexios is imprisoned, and refuses to participate in Thekla's scheme, hatched with Pankrates, to free him. Instead, he commits suicide, and his heroic death forces Thekla to leave and complete the mission. She does, and a fleet commanded by Eustathios Daphnomeles liberates Dyrrachion, before Thekla retires to the Stoudios

---

[10] Dragoumis *Martyron kai eroon aima*, 108.

Monastery in Constantinople. The novel ends with a précis of historical events up to Basil's victory in 1018.

In the time of the Bulgar-slayer develops the action and some of the characters introduced in the first novel. The story begins in 1004, as Adrianople fills with worshipers preparing to celebrate a holy festival. Among them is Pankrates, who is traveling to Vidin to deliver to Basil, who is besieging that city, his charge: Alexia, the four- or five-year-old daughter of Thekla and Alexios, the lead characters of the earlier novel. The Bulgarians, violating the sacred occasion, fall on the city, slaughtering and seizing Greeks. The Bulgarian commander, Ivatzes, kills the *katepano* of Adrianople, Krinites, before the eyes of his son Constantine, and his son's friend Michael. They swear vengeance, but are taken prisoner and become slaves of Tsar Samuel. Meanwhile, Alexia, who was captured but not kept prisoner, is wandering from Bulgarian village to Bulgarian village, without speaking. It is assumed that she is mute and Bulgarian. Following a victory of Basil's, the two boys are able to escape, but elect to remain in the Bulgarian camp as spies. For this they endure humiliation by the Bulgarians who cannot understand their choice to remain amongst Slavs. Mute Alexia is working behind the scenes to help the boys, without their knowledge. Both, nevertheless, fall in love with her. She falls in love with Constantine. At the time of the revolt of Vodena (Edessa), the two boys show their true colors. However, Michael suffers a serious wound, and confesses his love for Alexia, compelling Constantine to leave. He enrolls in Basil's army, under a false name, and is killed in battle by the anti-hero Ivatzes. Michael recovers, realizes the nature and extent of his friend's sacrifice, and swears to avenge his death. The novel ends with a letter from Michael to Alexia, in which he explains that he and the general Eustathios Daphnomeles have captured and blinded Ivatzes.[11]

When Delta completed *In the time of the Bulgar-slayer* she had not yet visited Macedonia. She was raised in Alexandria, and at the time she wrote these two novels lived in Frankfurt. She came to Byzantine history not through the texts being edited in Greece, nor even the historiography produced there, but through works of "foreign" authors. She corresponded regularly with Gustave Schlumberger, whose grand narratives she cited as her source for all historical information on Basil,[12] and with Kostis Palamas,

---

[11] The historical details ring true, as a glance at earlier chapters will demonstrate. See above pp. 17–18, 26, 34–6.

[12] P. Delta, *Ton kairo tou Voulgaroktonou* (Athens, 1911). The letters exchanged by Delta and Schlumberger have been published: X. Lefcoparidis, ed., *Lettres de deux amis. Une correspondance entre Pénélope S. Delta et Gustave Schlumberger, suivie de quelques lettres de Gabriel Millet* (Athens, 1962). See now M. Spanaki, "Byzantium and the novel in the twentieth century: from Penelope Delta to Maro Douka," in D. Ricks and P. Magdalino, eds., *Byzantium and the modern Greek identity*

who was not enamored of Delta's stories. He suggested in a letter to the author that they contained too much explicit historical instruction.[13] The slight is most uncharacteristic of the extremely polite letters exchanged by the two writers, and the sensitive Delta was clearly stung, not least since she valued Palamas' own work and opinions very highly. She had earlier written to request that she be permitted to use six lines from Palamas' *The king's flute* on the title page of her latest book, for he had "drawn in a few lines the image of the Bulgar-slayer... the hero whose passage shook the world." Palamas, belatedly, granted her request, and two of the six lines still feature on the title page. She wrote in response to his criticism that, "Once again [in writing *In the time of the Bulgar-slayer*] I have only one purpose: to teach the child to read history, and think the only value of the book, if it has any value at all, is where I follow faithfully historical events... The fictional characters have only one purpose: to allow me [to develop] a plot which excites the curiosity of the child." She continued, with excessive modesty, "I do not have the talent [as you do] to address literary matters! I do whatever is within my capabilities so that the Greek child may learn about historical events as they may not elsewhere."[14]

Palamas was to reply with his fullest letter to Delta, a gentle apology and critique of *In the time of the Bulgar-slayer*, which he characterized as driven by action not psychological development; by man not nature; by prosopography not topography; by dialogue not description. The fast pace drew, he believed, on the tradition of demotic songs: an inspiration to Palamas himself. Delta was a champion of the demotic form of the Greek language, *dimotiki*, which in any case is the only form of the language which her principal audience, young children, would know, before they were educated in the formal literary language, *katharevousa*. Indeed, the work, according to Palamas, avoided the pitfalls of many books for children which went in for cold moralizing and artistry beyond the comprehension of the reader. "Your psychology is simple: it is balanced by your boldness and the force of your proclamation of your patriotism (*patridalatreia*) which you pronounce fanatically, exclusively, placing it above every other feeling and virtue." Finally, Palamas noted, "The episode with Ivatzes reminded me

(Aldershot, 1998), 119–30; F. Tinnefeld, "Die Zeit Basileios II. in neugriechischen Romanen und Dramen des 20. Jahrhunderts," in E. Konstantinou, ed., *Byzantinische Stoffe und Motive in der europäischen Literatur des 19. und 20. Jahrhunderts*, Philhellenische Studien 6 (Frankfurt am Main, 1998), 317–36.

[13] X. Lefcoparides, ed., *Allilografia tis P. S. Delta 1906–40* (Athens, 1957), 42, letter 17 (23/4/1911). Cf. A. Hirst, "Two cheers for Byzantium: equivocal attitudes in the poetry of Palamas and Cafavy," in Ricks and Magdalino, eds., *Byzantium and the modern Greek identity*, 105–17 at 109: "It is no criticism of Palamas's poetry as poetry to say he is not concerned with historical accuracy."

[14] *Allilografia tis P. S. Delta*, 42–3, letter 18 (2/5/1911).

of the deep impression left on me when, as a young man, I first read the history of Paparrigopoulos. I planned then to write such a story – I even started it."[15] Palamas never completed his story.

A far more flattering response to Delta's history lesson slightly preceded Palamas'. In November 1911 the Metropolitan Archbishop of Amaseia, Germanos, reveled in his "transportation to a Byzantine world full of patriotic heroes, historical reverses, desperate wars of the nation, the glorious, valiant duels of our lion-hearted heroes for this sacred soil, where for seven whole years we have fought the same struggle with the same enemies."[16] Germanos (Karavangelis), who was from 1900 to 1907 the archbishop of Kastoria, played a full and active role in the Macedonian Struggle. In her reply Delta noted with delight that a school teacher had written to her, praising her book as "patriotic and educational" (*ethniko kai paidagogiko*).[17]

By the efforts, in no small part, of these writers, the story of the Bulgar-slayer re-entered the popular imagination, not least in the expanding city of Athens. A map of the city drawn in 1888 shows that the streets, which had begun to extend northeast from the University and Academy along the base of Lykavittos hill, were given predominantly classical names, for example the streets of Asklipios and Ippokrates (built in 1884).[18] However, the streets which ran at right-angles to these began suddenly, after 1910, to take on Byzantine imperial names: Tzimiskes, Komnenos, Vatatzes, Laskaris. Between Tzimiskes and Komnenos, in correct chronological order as one heads north (although Komnenos was built in 1915, before Tzimiskes in 1921) runs the street of Basil the Bulgar-slayer, *Odos Vasiliou Voulgaroktonou* (fig. Figure 13).[19] No other imperial street enjoys an epithet. Moreover, no other emperor enjoys the close company of so many contemporaries: streets named for two of his principal generals, Nikephoros Ouranos and

---

[15] *Allilografia tis P. S. Delta*, 44–6, letter 20 (27/1/1912). Cf. K. Paparrigopoulos, *Istoria tou ellinikou ethnous*, ed. P. Karolides, revised ed. (Athens, 1925), IV, 200–1.

[16] *Allilografia tis P. S. Delta*, 394, letter 4 (18/12/1911).

[17] *Allilografia tis P. S. Delta*, 395, letter 5 (8/1/1912). See also V. Laourdas, "O Kastorias Germanos Karavangelis (1866–1935)," in his *Makedonika analekta*, 49–52.

[18] E. Bastéa, *The creation of modern Athens: planning the myth* (Cambridge, 2000), 143 (map of 1888), 188 (naming 250 streets).

[19] See L. Kallivretakis, "I Athina tou 19ou aiona. Apo eparchiaki poli tis Othomanikis autokratorias, proteuousa tou Ellinikou vasileou," *Archaiologia tis polis Athinon. Epistimonikes-epimorfotikes dialexeis, Ianouarios – Martios 1994*, Eidikes morfotikes ekdiloseis 4 (Athens, 1994), 173–96 at 184–7. According to A. Verouka, *I onomatothesia odon kai plateion* (Athens, 1995), 70–1, 80, there are twelve streets in the modern city of Athens named *Voulgaroktonou*, but none at all in Thessaloniki. However, a contemporary A–Z of greater Athens lists fifteen distinct streets named *Vasileiou Voulgaroktonou*. See *Athina-Peraias proasteia. Chartis – odigos* (Athens, 1994), 39.

Figure 13   Four streets in modern Athens, named after Basil the Bulgar-slayer, his patriarch Sergios, and two of his generals, Nikephoros Ouranos and Eustathios Daphnomeles. Photos: Paul Stephenson.

Eustathios Daphnomeles, terminate at Voulgaroktonos, and join the emperor to his patriarch, Sergios.[20] Skylitzes, whose chronicle provided these names, is a little out of place behind the Strefi hill, joined to Voulgaroktonos by Justinian. This may suggest that officials did not use Skylitzes' work directly in planning the area, but perhaps favored the modern interpretation by Paparrigopoulos, who lived on Asklipios street. Of course, few Greeks, even those living on Bulgar-slayer street, would have felt as passionately about Macedonia as did Dragoumis and Delta: clearly Palamas did not, for example. But, just as stories of Basil's battles were widely known at the time of St. Nikon, so they were again in the early years of the twentieth century. This much is clear from the images employed on propaganda posters issued during the Balkan Wars. One nicely drawn piece, signed by the artist S. Christidis, shows a Greek fighter, his rifle discarded,

[20] Justinian comes closest, with both Belisarius and Narses in attendance, but at some distance. There are fourteen streets named Ioustinianou listed in the *Athina-Peraias proasteia. Chartis – odigos*, 85.

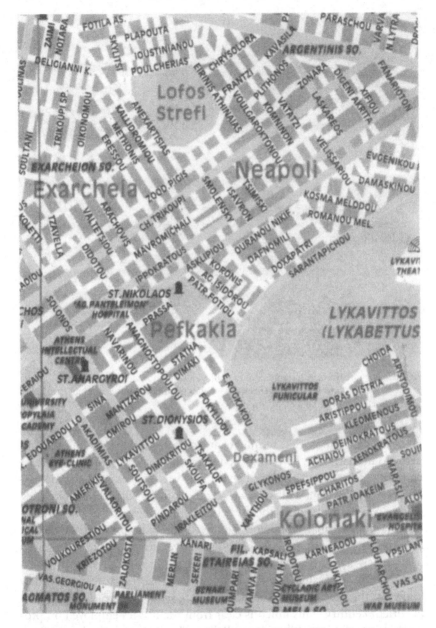

Figure 14   Map of modern Athens. Detail showing the district of Neapoli where one finds streets named after Basil II and his contemporaries. Reproduced from *Athina-Peraias proasteia. Chartis – odigos* (Athens, 1994).

gripping the wrists of his foe and biting a chunk from his right ear (plate 5). The caption above the image read "*O Voulgarophagos,*" the Bulgar-eater. Beneath the image, a verse caption by F. Panas reads, in rough prose translation: "The flaming sea which burns in my heart / with wild waves of anger – it shouts for vengeance – / Then the monsters of Sofia it will put to sleep, it will extinguish, when my hatred sucks up this blood of yours."[21] A second poster by Christidis has as its subject a Greek warrior wearing the foustanella, apart from his comrades in regular uniform, in the midst of a battle scene (plate 6). He holds a terrified Bulgarian by the throat with his left hand, and holds his dagger aloft in his right, about to plunge it into his foe's face. The image is accompanied by a longer and even more bloodthirsty poem by Panas, and by the caption "*Oi Voulgaroktonoi.*"[22]

A third poster in a cruder hand employs a direct allusion to Basil's supposed actions at Kleidion (plate 7). In the melée of a battle scene, a Greek soldier once again seizes a Bulgarian from behind in a similar pose to the first image, but now puts out his right eye with a dagger.[23] Thus we might also interpret the report that, at the battle of Sarantoporon in October 1912, Greeks "witnessed 'with their very eyes' the megalomartyrs, Saints George and Dimitrios, mounted on horseback and moving ahead of the Greek forces and inducing blindness in their enemies."[24]

Basil was established by 1913 in the popular imagination of Greeks, old and young, at war and at home, within and without the Greek state. Delta's novels and Palamas' poems swiftly went through more than a dozen impressions. Moreover, the story of the discovery and transferal of Basil's corpse, which was noted by Pachymeres and invoked in *The king's flute* was apparently shown to be true when, in August 1914, an underground burial chamber was discovered at the site of the Hebdomon Palace, at Bakırköy (Makrikeuy) in Istanbul. The circumstances of discovery, during the construction of barracks for mobilized troops, saw the site noted by

[21] Mazarakis-Ainian and Papaspyrou-Karadimitriou, *Valkanikoi polemoi*, 261, fig. 106; 367.
[22] Mazarakis-Ainian and Papaspyrou-Karadimitriou, *Valkanikoi polemoi*, 271, fig. 111; 370–1.
[23] Mazarakis-Ainian and Papaspyrou-Karadimitriou, *Valkanikoi polemoi*, 237, fig. 94.
[24] This is noted by R. Clogg, "The Byzantine legacy in the modern Greek world: the *megali idea,*" in L. Clucas, ed., *The Byzantine legacy in Eastern Europe* (Boulder, 1988), 253–81 at 267; repr. in R. Clogg, *Anatolica: studies in the Greek East in the 18th and 19th centuries* (Aldershot, 1996), no. IV. Clogg cites A. Adamantiou, *I vyzantini Thessaloniki* (Athens, 1914), 49[-50]. The enemies in this instance were the Turks. Clogg also notes that "When Halley's comet flashed across the sky in 1910 it was thought to point towards Macedonia and to be a portent of war," citing A. Wace and M. Thompson, *The nomads of the Balkans. An account of the life and customs among the Vlachs of the northern Pindus* (London, 1914; repr. 1972), 13. Such reflections were commonplace through the centuries, as we have seen in John Geometres' interpretation of the comet of 989, above in chapter two, p. 17. For representations of the battle without megalomartyrs see Mazarakis-Ainian and Papaspyrou-Karadimitriou, *Valkanikoi polemoi*, 81–3, figs. 16–17.

the directorate of the imperial museums in Istanbul, but largely untouched until after the armistice which followed World War I. Subsequently, with the barracks taken over by a French occupation force, excavations were urged by the director of the French School of Archaeology at Athens. Ten French troops were, therefore, set to work in July 1921 with shovels and the guidance of Th. Makrides (Makridy Bey), assistant director of the Istanbul museum, who had undertaken initial surveys in 1914 and 1915. Political affairs hindered further planned excavations in 1922, and in 1923 the French troops withdrew, interrupting the third and last "digging season." The burial chamber was enthusiastically, but prematurely pronounced to be the tomb of Basil the Bulgar-slayer.[25]

Further research by Makrides demonstrated that the hypogeum was an earlier structure, probably contemporary with the fifth-century sarcophagi it housed. Makrides continued to work on the Hebdomon, even after he had moved from Istanbul to become director of the Benaki Museum in Athens. In 1938–9 he published an extensive historical study of the complex, into which he slotted all archaeological material that had come to light. This contained a fuller refutation of the claim that the hypogeum was Basil II's tomb, but also proposed an alternative resting place for the Bulgar-slayer: a white marble sarcophagus, which had been removed, at an unspecified time, from the Church of St. John and converted into a water fountain. In 1939 it stood in a small square in Bakırköy (Makrikeuy); that is, in the eastern portion of what had been the Hebdomon Palace.[26] In fact, the supposition that the sarcophagus was removed from St. John cannot be demonstrated beyond the fact that it was found near the ruins of that church, and that other marble features were removed from that site during the construction of a stone jetty (Tas Iskelesi) and an Ottoman imperial textile mill.[27] Makrides' suggestion that the sarcophagus' grand size, its type and features corresponded, as far as he could tell, with those of imperial sarcophagi is hardly conclusive, particularly in the light of Yahya

[25] By J. Thibaut, "L'Hebdomon de Constantinople. Nouvel examen topographique," *EO* 21 (1922), 31–44. More circumspect is the fuller report published by T. Makridy [= Makrides] and J. Ebersolt, "Monuments funéraires de Constantinople," *BCH* 46 (1922), 356–93 at 363–93, who take issue with Thibaut. See also, J. Demangel, *Contribution à la topographie de l'Hebdomon* (Paris, 1945), 1–4, for an account of the discovery and early digging. It is further noted that in 1940 the entrance to the hypogeum had been covered with an iron gate and was obscured by earth as high as the vaulted ceiling.

[26] Th. K. Makrides, "To vyzantinon Evdomon kai ai par'autoi monai, I" *Thrakika* 10 (1938), 137–98; "To vyzantinon Evdomon kai ai par'autoi monai, II," *Thrakika* 12 (1939), 35–80.

[27] Makrides, "To vyzantinon Evdomon, II," 59–60. This suggestion was immediately accepted and repeated by F. Koukoules, "Ta kata tin tafin ton vyzantinon vasileon," *EEBS* 15 (1939), 52–78 at 67–9. See also, more skeptically, Demangel, *Contribution à la topographie de l'Hebdomon*, 53–4.

Figure 15   The lost sarcophagus of Basil II? A white marble sarcophagus, transformed into a fountain, which once stood in a square in Bakırköy (Makrikeuy), Istanbul. Photos: reproduced from Th. K. Makrides, "To vyzantinon Evdomon kai ai par'autoi monai, II," *Thrakika* 12 (1939), p. 59; J. Demangel, *Contribution à la topographie de l'Hebdomon* (Paris, 1945), p. 54.

of Antioch's claim that Basil demanded a simple, inexpensive burial.[28] The sarcophagus has, since 1939, disappeared.

Contemporary Balkan politics was a subject of passionate interest among Byzantinists and philhellenes in France and Britain as the nineteenth became the twentieth century. Gustave Schlumberger followed Balkan politics closely, and was vehemently pro-Greek.[29] One of his pieces for the French journal *Le Gaulois,* from which we have quoted above, proceeds to draw a direct comparison between Basil's "terrible war of forty-three years against these same Bulgars today so recently vanquished by the Greeks." Similarly, William Miller wrote regularly on Balkan politics from a Greek perspective for a number of journals in Britain, and was also writing a volume on the Greeks for the popular series *History of the peoples.* In the first chapter of this book he wrote "Modern Greece is politically... far more the child of the Byzantine Empire than she is the grandchild of the little classical republics." Miller adhered to the notion that the Great Idea implied no more than the restoration of the Hellenic empire to her appropriate limits, and stated in particular that "Modern Greek statesmen have dreamed of reviving... the exploits of... Basil II, the 'Bulgar-slayer,' in driving the Bulgarians from Macedonia."[30]

J. B. Bury, the foremost Byzantinist of his generation writing in English, remained studiously neutral on modern Balkan politics. Bury wrote not of the medieval Greek empire, nor often of the Byzantine, preferring the Eastern Roman empire.[31] He was also the author of articles and monographs on classical Greek history, but never sought to write a continuous history of the Greek people. According to Miller, in an obituary, Bury also "paid special attention to Bulgarian history, and was the first English historian to make use of the Russian excavations at Aboba, and which revealed the first Bulgarian capital at Pliska." This information he included in his monograph on the ninth century.[32] A footnote in this book, published

---

[28] *Histoire de Yahyā ibn Saʿīd d'Antioche*, fasc. 3, ed. I. Kratchkovsky, tr. F. Micheau and G. Tropeau, Patrologia Orientalis 47/4, no. 212 (Turnhout, 1997), [112–15], 480–3. Cf. *Yahyā al-Antakī, Cronache dell'Egitto fātimide e dell'impero bizantino 937–1033*, tr. B. Pirone (Milan, 1997), 336, §15:69. See above, chapter four, at p. 50.

[29] See, for example, his letter to Delta dated 7 April 1913, in Lefcoparidis, ed., *Lettres de deux amis,* 53–5, no. 17.

[30] W. Miller, *A history of the Greek people (1821–1921)* (London, 1922), 2, 6.

[31] J. B. Bury, *A history of the Eastern Roman empire from the fall of Irene to the accession of Basil I (A.D. 802–67)* (London, 1912).

[32] W. Miller, "John Bagnell Bury," *EHR* 43 (1928), 66–72 at 70, where we also learn that Bury cast his dispassionate eye over the literature stirred up by Fallmerayer's thesis. See Bury, *Eastern Roman empire*, 332–74, "Bulgaria."

in 1912, demonstrates his strictly scholastic interest in Macedonia.[33] Bury wrote on Basil II only to draw attention to the account presented by Psellos, then recently edited by K. Sathas.[34] Therefore, he does not focus, as Psellos does not, on Basil's Bulgarian wars and extension of the frontiers. This is unfortunate, as Bury had already cast his critical gaze upon traditional interpretations of the reign of Justinian I (527–65), concluding that the notion that a ruler who extends his frontiers increases the happiness of his subjects was a "capital error."[35]

It fell, some might later have felt inevitably, to Arnold Toynbee to reconsider the historical Basil, and point out some cracks in the veneer of Hellenic historical continuity, in his inaugural lecture in the Koraes Chair of King's College, London, in October 1919. Toynbee saw the rupture in Greek history as the period of the Avar, Slavic and Bulgar invasions which were "contemporary with, and comparable to our Western Dark Age."[36] In making this point, Toynbee compared Basil II with Justinian, who, he concluded, by waging protracted wars in Italy, had exhausted the resources and resolve of his people, and thus sacrificed the Balkans to the Avars twenty-five years later. Similarly, "Because Basil II fought a twenty-three years war against the Bulgars to reconquer the Balkans (996–1019), Anatolia, fifty years afterwards, had to be yielded to the Seljuk Turk."[37] Toynbee invited his audience to compare the Balkan peninsula in 565, the year of Justinian's death, with the same lands after Basil II's reconquests. The frontiers of the empire, he observed, would be the same, and this might support a notion of continuity. "But if we had an atlas depicting changes not of governments, but of language and nationality, we should receive a contrary impression."[38] Indeed, he continued, "Basil the slayer of Bulgars ... could not restore Justinian's Balkan world, and his statesman-like respect for the national individuality of the conquered Slav populations was an admission that the forces of racial change were stronger than the Imperial restoration."[39]

Toynbee's inaugural was delivered in London even as the Paris peace conferences following World War I were underway, and his opinions on the place of modern Greece, as distinct from medieval Greece, in history

[33] Bury, *Eastern Roman empire*, 370, n. 3.

[34] J. B. Bury, "Roman emperors from Basil II to Isaak Komnenos," *EHR* 4 (1889), 41–64, 251–85 at 47–52.

[35] Miller, "John Bagnell Bury," 70.

[36] A. Toynbee, *The place of mediaeval and modern Greece in history. Inaugural lecture of the Koraes Chair of Modern Greek and Byzantine Language, Literature and History* (London, 1919), 14.

[37] Toynbee, *Mediaeval and modern Greece*, 22–3.

[38] Toynbee, *Mediaeval and modern Greece*, 11. Toynbee was well aware that several such maps had been produced in the preceding years.

[39] Toynbee, *Mediaeval and modern Greece*, 12.

were intended to be understood in that context. He made this clear in his conclusion, where he referred to the peace conferences, and suggested that the new Greece should be the intermediary between Europe and the Middle East. Toynbee was rapidly disabused of that notion when, shortly afterwards, he traveled extensively in Asia Minor as special correspondent for the *Manchester Guardian*. His inimical reports on Greek activities led to his resignation from the Koraes Chair, and his withdrawal, for more than forty years, from the study of medieval Greece.[40] Numerous scholars of international distinction, however, remained active in the field. Indeed, the years between the two world wars represented the crucial phase in the consolidation of Byzantine studies in Greece, where chairs in Byzantine art and history were established at the University of Athens in 1914 and 1924 respectively, in European universities and, largely by the efforts of European emigrants, American universities.[41] Following *Byzantinische Zeitschrift* (1892) and *Vizantiiskii vremennik* (1894), three further important journals were founded to promote the publication of scholarship principally in French, but also Slavic languages, German and English: *Byzantion* (1924), *Byzantinoslavica* (1929) and *Revue des études byzantines* (1944). There appeared also, as we have seen in our introduction, a number of general histories, including those by Vasiliev (1913, 1932), Diehl (1919), Runciman (1933) and Iorga (1934), which universally regarded Basil's reign as a "golden age."

Despite the early domination of French-language scholarship, the twentieth century's most influential history of the Byzantine empire was originally published in German, by George Ostrogorsky. Born in St. Petersburg, Ostrogorsky was educated in the interwar period in Heidelberg and Paris.[42] In 1933 he arrived in Belgrade, capital of the Kingdom of Serbs, Croats and Slovenes. That part of Macedonia granted to Belgrade was then known as Southern Serbia, and comprised the administrative district of Vardarska. Subsequently, during World War II, Macedonia and Kosovo

---

[40] R. Clogg, *Politics and the academy. Arnold Toynbee and the Koraes Chair* (London, 1986). Toynbee rapidly revised his findings for publication as *The Western Question in Greece and Turkey. A study in the contact of civilisations* (London, 1922). Given the clear discrepancy between Toynbee's and Miller's sentiments at this time it is interesting to note that Miller had been the first-choice candidate for the Koraes Chair.

[41] T. Kiousopoulou, "I proti edra vyzantinis istorias sto Panepistimiou Athinon," *Mnimon* 15 (1993), 257–76; A. A. Vasiliev, *History of the Byzantine empire 324–1453*, 2nd English ed. (Madison, 1952), 13–42.

[42] On Ostrogorsky's life and works, see R. Syme, *Gedenkworte für Georg Ostrogorsky. Orden pour le merité für Wissenschaften und Künste. Reden und Gedenkworte, vierzehnter Band* (Heidelberg, 1978). Also, at greater length, see the posthumous tributes by his Belgrade colleagues in *ZRVI* 18 (1978), 269–85.

were partitioned between Bulgaria and Albania. Then, when in March 1945 the new federal Republic of Yugoslavia came into existence, Macedonia became a full republic. Immediately concerted efforts were made to establish the region's independent Slavic culture: independent, that is, of Greek and Bulgarian influences. In the intervening period Ostrogorsky had published the first German version of his general history.[43]

Ostrogorsky considered the reign of Basil II to be the high-water mark of imperial fortunes, to be contrasted with the weakness and folly of his "civilian" successors. However, Ostrogorsky's principal interest in Basil's reign was not his foreign policy, on or off the field of battle, but rather his domestic and agrarian policy. In a close study of Basil's surviving land legislation, and accounts of it provided by contemporary chroniclers, Ostrogorsky presented Basil as a champion and defender of the interests of small landholders against the depredations of the powerful military aristocracy. Basil's policies were, he determined, slanted against emergent western "feudal" tendencies which, once promoted by Basil's successors, led to the internal collapse of the state system, and thus the external collapse of its borders. The empire's internal "decline" in the eleventh century had been a principal concern of Russian historians following V. G. Vasilevskii, and Ostrogorsky has been called "the most representative member of the school founded by Vasil'evskij."[44] Recent scholarship has shown how erroneous was this interpretation; that the Byzantine economy expanded rapidly throughout the eleventh century; and that the "civilian" emperors presided over a period of social and cultural enrichment which was brought to an end by the re-establishment of military government by the Komnenoi.[45] Nevertheless, Ostrogorsky's general history has remained the single most influential volume in Byzantine history, and his representation of Basil's reign and achievements has complemented the notion that Basil's reign was a "golden age." This notion was devised, as we have seen, for quite different reasons, by Greek and philhellene sholars.

At Dumbarton Oaks in 1957 Ostrogorsky announced that "the frontiers between the Byzantine and Slavic spheres [in the Balkans] in the middle

---

[43] G. Ostrogorski, *Geschichte des byzantinischen Staates*. Handbuch der Altertumswissenschaft, 2, III (Munich, 1940). This was subsequently translated into numerous languages, the latest English version being: G. Ostrogorsky, *History of the Byzantine state*, tr. J. Hussey, 2nd ed. (Oxford, 1968).

[44] A. Kazhdan, "Russian pre-revolutionary studies on eleventh-century Byzantium," in S. Vryonis, Jr., ed., *Byzantine studies: essays on the Slavic world and the eleventh century* (New Rochelle, NY, 1992), 111–25 at 121.

[45] The most forceful sustained defence of the eleventh century was presented by P. Lemerle, *Cinq études sur le XIe siècle byzantin* (Paris, 1977). See also P. Lemerle, ed., *Recherches sur le XIe siècle*, being *TM* 6 (Paris, 1976).

of the ninth century correspond fairly exactly to the cultural zones which the eminent Yugoslav geographer Cvijić has defined in modern times."[46] Ostrogorsky's opinions on Macedonia and the cultural limits of *Slavia Orthodoxa* had been formulated over long years in the Academy in Belgrade, where he had risen to be Professor of Byzantinology. It is quite natural that he would cite a near contemporary and Belgrade authority on ethnography. However, Cvijić's vision was far from neutral, for it was formulated and developed in the first two decades of the twentieth century.[47] Ostrogorsky cannot have been unaware of this, but nevertheless his statement in 1957 was not a Serbian claim to northern Macedonia. Rather, it was a rare explicit reference to a desire which underpinned his scholarship, as it did that of the entire Russian school. The desire, and one in which he was quite justified, was to challenge the historiographical myth that Byzantine history was exclusively Greek history. This view of Byzantium, rejected by eastern Slavs, was accepted by many south Slavic scholars, who were willing to regard Byzantium as a Greek power opposed to their own nascent nation states. Ostrogorsky did not regard the history of Byzantium as the story only of Greek speakers, nor did he consider the history of the Balkan Slavs to be merely a chronicle of resistance to Greek hegemony. He saw Slavic society and culture as both a product of, and contributor to, Byzantine society and culture.[48] This vision found its fullest expression in D. Obolensky's *The Byzantine commonwealth*, which exposes the poverty of narrow,

---

[46] G. Ostrogorsky, "Byzantium in the seventh century," *DOP* 13 (1959), 5–21 at 7. Cf. Ostrogorsky, *History of the Byzantine state*, 93–4, 217–18, for authoritative statements on Byzantine relations with the Slavs in the seventh to ninth centuries. His reference was to J. Cvijić, *La péninsule balkanique. Géographie humaine* (Paris, 1918). See also, more explicitly, J. Cvijić, *Remarques sur l'ethnographie de la Macédoine. Deuxième édition augmentée d'une carte de la Vieille-Serbie* (Paris, 1907). Cvijić clearly intended for his work to reach an international audience, since it was also published in English, German, Russian and Serbo-Croat. A Bulgarian riposte to his treatise was swiftly published by A. Ichircoff [= Ishirkov], *Etude ethnographique sur les Slaves de Macédoine. Réponse à M. J. Zvijitch* (Paris, 1908). An influential Greek text employing similar historical and ethnographical arguments: V. Colocotronis, *La Macédoine et l'Hellénisme. Etude historique et ethnologique* (Paris, 1919).

[47] For a dismissive assessment of Cvijić's ethnographic mapping from a Bulgarian perspective, see P. Koledarov, "Ethnography in Great Britain and the Bulgarian Question," *Macedonian Studies* 9 (1992), 3–34 at 20–1, 28. In contrast, P. Kitromilides, "'Balkan mentality': history, legend, imagination," *Nations and Nationalism* 2 (1996), 163–91, contains a fine and balanced overview of Cvijić's contribution to Balkan scholarship and thought.

[48] Ostrogorsky, *Byzantine state*, vii. For a list of his publications 1926–62 see *Mélanges Georges Ostrogorsky*, 2 vols. (Belgrade, 1968) [= *ZRVI* 8], I, vii–xviii. However, Ostrogorsky broke with earlier Russian scholarship which placed Slavic settlement at the core of Byzantine economic and agrarian history, and argued for decline after the eleventh century under the influence of "German" feudal practices. This view must be understood in the light of a wider discussion of Slavic and German historical antagonism.

nationalist interpretations of medieval cultures in eastern and southeastern Europe.[49]

Since Ostrogorsky, and indeed Obolensky, Basil's reign has featured in a number of works by medievalists devoted to Macedonia. As with all works of history, they betray signs of the political and social contexts in which they were produced, and many betray clear national biases or prejudices. The legend of the Bulgar-slayer also remains a subject of contemporary interest in works of fiction. In Greece today, books by Palamas and Delta remain popular, and further works have been written, which remain in print. In 1964 a novel appeared with the straightforward title *Basil the Bulgar-slayer*. The author, Kostas Kyriazes, at the time editor of the daily newspaper *Ethnos*, took liberties with available historical data: he gave the notorious bachelor emperor a lifelong, female lover, Arete; he "discovered" three lost sources, as historians would love to, which provided details of Basil's private life (as penned by Arete), and both Bulgarian and Greek perspectives on his campaigns. These texts, discovered like Basil's flute-bearing body in the ruins of the Church of St. John at the Hebdomon, are presented to the reader by a fictional narrator, Kyrillos.[50]

A sense of the popular understanding of Basil's reign today can be gained by browsing personal pages on the World Wide Web. A search on "bulgarslayer" turns up dozens of documents devoted to establishing the "true history" of Macedonia from diametrically opposed perspectives. However, alternative visions of Basil and his empire have been presented by writers in Greece seeking to articulate a common identity for all the peoples of the southern Balkans. For example, Basil and his deeds have been invoked, amongst other characters and episodes of Byzantine history, in the historical poems published in Greek by the distinguished Byzantinist, Hélène Ahrweiler, who has stated that Basil acted with great cruelty during his Bulgarian wars, whereas his counterpart, Tsar Samuel, was a most sympathetic ruler.[51] The articulation of a common Balkan consciousness which transcends national borders may, therefore, lead to the vilification of Basil as a reaction to his reputation as the "Bulgar-slayer." However, Basil is not

---

[49] Subtitled: *Eastern Europe, 500–1453* (London, 1971).
[50] F. Tinnefeld, "Die Zeit Basileios II. in neugriechischen Romanen," 322–3.
[51] E. Arveler [H. Ahrweiler], *Elliniki synecheia. Poiimata istorias* (Athens, 1998), 22–3, 28–9. Ahrweiler explained her views in an interview in *To Vima*, 6 December 1998. I am grateful to Despina Christodoulou for drawing this to my attention, and for supplying me with the most recent treatment of Basil's reign, which is presented traditionally as the "apogee of Byzantine power." This is a glossy, illustrated military history by a doctoral candidate at the University of Ioannina, A. Kardaras, *Vasileios II o Voulgaroktonos. To apogeio tis Vyzantinis dynamis* (Athens, 2002), a supplement to the magazine *Stratiotiki Istoria* (military history).

only subject to censure by liberal intellectuals in Greece. In the former Yugoslav Republic of Macedonia, Samuel is widely held to have been the ruler of the first Slavic Macedonian state. Moreover, his battles with Basil have been cited as proof of Greek hostility to that state through the ages.[52]

In July 1998 I was sitting in front of the Church of Sv. Kliment (St. Clement), a thirteenth-century foundation on a hill which overlooks Ohrid in the Republic of Macedonia. The crest of the hill on the opposite side of the town is dominated by the ruins of an eleventh-century citadel, which Brailsford called "The Bulgarian Tsar's fortress," and modern tourist maps call more simply "Samuil's Fortress." As I sat a local tour guide explained how this came to be. He told a version of the story of the battle of Kleidion, after which the blinded troops marched back to Samuel's fortress, and the cruel "Greek king" Basil ever after was known as the "Macedonian-slayer." A similar account is included in a recent national history, compiled by two journalists from Skopje, which includes a translation into Macedonian Slavic of Skylitzes' account of the battle of Kleidion, with all references to Bulgaria and Bulgarians excised.[53] This was my reason for beginning this study, and so here also it will end.

---

[52] S. Antoljak, *Samuel and his state* (Skopje, 1985); D. Tashkovski, *The Macedonian nation* (Skopje, 1976) 28–56. For a critical slant: S. Troebst, "IMRO + 100 = FYROM? The politics of Macedonian historiography," in J. Pettifer, ed., *The new Macedonian Question* (London, 1999), 60–78.

[53] J. Pavlovski and M. Pavlovski, *Makedonija včera i denes* (Skopje, 1996), 83–4.

Conclusion

There is nothing exceptional about the legend of Basil the Bulgar-slayer, nor about the functions that it has served in the distant or more recent past. Legends which emphasize military victories and the martial achievements of past rulers have been identified as the most common type of national, and nationalist, myth.[1] Moreover, the legend of the Bulgar-slayer had less potency and longevity than other tales of dead emperors. For example, unlike that of Basil II, the story of the last emperor, Constantine XI, survived and was adapted throughout the *Tourkokratia*, and is still occasionally told. Nor could Basil's legend match those which adhered to Constantine the Great, and his emulators, either within or without the eastern empire. Constantine I's only challenger for legendary preeminence is Charlemagne.[2] However, Basil's legend was significant, and as a result of his perceived martial prowess, the Bulgar-slayer has had more than one posthumous moment in the sun. Like the battle of Bouvines for the French, who knew many more and several greater battles,[3] the episode at Kleidion was especially resonant for readers of Greek literature, who knew of several past battles in mountain passes. This victory and its aftermath became a motif for those pursuing military agendas, in the later twelfth and early twentieth centuries, and at points in between. Furthermore, the notion that Basil's reign was the

[1] G. Schöpflin, "The functions of myth and a taxonomy of myths," in G. Hosking and G. Schöpflin, eds., *Myths and nationhood* (London, 1997), 19–35. For a powerful African parallel, one may examine the significance of Shaka Zulu and his battles in the formation of Zulu national consciousness: C. Hamilton, *Terrific majesty: the powers of Shaka Zulu and the limits of historical invention* (Cambridge, MA, 1997). This is noted also in a pertinent new synthesis by P. Geary, *The myth of nations* (Princeton, 2002).

[2] *Eusebius, Life of Constantine*, tr. Averil Cameron and S. G. Hall (Oxford, 1999), 49–50, for references to literature on Constantine's later legends. One might then start with S. Lieu and D. Montserrat, eds., *Constantine. History, historiography and legend* (London and New York, 1998); and P. Magdalino, ed., *New Constantines: the rhythm of imperial renewal in Byzantium, 4th–13th centuries* (Aldershot, 1994). On Charlemagne, see R. Folz, *Le souvenir et la légende de Charlemagne dans l'empire germanique médiéval* (Paris, 1950).

[3] G. Duby, *The legend of Bouvines. War, religion and culture in the Middle Ages*, tr. C. Tihanyi (Cambridge, 1990).

culmination of a "golden age" served a similar purpose in both medieval and modern contexts.

It is possible, indeed likely, that for much of the period 1001–14, a period traditionally interpreted as one of constant warfare, Basil II was willing to recognize the independence of Samuel's Bulgaria. He may even have contemplated, in 1005, establishing a client state between Thessalonika, Dyrrachion and Dalmatia. Ring-fenced by strategic alliances with potentates to the north and west, and by Basil's standing army to the south and east, Bulgaria was no longer a threat to the empire. But Samuel's death in October 1014, and the belligerent stance adopted by his successors, not without success, provoked a sustained martial response from Basil. Consequently, the emperor was obliged to annex Bulgaria following the general surrender by potentates in 1018, and to consider a radical reorganization of the northwestern Balkans. The annexation of Bulgaria was not, however, an exercise in suppressing Bulgarians and Bulgarian national feeling, as later accounts would have us believe. Indeed, the carrot played a larger role than the stick in persuading Bulgarian potentates to surrender, and many were allowed to continue in power, their authority bolstered by imperial titles, robes of office and cash payments. Only decades after Basil's death did the new administrative district of Bulgaria acquire a more evolved civilian and fiscal administration, as well as a Greek-speaking prelate for the Bulgarian Church.

After 1018, Bulgarians were both subjects of the emperor and Christians, and as such they required no slayer. Nor was the emperor as slayer a familiar motif in the century after Basil's death, when pacific characteristics dominated imperial descriptions. However, this began to change as a new military dynasty gained power in Constantinople. For the Komnenian emperors, beginning with the reign of Isaak I, and extending through those of Alexios I, John II and Manuel I, Basil's age was considered golden because of his military successes, which saw the empire's frontiers extended to the east and west. The rebellion of Peter and Asen in Bulgaria during the reign of Isaak II gave a particular boost to Basil's image, and led to his being called for the first time "the Bulgar-slayer." Thereafter, Basil was always known by the cognomen *Voulgaroktonos*, but his memory and example were also invoked in wars against the Latins and Turks, ultimately unsuccessfully. The former, after 1204, shattered the multicultural character of the empire, the latter subjected the empire's lands, peoples and, after 1453, the capital to their rule.

For Greek historians of the nineteenth and early twentieth centuries the legend of Basil the Bulgar-slayer played a vital role in "mobilizing, unifying and directing the energies of 'the [Greek] people' to meet the challenges of nation formation [as] a myth of national history and destiny."[4] Basil's particular association with Athens, as well as Constantinople, made him the ideal figure to join what had been described as the two poles of Hellenism. Moreover, the facts that Basil's best known struggles were against the Bulgarians, and that they took place in Macedonia, made him a compelling figure to Greeks who were engaged in the modern struggle against the Bulgarians for control of Macedonia. Since 1918, Basil's Bulgarian campaigns, his victory over the Bulgarians and its apparent representation in the emperor's psalter illumination, have been incorporated wholly into the traditional narrative of Greek national, political and military history. This much is evident from the fine reproduction of the psalter illumination which graces the first hall of the Greek National Historical Museum in Athens. A greatly enlarged reproduction of this reproduction, not of the original, may be seen in the nearby Hellenic War Museum.[5] Here, Basil is the only Byzantine emperor whose campaigns, notably only those he fought in the Balkans, are illustrated with schematic maps. One may compare these with displays in adjoining rooms devoted to the Struggle for Macedonia and the Balkan Wars. This may, of course, be attributed to the conservatism or inertia associated with permanent exhibitions in national museums, and we might expect that, as the critical revisionism which has come to dominate Greek national historical scholarship in recent decades permeates more fully into public conceptions of the past, this will be reflected in the War Museum. Already, this has been the case in temporary exhibitions in the splendid new wing of the Byzantine and Christian Museum. It remains to be seen whether such developments will bring Basil back into the limelight, or, more likely, will allow him to fade further into the background, until such a time as his particular achievements are once more reconsidered.

---

[4] A. D. Smith, "The 'golden age' and national renewal," in Hosking and Schöpflin, eds., *Myths and nationhood*, 36–59 at 59. Cf. A. D. Smith, *National identity* (London, 1991), 71–98.

[5] I. Mazarakis-Ainian, general secretary of the Historical and Ethnological Society of Greece, informs me that this is one of 395 images of Byzantine emperors in the collection of the National Historical Museum in Athens. Copied at the urging of Spyridon Lambros, these images were published posthumously in his name as S. Lambros, *Leukoma Vyzantinon autokratoron* (Athens, 1930). The reproduction of the psalter portrait is picture 56 in this catalogue, and plate 3 below.

Bibliography

UNPUBLISHED LITERATURE

Argoe, K., "John Kyriotes Geometres, a tenth century Byzantine writer," Ph.D. thesis, University of Wisconsin (Madison, 1938)

Farag, W. A., "Byzantium and its Muslim neighbours during the reign of Basil II (976–1025)," Ph.D. thesis, University of Birmingham (Birmingham, 1976)

Fatalas-Papadopoulos McGrath, S., "A study of the social structure of Byzantine aristocracy as seen through Ioannes Skylitzes' *Synopsis historion*," Ph.D. thesis, Catholic University of America (Washington, DC, 1996)

Forsyth, J. H., "The Byzantine-Arab chronicle (938–1034) of Yahyā b. Saʻid al-Antākī," Ph.D. thesis, University of Michigan, 2 vols. (Ann Arbor, 1977)

Holmes, C. J., "Basil II and the government of empire (976–1025)," D.Phil. dissertation, University of Oxford (Oxford, 1999)

Jeffreys, E. and M. Jeffreys, The poems of Manganeios Prodromos, an edition and English translation, in progress.

PRIMARY SOURCES

Actes de Lavra, première partie des origines à 1204, eds. P. Lemerle, A. Guillou, N. Svoronos and D. Papachryssanthou, Archives de l'Athos V (Paris, 1970)

Ademari Cabannensis opera omnia, I, eds. P. Bourgain, R. Landes and G. Pon, Corpus Christianorum 129 (Turnhout, 1999)

The Alexiad of Anna Comnena, tr. E. R. A. Sewter (Harmondsworth, 1969)

Annae Comnenae Alexias, eds. D. Reinsch and A. Kambylis, CFHB 40/1 (Berlin and New York, 2001)

Anne Comnène, Alexiade, ed. B. Leib, 3 vols. (Paris, 1937–45)

Anthologia Graeca, ed. H. Beckby, 4 vols., 2nd ed. (Munich, 1965)

Aristakïs Lastivercʻi's History, tr. R. Bedrosian (New York, 1985)

Cecaumeni Strategicon, eds. B. Wassiliewsky and P. Jernstedt (St. Petersburg, 1896)

Constantine Porphyrogenitus De Administrando Imperio, ed. G. Moravcsik, tr. R. J. H. Jenkins, CFHB 1 (Washington, DC, 1967)

Constantine Porphyrogenitus. Three military treatises on imperial military expeditions, ed. and tr. J. F. Haldon, CFHB 28 (Vienna, 1990)

Constantini Manasses Breviarum Chronicum, ed. O. Lampsidis, CFHB 36 (Athens, 1996)

Constantini Porphyrogeniti De Cerimoniis Aulae Byzantinae, ed. J. Reiske, CSHB, 2 vols. (Bonn, 1829)

Constantinople in the eighth century. Parastaseis Syntomoi Chronikai, eds. and tr. A. Cameron and J. Herrin (Leiden, 1984)

La cronaca Siculo-Saracena di Cambridge con doppio testo greco, ed. G. Cozza-Luzi (Palermo, 1890)

Cumont, F., *Anecdota Bruxellensia*, I: *Chroniques byzantines du manuscrit 11376* (Gand, 1894)

Darrouzès, J., "Deux lettres de Grégoire Antiochos écrites de Bulgarie vers 1173," I, *BSl* 23 (1963), 276–84; II, *BSl* 24 (1963), 65–86

Darrouzès, J., ed., *Documents inédits d'ecclésiologie byzantine* (Paris, 1966)

Delehaye, H., *Les saints stylites*, Studia hagiographica 14 (Paris, 1923)

Downey, G., "Nikolaos Mesarites: description of the Church of the Holy Apostles at Constantinople," *Transactions of the American Philosophical Society*, N.S. 47, part 6 (1957), 855–924

Ephraem Aenii historia chronica, ed. O. Lampsides, CFHB 27 (Athens, 1990)

Eusebius, Life of Constantine, tr. Averil Cameron and S. G. Hall (Oxford, 1999)

Eusebius, Werke, I.1. Über das Leben des Kaisers Konstantin, ed. F. Winkelmann, 2nd ed. (Berlin, 1992)

Ex miraculis Sancti Symeonis auctore Ebervino, ed. G. Waitz, *MGH* Scriptores 8 (Hanover, 1868)

Fontes Byzantini historiae Hungariae aevo ducum et regum ex stirpe Árpád descendentium, ed. G. Moravcsik (Budapest, 1984)

Fontes Graeci historiae Bulgaricae, eds. G. Cankova-Petkova, I. Dujčev, L. Jončev, V. Tăpkova-Zaimova and P. Tivčev [= Fontes historiae Bulgaricae, XI] (Sofia, 1965)

Die Gedichte des Christophoros Mitylenaios, ed. E. Kurtz (Leipzig, 1903)

Gelzer, H., ed., "Ungedruckte und wenig bekannte Bistümerverzeichnisse der orientalischen Kirche," *BZ* 2 (1893), 22–72

Genesios on the reigns of the emperors, tr. A. Kaldellis, Byzantina Australiensia 11 (Canberra, 1998)

Geometres, John, PG 106, 806–1002

Georges Pachymérès. Relations historiques, ed. A. Failler, tr. V. Laurent, 5 vols., CFHB 24 (Paris, 1984–2000)

Georgii Acropolitae opera, ed. A. Heisenberg, 2 vols. (Leipzig, 1903)

Georgii Monachi, dicti Hamartoli chronicon ab orbe condito usque ad annum p. Chr. n. 842 et diversis scriptoribus usque ad a. 1143 continuatum, ed. E. de Muralto (St. Petersburg, 1859)

Georgio di Pisidia poemi, ed. and tr. A. Pertusi (Ettal, 1959)

Herodotus, Histories, tr. A. de Selincourt (Harmondsworth, 1954)

Histoire de Yahya-Ibn-Saïd d'Antioche, fasc. 2, ed. and tr. I. Kratchkovsky and A. Vasiliev, Patrologia Orientalis 23/2 (Paris, 1932)

Histoire de Yahyā ibn Saʿīd' d'Antioche, fasc. 3, ed. I. Kratchkovsky, tr. F. Micheau and G. Tropeau, Patrologia Orientalis 47/4, no. 212 (Turnhout, 1997)

Historia martyrii XV martyrum, PG 126, 152–221

Ioannis Cinnami epitome rerum ab Ioanne et Alexio Comnenis gestarum, ed. A. Meinecke, CSHB (Bonn, 1836)

Ioannis Euchaitorum metropolitae quae in cod. Vat. gr. 676 supersunt, eds. J. Bollig and P. de Lagarde (Göttingen, 1882)

Ioannis Scylitzes Synopsis Historiarum, ed. J. Thurn, CFHB 5 (Berlin and New York, 1973)

Ioannis Tzetzae Historiae, ed. P. M. Leone (Naples, 1968)

Ioannis Zonarae epitome historiarum, eds. M. Pinder and T. Büttner-Wobst, 3 vols., CSHB (Bonn, 1841–97)

Lambros, S., "O Markianos kodiks 524," *Neos Ellin.* 8/2 (1911), 123–92

Legenda Sancti Gerhardi Episcopi, ed. I. Madzsar, in E. Szentpétery, ed., *Scriptores Rerum Hungaricarum*, 2 vols. (Budapest, 1937–8), II, 461–506

Leib, B., *Deux inédits byzantins sur les azymes au début du XIIe siècle*, Orientalia Christiana 9 (Paris, 1924)

Leonis Diaconi Caloensis historiae libri decem, ed. C. B. Hase, CSHB (Bonn, 1828)

Letopis Popa Dukljanina, ed. F. Šišić, Posebno Isdanje Srpske kr. akademije, knj. 67 (Belgrade and Zagreb, 1928)

The letters of John Mauropous metropolitan of Euchaita, ed. and tr. A. Karpozilos, CFHB 34 (Thessaloniki, 1990)

"Life of St. Mary the Younger," tr. A. Laiou, in A.-M. Talbot, ed., *Holy women of Byzantium* (Washington, DC, 1996), 239–89

The life of St. Nikon, ed. and tr. D. F. Sullivan (Brookline, 1987)

Les listes de préséance byzantines des IXe–Xe siècles, ed. N. Oikonomides (Paris, 1972)

Mai, A., ed., *Novae Patrium bibliothecae*, 10 vols. (Rome, 1853–1905)

Mango, C., "The conciliar edict of 1166," *DOP* 17 (1963), 317–30

McGeer, E., *Sowing the dragon's teeth. Byzantine warfare in the tenth century*, DOS 23 (Washington, DC, 1995)

The land legislation of the Macedonian emperors (Toronto, 2000)

Mercati, S. G., "Sull'epitafio di Basilio II Bulgaroctonos," *Bessarione* 25 (1921), 137–42; repr. in his *Collectanea Byzantina*, 2 vols. (Bari, 1970), II, 226–31

"L'epitafio di Basilio Bulgaroctonos secondo il codice Modense Greco 144 ed Ottoboniano Greco 344," *Bessarione* 26 (1922), 220–2; repr. in his *Collectanea Byzantina*, 2 vols. (Bari, 1970), II, 232–4

Michaeli Pselli orationes panegyricae, ed. G. T. Dennis (Stuttgart and Leipzig, 1994)

Michaeli Pselli poemata, ed. L. G. Westerink (Stuttgart and Leipzig, 1992)

Michaelis Attaliotae historia, ed. I. Bekker, CSHB (Bonn, 1853)

Michaelis Choniatae epistulae, ed. F. Kolovou, CFHB 41 (Berlin and New York, 2001)

Michaelis Pselli scripta minora, eds. E. Kurtz and F. Drexl, 2 vols. (Milan, 1936–41)

Michail Akominatou tou Choniatou ta sozomena, ed. S. Lambros, 2 vols. (Athens, 1879–80)

Michel Psellos Chronographie, ou histoire d'un siècle de Byzance (976–1077), ed. E. Renauld, 2 vols. (Paris, 1926–8)

Monumenta ad SS Cyrilli et Methodii successorum vitas resque gestas pertinentia, ed. N. L. Tunickij (London, 1972)

Nicéphore Bryennios histoire, ed. and tr. P. Gautier, CFHB 9 (Brussels, 1979)

Nicephori Gregorae Byzantina historia, eds. B. Niebuhr and L. Schopen, 3 vols., CSHB (Bonn, 1829–55)

Nicetae Choniatae orationes et epistolae, ed. J.-L. van Dieten, CFHB 3 (Berlin and New York, 1972)

Nicetae Choniatae historiae, ed. J.-L. van Dieten, CFHB 11/1 (Berlin, 1975)

Nicétas Stéthatos, opuscules et lettres, ed. J. Darrouzès (Paris, 1961)

Notitiae episcopatuum ecclesiae Constantinopolitanae, ed. J. Darrouzès (Paris, 1981)

Panagiotakes, N. M., "Fragments of a lost eleventh century Byzantine historical work," in *ΦΙΛΕΛΛΗΝ. Studies in honour of Robert Browning*, ed. C. N. Constantinides et al. (Venice, 1996), 321–57

Plutarchi Moralia, ed. and tr. F. C. Babbitt et al., 15 vols. (Cambridge, MA, 1927–69)

Povest' vremennykh let. Po Lavrent'evskoj letopisi 1377 goda, eds. D. S. Likhachev and V. Adrianova-Perets, I (Moscow and Leningrad, 1950)

Procopius IV. De aedificiis libri IV, ed. J. Haury (Leipzig, 1964)

Rallis, G. and M. Potlis, eds., *Syntagma ton theion kai hieron kanonon ton te hagion kai paneuphimon apostolon*, 6 vols. (Athens, 1852–9)

The Russian primary chronicle, tr. S. H. Cross and O. Sherbowitz-Wetzor (Cambridge, MA, 1953)

Sathas, K., ed., *Mesaioniki vivliothiki*, 7 vols. (Athens, Paris and Venice, 1872–94)

Sathas, K., ed., *Anonymou synopsis chroniki*, vol. VII of his *Mesaioniki vivliothiki* (Venice, 1894)

Schreiner, P., ed., *Die byzantinischen Kleinchroniken*, CFHB 12/1–3 (Vienna, 1975–9)

Sovety i rasskazy Kekavmena. Sochinenie vizantiiskogo polkovodtsa XI veka, ed. G. G. Litavrin (Moscow, 1972)

Des Stephanos von Taron armenische Geschichte, tr. H. Gelzer and A. Burckhardt (Leipzig, 1907)

Suidae Lexicon, ed. A. Adler, 5 vols. (Leipzig, 1928–38)

Svoronos, N., ed., *Les novelles des empereurs macédoniens concernant la terre et les stratiotes* (Athens, 1994)

Sykoutres, I., "Leontos tou diaconou anekdoton enkomion eis Vasileion ton II," *EEBS* 10 (1933), 425–34

Theodoros Prodromos, historische Gedichte, ed. W. Hörandner (Vienna, 1974)

Theodosius Diaconus de Creta capta, ed. H. Criscuolo (Leipzig, 1979)

Theophanes continuatus, Ioannes Caminiata, Symeon Magister, Georgius Monachus continuatus, ed. I. Bekker, CSHB (Bonn, 1825)

Théophylacte d'Achrida, I, discours, traités, poésies, ed. and tr. P. Gautier, CFHB 16/1 (Thessaloniki, 1980)

Théophylacte d'Achrida, II, lettres, ed. and tr. P. Gautier, CFHB 16/2 (Thessaloniki, 1986)

Vie de Saint Luc le Stylite (879–979), ed. F. Vanderstuyf, Patrologia Orientalis 11 (Paris, 1915), 145–299

Yahyā al-Antakī, Cronache dell'Egitto fâtimide e dell'impero bizantino 937–1033, tr. B. Pirone (Milan, 1997)

Zepos, I., *Vasilika kata tin en Leipsia ekdosin tou G.E. Heimbach kai to sympliroma tou Z. Lingenthal*, 5 vols. (Athens, 1896–1900)

SECONDARY LITERATURE

Adamantiou, A., *I vyzantini Thessaloniki* (Athens, 1914)

Adontz, N., "Samuel l'Arménien, roi des Bulgares," in his *Études armeno-byzantines* (Lisbon, 1965), 347–407

Agapitos, P., "Byzantine literature and Greek philologists in the nineteenth century," *Classica et Medievalia* 43 (1992), 231–60

"Byzantium in the poetry of Kostis Palamas and C. P. Cafavy," *Kampos* 2 (1994), 1–20

Ahrweiler, H., "Recherches sur l'administration de l'empire byzantin aux IX–XI siècles," *BCH* 84 (1960), 1–109

Études sur les structures administratives et sociales de Byzance (London, 1971)

[Arveler, E.], *Elliniki synecheia. Poiimata istorias* (Athens, 1998)

Alexiou, M., "Writing against silence: antithesis and ekphrasis in the prose fiction of Georgios Vizyenos," *DOP* 47 (1993) 263–86

Angold, M., "Byzantine 'nationalism' and the Nicaean Empire," *BMGS* 1 (1975), 49–70

The Byzantine empire, 1025–1204: a political history, 2nd ed. (London, 1997)

Antoljak, S., *Samuel and his state* (Skopje, 1985)

Srednovekovna Makedonija, 3 vols. (Skopje, 1985)

"Dali sa avtentički onie tri ispravi na tsarot Vasilij II izdadeni vo korist na Ohridsakata arhiepiskopija," in his *Srednovekovna Makedonija* (Skopje, 1985), I, 69–108

Arbagi, M., "The celibacy of Basil II," *ByzSt* 2 (1975), 41–5

Athina-Peraias proasteia. Chartis – odigos (Athens, 1994)

Bálint, C., *Südungarn im 10. Jahrhundert* (Budapest, 1991)

Banduri, A., *Imperium Orientale sive antiquitates Constantinopolitanae*, 2 vols. (Paris, 1711)

Bănescu, N., *Les duchés byzantins de Paristrion (Paradounavon) et de Bulgarie* (Bucharest, 1946)

Bănescu, N. and P. Papahagi, "Plombs byzantins découverts à Silistra," *Byzantion* 10 (1935), 601–6

Baraschi, S. and O. Damian, "Considérations sur la céramique émaillée de Nufăru," *Dacia* 37 (1993), 237–77

Barker, J. W., *Justinian and the later Roman empire* (Madison, WI, 1966)

Barnea, I., "Sceaux de deux gouverneurs inconnus du thème de Paristrion," *Dacia* 8 (1964), 239–47

"Dinogetia et Noviodunum, deux villes byzantines du Bas-Danube," *RESEE* 9 (1971), 343–62

"Les sceaux byzantins mis au jour à Noviodunum," in N. Oikonomides, ed., *Studies in Byzantine sigilliography*, II (Washington, DC, 1990), 153–61

Bastéa, E., *The creation of modern Athens: planning the myth* (Cambridge, 2000)

Bauer, J. B., ed., *A reverse index of Patristic Greek* (Graz, 1983)

Baumstark, R., ed., *Rom und Byzanz. Schatzkammerstücke aus bayerischen Sammlungen* (Munich, 1998)

Beck, H.-G., *Kirche und theologische Literatur im byzantinischen Reich* (Munich, 1959)

Bel, G., "Classical Greece, Byzantium and the struggle for Greek national identity," in *Polyphonia Byzantina. Studies in honour of William J. Aerts* (Groningen, 1993), 325–37

Berger, A., *Untersuchungen zu den Patria Konstantinupoleos*, Poikila Byzantina 8 (Bonn, 1988)

Brailsford, H. N., *Macedonia: its races and their future* (London, 1906)

Braun, M., *Die Schlacht auf dem Amselfelde in geschichtlicher und epischer Überlieferung* (Leipzig, 1937)

Brehier, L., *Le monde byzantin, I. Vie et mort de Byzance* (Paris, 1948)

Brubaker, L., *Vision and meaning in ninth-century Byzantium. Image as exegesis in the homilies of Gregory of Nazianzus* (Cambridge, 1999)

Buck, C. D. and W. Petersen, *A reverse index of Greek nouns and adjectives* (Chicago, 1944)

Bulow, G. von, and A. Milcheva, eds., *Der Limes an der unteren Donau von Diokletian bis Heraklios. Vorträge der internationalen Konferenz Svishtov, Bulgarien (1.–5. September 1998)* (Sofia, 1999)

Bury, J. B., "Roman emperors from Basil II to Isaac Komnenos," *EHR* 4 (1889), 41–64, 251–85

A history of the Eastern Roman empire from the fall of Irene to the accession of Basil I (A.D. 802–67) (London, 1912)

Charitakis, G., ed., *Eis mnimin Spyridonos Lambrou* (Athens, 1935)

Cheynet, J.-C., "Du stratège du thème au duc: chronologie de l'évolution au cours du XIe siècle," *TM* 9 (1985), 181–94

Pouvoir et contestations à Byzance (963–1210) (Paris, 1990)

Cirac Estopañan, S., *Skyllitzes Matritensis, I. Reproducciones et minituras* (Barcelona and Madrid, 1965)

Clogg, R., "Aspects of the movement for Greek independence," in his *The struggle for Greek independence. Essays to mark the 150th anniversary of the Greek War of Independence* (London, 1973), 1–40

Politics and the academy. Arnold Toynbee and the Koraes Chair (London, 1986)

"The Byzantine legacy in the modern Greek world: the *megali idea*," in L. Clucas, ed., *The Byzantine legacy in Eastern Europe* (Boulder, 1988), 253–81; repr. in R. Clogg, *Anatolica: studies in the Greek East in the 18th and 19th centuries* (Aldershot, 1996), no. IV

A concise history of Greece (Cambridge, 1992)

Colocotronis, V., *La Macédoine et l'Hellénisme. Étude historique et ethnologique* (Paris, 1919)

Cormack, R., *Writing in gold. Byzantine society and its icons* (London, 1985)

Crampton, R. J., *A concise history of Bulgaria* (Cambridge, 1997)

Curta, F., "Transylvania around A.D. 1000," in P. Urbanczyk, ed., *Europe around the year 1000* (Warsaw, 2001), 141–65

Custarea, G., "Catalogul monedelor bizantine anonime descoperite la Capidava," *Pontica* 28–9 (1995–6), 301–7

Circulaţia monedei bizantine în Dobrogea (sec. IX–XI) (Constanţa, 2000)

Cutler, A., "The psalter of Basil II," *Arte Veneta* 30 (1976), 9–19

"The psalter of Basil II (part II)," *Arte Veneta* 31 (1977), 9–15

Cvijić, J., *La péninsule balkanique. Géographie humaine* (Paris, 1918)

Remarques sur l'ethnographie de la Macédoine. Deuxième édition augmentée d'une carte de la Vieille-Serbie (Paris, 1907)

Danforth, L., " 'How can a woman give birth to one Greek and one Macedonian?' The construction of national identity among immigrants to Australia from northern Greece," in J. Cowan, ed., *Macedonia: the politics of identity and difference* (London, 2000), 85–103

Darrouzès, J., *Recherches sur les Offikia de l'église byzantine* (Paris, 1970)

Daskalakis, A., ed., *To politeuma tou Riga Velestinli. Proton syntagma Ellinikis Dimokratias kai eleutheras diaviossios ton Valkanikon laon* (Athens, 1976)

Déer, J., *Die heilige Krone Ungarns* (Vienna, 1966)

Delta, P., *Gia tin patrida* (Athens, 1909)

Ton kairo tou Voulgaroktonou (Athens, 1911)

Demangel, J., *Contribution à la topographie de l'Hebdomon* (Paris, 1945)

Dennis, G., "Imperial panegyric: rhetoric and reality," in H. Maguire, ed., *Byzantine court culture from 829 to 1204* (Washington, DC, 1997), 131–40

Der Nersessian, S., "Remarks on the date of the menologion and the psalter written for Basil II," *Byzantion* 15 (1940–1), 104–25

Diaconu, P., "De nouveau à propos de Presthlavitza," *SüdostF* 46 (1987), 279–93

Diaconu, P. and D. Vîlceanu, *Păcuiul lui Soare, cetatea bizantină*, I (Bucharest, 1972)

Diehl, C., *Histoire de l'empire byzantin* (Paris, 1919)

Dimitrakopoulos, F., *Vyzantio kai neoelliniki dianoisi sta mesa tou dekatou enatou aionos* (Athens, 1996)

Downey, G., "The tombs of the Byzantine emperors at the Church of the Holy Apostles in Constantinople," *JHS* 79 (1959), 27–51

Dragoumis, I., *Martyron kai eroon aima* (Athens, 1907)

Duby, G., *The legend of Bouvines. War, religion and culture in the Middle Ages*, tr. C. Tihanyi (Cambridge, 1990)

Du Cange, C., *Historia Byzantina duplici commentario illustrata*, 2 vols. [in one]: I, *Familias ac stemmata imperatorum Constantinopolitanorum*; II, *Constantinopolis Christiana* (Paris, 1680)

Ducellier, A., *Byzance et le monde orthodoxe* (Paris, 1986)

Dujčev, I., "Recherches sur le Moyen Age bulgare [sommaire par V. Grumel]," *REB* 7 (1949), 129–32

Minijaturite na Manasjevata Letopis (Sofia, 1962)

"La chronique byzantine de l'an 811," *TM* 1 (1965), 205–55

Dvornik, F., *The Photian Schism, history and legend* (Cambridge, 1948)

Evans, H. C. and W. D. Wixom, eds., *The glory of Byzantium: art and culture in the middle Byzantine era, A.D. 843–1261* (New York, 1997)

Falkenhausen, V. von, "Eine byzantinische Beamtenurkunde aus Dubrownik," *BZ* 63 (1970), 10–23

La dominazione bizantina nell'Italia dal IX all'XI secolo, 2nd ed. (Bari, 1978)

"Bishops," in G. Cavallo, ed., *The Byzantines* (Chicago, 1997), 172–96

Fallmerayer, J. P., *Geschichte der Halbinsel Morea während des Mittelalters*, 2 vols. (Stuttgart, 1830–6)

Ferluga, J., "Vreme podizanje Crkve Sv. Ahileja na Prespi," *Zbornik za likovne umetnosti* 2 (1966), 3–7

"Le soulèvement des Cometopoules," *ZRVI* 9 (1966), 75–84

"John Skylitzes and Michael of Devol," *ZRVI* 10 (1967), 163–70

Byzantium on the Balkans. Studies on the Byzantine administration and the southern Slavs from the VIIth to the XIIth centuries (Amsterdam, 1976)

"Die Chronik des Priesters von Diokleia als Quelle für die byzantinische Geschichte," *Vyzantina* 10 (1980), 429–60

Fine, Jr., J. V. A., "A fresh look at Bulgaria under Tsar Peter (927–69)," *ByzSt* 5 (1978), 88–95

The early medieval Balkans: a critical survey from the sixth to the late twelfth century (Ann Arbor, 1983)

Finlay, G., *A history of Greece from its conquest by the Romans to the present time, B.C. 146 to A.D. 1864*, 2nd ed., ed. H. F. Tozer, 7 vols. (Oxford, 1877)

History of the Byzantine empire from DCCXVI to MLVII (London, 1906)

Folz, R., *Le souvenir et la légende de Charlemagne dans l'empire germanique médiéval* (Paris, 1950)

Franklin, S. and J. Shepard, *The emergence of Rus, 750–1200* (London and New York, 1996)

Frankopan, P. Doimi de, "The workings of the Byzantine provincial administration in the 10th–12th centuries: the example of Preslav," *Byzantion* 71 (2001), 73–97

Freeman, E. A., *Historical essays*, 3rd series (London, 1892)

Garland, L., "Basil II as humorist," *Byzantion* 69 (1999), 321–43

Geary, P., *The myth of nations* (Princeton, 2002)

Glück, H., *Das Hebdomon und seine Reste in Makriköi* (Vienna, 1920)

Gounaris, B., "Reassessing ninety years of Greek historiography on the 'Struggle for Macedonia 1904–1908'," *JMGS* 14 (1996), 235–51; repr. in P. Mackridge and E. Yannakakis, eds., *Ourselves and others. The development of Greek Macedonian identity since 1912* (Oxford, 1997).

Grabar, A., *L'empereur dans l'art byzantin* (Strasbourg, 1936)

"La soie byzantine de l'évêque Gunther à la cathédrale de Bamberg," *L'art de la fin de l'antiquité et du Moyen Age* (Paris, 1968), I, 213–27; repr. with new pagination from *Münchner Jahrbuch der bildenden Kunst*, n.f. 8 (1956)

Grabar, O. and M. Manoussacas, *L'illustration du manuscrit de Skylitzès de la Bibliothèque Nationale de Madrid* (Venice, 1979)

Gregorovius, F., *Geschichte der Stadt Athen im Mittelalter von der Zeit Justinians bis zur türkischen Eroberung*, 2 vols. (Stuttgart, 1889)

Grierson, P., "The tombs and obits of the Byzantine emperors (337–1042)," *DOP* 16 (1962), 3–60

Catalogue of Byzantine coins in the Dumbarton Oaks collection, III: Leo III to Nicephorus III, 717–1081 (Washington, DC, 1973)

Grumel, V., *Les regestes des actes du patriarchat de Constantinople, I. Les actes des patriarches, II–III: Les regestes de 715 à 1206*, 2nd ed., ed. J. Darrouzès (Paris, 1989)

Grünbart, M., "Die Familie Apokapes im Licht neuer Quellen," in N. Oikonomides, ed., *Studies in Byzantine sigillography*, V (Washington, DC, 1998), 29–41

Györffy, G., "Das Güterverzeichnis des Klosters zu Szávaszentdemeter (Sremska Mitrovica) aus dem 12. Jahrhundert," *Studia Slavica* 5 (1959), 9–74

"Zur Geschichte der Eroberung Ochrids durch Basileios II.," in *Actes du XIIe congrès international des études byzantines, Ochride, 10–16 septembre 1961*, II (Belgrade, 1964), 149–54

Haase, W., "'Si vis pacem, para bellum': Zur Beurteilung militärischer Stärke in der römischen Kaiserzeit," in J. Fitz, ed., *Limes. Akten des XI. Internationalen Limeskongresses (Székesfehérvár, 30.8.–6.9.1976)* (Budapest, 1977), 721–55

Haldon, J., *Warfare, state and society in the Byzantine world, 565–1204* (London, 1999)

Hamilton, C., *Terrific majesty: the powers of Shaka Zulu and the limits of historical invention* (Cambridge, MA, 1997)

Heisenberg, A., *Grabeskirche und Apostelkirche. Zwei Basiliken Konstantins. Untersuchungen zur Kunst und Literatur des ausgehenden Altertums, II: Die Apostelkirche in Konstantinopel* (Leipzig, 1908), 84–5.

Hendy, M., *Studies in the Byzantine monetary economy, 300–1450* (Cambridge, 1985)

Hergenröther, J., *Photius, Patriarch von Constantinopel sein Leben, seine Schriften und das griechische Schisma*, 3 vols. (Regensberg, 1867–9)

ed., *Monumenta Graeca ad Photium ejusque historiam pertinentia* (Regensberg, 1869; repr. 1969)

Herrin, J., "Blinding in Byzantium," in ΠΟΛΥΠΛΕΥΡΟΣ ΝΟΥΣ. *Miscellanea für Peter Schreiner zu seinem 60. Geburtstag*, eds. C. Scholz and G. Makris (Leipzig, 2000)

Hirst, A., "Two cheers for Byzantium: equivocal attitudes in the poetry of Palamas and Cafavy," in D. Ricks and P. Magdalino, eds., *Byzantium and the modern Greek identity* (Aldershot, 1998), 105–17

Holmes, C., "Byzantium's eastern frontier in the tenth and eleventh centuries," in N. Berend and D. Abulafia, eds., *Medieval frontiers: concepts and practices* (Aldershot, 2002), 83–104

Hunger, H., "Zehn unedierte byzantinischen Beamten-Siegel," *JÖB* 17 (1968), 179–95

"Reditus Imperatoris," in G. Prinzing and D. Simon, eds., *Fest und Alltag in Byzanz* (Munich, 1990), 17–35

Hussey, J. M., "George Finlay in perspective – a centenary reappraisal," *Annual of the British School at Athens* 70 (1975), 135–44

Hutter, I., "Theodorupolis," in *AΕΤΟΣ. Studies in honour of Cyril Mango*, ed. I. Ševčenko et al. (Stuttgart and Leipzig, 1998), 181–90

Huxley, G., "Aspects of modern Greek historiography of Byzantium," in D. Ricks and P. Magdalino, eds., *Byzantium and the modern Greek identity* (Aldershot, 1998), 15–25

Ichircoff [= Ishirkov], A., *Étude ethnographique sur les Slaves de Macédoine. Réponse à M. J. Zvijitch* (Paris, 1908)

Ingham, N. W., "The martyrdom of Saint John Vladimir of Dioclea," *International Journal of Slavic Linguistics and Poetics* 35–6 (1987), 199–216

Iordanov, I., "Neizdadeni vizantiiski olovni pechati ot Silistra (I)," *Izvestiia na Narodniia Muzei Varna* 19 [34] (1983), 97–110

"Neizdadeni vizantiiski olovni pechati ot Silistra (II)," *Izvestiia na Narodniia Muzei Varna* 21 [36] (1985), 98–107

"Neizdadeni vizantiiski olovni pechati ot Silistra (III)," *Izvestiia na Narodniia Muzei Varna* 24 [39] (1988), 88–103

"Neizdadeni vizantiiski olovni pechati ot Silistra (IV)," *Izvestiia na Narodniia Muzei Varna* 28 [43] (1992), 229–45

Pechatite ot strategiiata v Preslav (971–1088) (Sofia, 1993)

Iorga, N., *Histoire de la vie byzantine. Empire et civilisation, II. L'empire moyen de civilisation hellénique* (Bucharest, 1934)

Byzance après Byzance (Bucharest, 1935; repr. 1971)

Ivaniševič, V., "Vizantijski novac (491–1092) iz zbirke Narodnog Muzeja u Požarevcu," *Numizmatičar* 11 (1988), 87–99

"Optičaj Vizantijski folisa XI. veka na prostoru centralnog Balkana," *Numizmatičar* 16 (1993), 79–92

Ivaniševič, V. and V. Radić, "Četiri ostave vizantijskog novca iz zbirke Narodnog Muzeja u Beogradu," *Numismatičar* 20 (1997), 131–46

Ivanov, J., "Le costume des anciens Bulgares," in *L'art byzantin chez les Slaves, II. Les Balkans* (Paris, 1930)

Janin, R., *La géographie ecclésiastique de l'empire byzantin, I. Le siège de Constantinople et la patriarcat oecuménique, III. Les églises et les monastères* (Paris, 1953)

Janković, M., *Srednjovekovno naselje na Velikom Gradcu u X–XI veku* (Belgrade, 1981)

Jenkins, R. and C. Mango, "A synodicon of Antioch and Lacedaemonia," *DOP* 15 (1961), 225–42

Jireček, C. and V. Jagić, "Die cyrillische Inschrift vom Jahre 993," *Archiv für slavische Philologie* 21 (1899), 543–57

Jolivet-Lévy, C., "L'image du pouvoir dans l'art byzantin à l'époque de la dynastie macédonienne (867–1056)," *Byzantion* 57 (1987), 441–70

Kalavrezou-Maxeiner, I., "The portraits of Basil I in Paris gr. 510," *JÖB* 27 (1978), 19–24

Kalić, J., "La région de Ras à l'époque byzantine," in H. Ahrweiler, ed., *Géographie historique du monde méditerranéan*, Byzantina Sorbonensia 7 (Paris, 1988), 127–40

Kallivretakis, L., "I Athina tou 19ou aiona. Apo eparchiaki poli tis Othomanikis autokratorias, proteuousa tou Ellinikou vasileou," *Archaiologia tis polis Athinon. Epistimonikes-epimorfotikes dialexeis, Ianouarios – Martios 1994*, Eidikes morfotikes ekdiloseis 4 (Athens, 1994), 173–96

Kardaras, A., *Vasileios II o Voulgaroktonos. To apogeio tis Vyzantinis dynamis* (Athens, 2002)

Kazhdan, A., "The aristocracy and the imperial ideal," in M. Angold, ed., *The Byzantine aristocracy IX to XIII centuries* (Oxford, 1984), 43–57

"Russian pre-revolutionary studies on eleventh-century Byzantium," in S. Vryonis, Jr., ed., *Byzantine studies: essays on the Slavic world and the eleventh century* (New Rochelle, NY, 1992), 111–25

Kiousopoulou, T., "I proti edra vyzantinis istorias sto Panepistimiou Athinon," *Mnimon* 15 (1993), 257–76

Kitromilides, P., " 'Imagined communities' and the origins of the national question in the Balkans," *European History Quarterly* 19/ii (1989), 149–92; repr. in his *Enlightenment, nationalism, orthodoxy. Studies in the culture and political thought of south-eastern Europe* (Aldershot, 1994), no. XI

" 'Balkan mentality': history, legend, imagination," *Nations and Nationalism* 2 (1996), 163–91

"On the intellectual content of Greek nationalism: Paparrigopoulos, Byzantium and the Great Idea," in D. Ricks and P. Magdalino, eds., *Byzantium and the modern Greek identity* (Aldershot, 1998), 25–33

Koder, J., "Macedonia and Macedonians in Byzantine spatial thinking," in J. Burke and R. Scott, eds., *Byzantine Macedonia. Identity, image and history*, Byzantina Australiensia 13 (Melbourne, 2000), 12–28

Koledarov, P., "Ethnography in Great Britain and the Bulgarian Question," *Macedonian Studies* 9 (1992), 3–34

Kolias, T. G., *Byzantinische Waffen. Ein Beitrag zur byzantinischen Waffenkunde von den Anfängen bis zur lateinischen Eroberung*, Byzantina Vindobonensia 17 (Vienna, 1988)

Konstantinou Tegiou-Stergiadou, E., *Ta schetika tin Archiepiskopi Achridas sigillia tou Vasileiou II* (Thessaloniki, 1988)

Korpela, J., *Prince, saint and apostle. Prince Vladimir Svjatoslavič of Kiev, his posthumous life, and the religious legitimization of the Russian great power* (Wiesbaden, 2001)

Koukoules, F., "Ta kata tin tafin ton vyzantinon vasileon," *EEBS* 15 (1939), 52–78

Kravari, V., *Villes et villages de Macédoine occidentale*, Réalitiés byzantines (Paris, 1989)

Kristó, G., "Ajtony and Vidin," in G. Káldy-Nagy, ed., *Turkic-Bulgarian-Hungarian relations (VIth–XIth Centuries)*, Studia Turco-Hungarica 5 (Budapest, 1981), 129–35

Krumbacher, K., *Geschichte des byzantinischen Litteratur von Justinian bis zum Ende des oströmischen Reiches (527–1453)*, 2 vols. (Munich, 1897)

Kubinyi, A., "Handel und Entwicklung der Städte in der ungarischen Tiefebene im Mittelalter," in *Europa Slavica – Europa Orientalis. Festschrift für K. Ludat*, eds. K. D. Grothusen and K. Zernack (Berlin, 1980), 423–44

Kühn, H.-J., *Die byzantinische Armee im 10. und 11. Jahrhundert. Studien zur Organisation der Tagmata* (Vienna, 1991)

Külzer, A., "Studium zum Chronicon Bruxellense," *Byzantion* 61 (1991), 413–47

Lambros, S., *Ai Athinai peri ta teli tou dodekatou aionos* (Athens, 1878)

  Leukoma vyzantinon autokratoron (Athens, 1930)

Laourdas, V., *I Pinelopi Delta kai i Makedonia* (Thessaloniki, 1958); repr. in his *Makedonika analekta* (Thessaloniki, 1980), 67–94

  "O Ion Dragoumis kai i epochi tou," in his *Makedonika analekta* (Thessaloniki, 1980), 95–110

  "O Kastorias Germanos Karavangelis (1866–1935)," in his *Makedonika analekta* (Thessaloniki, 1980), 49–52

Laurent, V., "Le thème byzantin de Serbie au XIe siècle," *REB* 15 (1957), 185–95

  Le corpus de sceaux de l'empire byzantin, V. L'église (Paris, 1965)

L[aurent], V., "Short note," *BZ* 58 (1965), 220

Lauxtermann, M., "Byzantine poetry and the paradox of Basil II's reign," in P. Magdalino, ed., *Byzantium in the year 1000* (Leiden, 2003), 199–216

Lefcoparides, X., ed., *Allilografia tis P. S. Delta 1906–40* (Athens, 1957)

  Lettres de deux amis. Une correspondance entre Pénélope S. Delta et Gustave Schlumberger, suivie de quelques lettres de Gabriel Millet (Athens, 1962)

Lefort, J., "Rhétorique et politique: trois discours de Jean Mauropous en 1047," *TM* 6 (1976), 265–303

Legrand, E., "Description des oeuvres d'art et de l'Eglise des Saints Apôtres à Constantinople par Constantin le Rhodien," *REG* 9 (1896), 36–65

Lemerle, P., ed., *Recherches sur le XIe siècle*, = *TM* 6 (Paris, 1976).

  Cinq études sur le XIᵉ siècle byzantin (Paris, 1977)

Liakos, A., "The construction of national time: the making of the modern Greek historical imagination," *Mediterranean Historical Review* 16 (2001), 27–42

Lieu, S. and D. Montserrat, eds., *Constantine. History, historiography and legend* (London and New York, 1998)

Loos, M., "Symposium historique «l'insurrection des comitopules de la création de l'Etat de Samuel.» Prespa, 10–15 Octobre 1969," *BSl* 31 (1970), 292–4

Loparev, Ch., "Opisanie nekotorykh grecheskykh zhit'ii sviat'ikh," *VV* 4 (1897), 337–401

Macartney, C. A., "Studies on the earliest Hungarian historical sources, I: the Lives of St. Gerard," *Archivum Europae Centro-Orientalis* 18 (1938), 1–35
    Early Hungarian and Pontic history, eds. L. Czigány and L. Péter (Aldershot, 1999)
Mackridge, P., "Macedonia and Macedonians in *Sta mystika tou valtou* (1937) by P. S. Delta," *Dialogos* 7 (2000), 41–55
Madgearu, A., "The military organization of Paradunavon," *BSl* 60 (1999), 421–46
Magdalino, P., "Aspects of twelfth-century Byzantine Kaiserkritik," *Speculum* 58 (1983), 326–46
    "Hellenism and nationalism in Byzantium," in his *Tradition and transformation in medieval Byzantium* (Aldershot, 1991), no. XIV, 1–29 at 10; repr. with same pagination, in J. Burke and S. Gauntlett, eds., *Neohellenism*, Australian National University: Humanities Research Monograph 5 (Melbourne, 1992)
    The empire of Manuel I Komnenos, 1143–1180 (Cambridge, 1993)
    ed., *New Constantines: the rhythm of imperial renewal in Byzantium, 4th–13th centuries* (Aldershot, 1994)
Magdalino, P. and R. Nelson, "The emperor in Byzantine art of the twelfth century," *ByzF* 8 (1982), 123–83
Maguire, H., "Imperial gardens and the rhetoric of renewal," in P. Magdalino, ed., *New Constantines. The rhythm of imperial renewal in Byzantium, 4th to 13th centuries* (Aldershot, 1994), 181–98
    "Images of the court," in H. C. Evans and W. D. Wixom, eds., *The glory of Byzantium: art and culture in the middle Byzantine era, A.D. 843–1261* (New York, 1997), 182–91
Makk, F., "Relations Hungaro-Bulgares au temps du Prince Géza und du Roi Etienne 1er," in *Szegedi Bolgarisztika*, Hungaro-Bulgarica 5 (Szeged, 1994), 25–33
Makrides, Th. K., "To vyzantinon Evdomon kai ai par'autoi monai, I," *Thrakika* 10 (1938), 137–98
    "To vyzantinon Evdomon kai ai par'autoi monai, II," *Thrakika* 12 (1939), 35–80
Makridy, T. [= Th. K. Makrides] and J. Ebersolt, "Monuments funéraires de Constantinople," *BCH* 46 (1922), 356–93
Maksimović, L., *The Byzantine provincial administration under the Palaiologoi* (Amsterdam, 1988)
    "Organizacija Vizantijske vlasti u novoosvojenim oblastima posle 1018. godine," *ZRVI* 36 (1997), 31–43
Maksimović, L. and M. Popović, "Les sceaux byzantins de la région danubienne en Serbie, II," in N. Oikonomides, ed., *Studies in Byzantine sigillography*, III (Washington, DC, 1993), 113–42
Malamut, E., "L'image byzantine des Petchénègues," *BZ* 88 (1995), 105–47
    "Concepts et réalitiés: recherches sur les termes désignant les Serbes et les pays Serbes dans les sources byzantines des Xe–XIIe siècles," in *EYΨYXIA. Mélanges offerts à Hélène Ahrweiler*, ed. M. Balard et al. (Paris, 1998), 439–57

Malingoudis, P., *Die mittelalterlichen kyrillischen Inschriften der Hämus-Halbinsel, I. Die bulgarischen Inschriften* (Thessaloniki, 1979)

Mandić, L. and R. Mihajlovski, "A XIth century Byzantine seal from Heraclea near Bitola," *REB* 58 (2000), 273–7

Mango, C., "Letter to the editor," *ArtB* 41 (1959), 351–6; repr. as "Justinian's equestrian statue," in his *Studies in Constantinople* (Aldershot, 1993), no. XI, with new pagination, 1–16

"The legend of Leo the Wise," *ZRVI* 6 (1960), 59–93, 78; repr. in his *Byzantium and its image* (London, 1984), no. XVI

"Byzantinism and Romantic Hellenism," *Journal of the Warburg and Courtauld Institutes* 28 (1965), 29–43; repr. in his *Byzantium and its image* (London, 1984), no. I

"A Byzantine inscription relating to Dyrrhachium," *Archäologischer Anzeiger* 3 (1966), 410–14

The art of the Byzantine empire (Englewood Cliffs, NJ, 1972)

"The Phanariots and the Byzantine tradition," in R. Clogg, ed., *The struggle for Greek independence. Essays to mark the 150th anniversary of the Greek War of Independence* (London, 1973), 41–66

"The columns of Justinian and his successors," in his *Studies in Constantinople* (Aldershot, 1993), no. X, 1–20

"The triumphal way of Constantinople and the Golden Gate," *DOP* 54 (2000), 173–88

Mănucu-Adameşteanu, G., "Aspecte privind circulaţia monetară la Mangalia în secolele X–XI (969–1081)," *Pontica* 28–9 (1995–6), 287–300

Maricq, A., "Notes philologiques, 4: Les sarcophages impériaux de Constantinople," *Byzantion* 22 (1952), 370–2

Mathews, T., *Byzantium from Antiquity to the Renaissance* (New York, 1998)

Mattern, S., *Rome and the enemy. Imperial strategy in the Principate* (Berkeley, 1999)

Mazarakis-Ainian, I. and E. Papaspyrou-Karadimitriou, *Valkanikoi polemoi 1912–1913. Elliniki laiki eikonografia*, 2nd ed. (Athens, 1999)

Mazower, M., "Introduction to the study of Macedonia," *JMGS* 14 (1996), 229–35

McCormick, M., *Eternal victory. Triumphal rulership in Late Antiquity, Byzantium and the early medieval West* (Cambridge and Paris, 1986)

McGrath, S., "The battles of Dorostolon (971): rhetoric and reality," in *Peace and war in Byzantium. Essays in honor of George T. Dennis, S. J.*, eds. T. S. Miller and J. Nesbitt (Washington, DC, 1995), 152–64

Mélanges Georges Ostrogorsky, 2 vols. (Belgrade, 1968) [= *ZRVI* 8]

Il menologio di Basilio II (Cod. Vaticano Greco 1613) (Turin, 1907)

Michel, A., *Humbert und Kerullarios*, 2 vols. (Paderborn, 1924–30)

Mikulčić, I., *Srednovekovni gradovi i tvrdini vo Makedonija* (Skopje, 1996)

Miller, W., *Essays in the Latin Orient* (Cambridge, 1921)

A history of the Greek people (1821–1921) (London, 1922)

"The Finlay papers," *EHR* 39 (1924), 386–98

"The journals of Finlay and Jarvis," *EHR* 41 (1926), 514–25

"John Bagnell Bury," *EHR* 43 (1928), 66–72

Mitsakis, K., "Byzantium in modern Greek historical fiction," in E. Konstantinou, ed., *Byzantinische Stoffe und Motive in der europäischen Literatur des 19. und 20. Jahrhunderts*, Philhellenische Studien 6 (Frankfurt am Main, 1998), 239–51

Moravcsik, G., *Byzantinoturcica*, 2 vols., 2nd ed. (Berlin, 1958)

Morrisson, C., *Catalogue des monnaies byzantines de la Bibliothèque Nationale, I. 491–711* (Paris, 1970)

Moutsopoulos, N., *Anaskafi tis vasilikis tou agiou Achilleiou*, 5 vols. (Thessaloniki, 1966–72)

"Le tombeau du Tsar Samuil dans la Basilique de Saint Achille à Prespa," *Études Balkaniques* 3 (1984), 114–26

Müller-Christensen, S., "Beobachtungen zum Bamberger Gunthertuch," *Münchner Jahrbuch der bildenden Kunst*, n.f. 17 (1966), 9–16.

Das Guntertuch im Bamberger Domschatz (Bamberg, 1984)

Mullett, M., *Theophylact of Ochrid. Reading the letters of a Byzantine archbishop*, Birmingham Byzantine and Ottoman Monographs 2 (Birmingham, 1997)

Nesbitt, J. and N. Oikonomides, *Catalogue of Byzantine seals at Dumbarton Oaks and in the Fogg Museum of Art, I: Italy, north of the Balkans, north of the Black Sea* (Washington, DC, 1991)

Niavis, P., *The reign of the Byzantine emperor Nicephorus I (A.D. 802–811)* (Athens, 1987)

Nikolov, G., "The Bulgarian aristocracy in the war against the Byzantine empire (971–1019)," in M. Salamon and G. Prinzing with P. Stephenson, eds., *Byzantium and East-Central Europe*, Byzantina et Slavica Cracoviensia 3 (Cracow, 2001), 141–58

Nystazopoulou-Pelekidou, M., "Oi vizantines istorikes spoudes stin Ellada. Apo ton Spyridona Zambelio ston Dionysio Zakythino," *Symmeikta. Ethniko Idryma Ereunon, Kentro Vyzantinon Ereunon* 9, 2 vols. (1994), II, 153–76

Obolensky, D., *The Byzantine commonwealth. Eastern Europe, 500–1453* (London, 1971)

"Theophylaktos of Ohrid and the authorship of the Vita Clementis," in *Byzantium. A tribute to Andreas N. Stratos*, 2 vols. (Athens, 1986), II, 601–18

Six Byzantine portraits (Oxford, 1988)

Oikonomides, N., "Recherches sur l'histoire du Bas-Danube au Xe–XIIe siècles: Mésopotamie d'Occident," *RESEE* 3 (1965), 57–79

"L'évolution de l'organisation administrative de l'empire byzantin au XIe siècle (1025–1118)," *TM* 6 (1976), 125–52

"Presthlavitza, the Little Preslav," *SüdostF* 42 (1983), 1–9

"À propos de la première occupation byzantine de la Bulgarie (971–ca 986)," in *EYΨYXIA. Mélanges offerts à Hélène Ahrweiler*, ed. M. Balard et al., Byzantina Sorbonensia 16, 2 vols. (Paris, 1998), II, 581–9

Omont, H., *Inventaire sommaire des manuscrits grecs de la Bibliothèque Nationale*, 4 vols. (Paris, 1883–98)

Les manuscrits grecs datés des XVe et XVIe siècles de la Bibliothèque Nationale et des autres bibliothèques de France (Paris, 1892)

Ostrogorski [= Ostrogorsky], G., *Geschichte des byzantinischen Staates*. Handbuch der Altertumswissenschaft, 2, III (Munich, 1940)

Ostrogorsky, G., "Une ambassade Serbe auprès de l'empereur Basile II," *Byzantion* 19 (1949), 187–94

"Byzantium in the seventh century," *DOP* 13 (1959), 5–21

History of the Byzantine state, tr. J. Hussey, 2nd English ed. (Oxford, 1968)

Mélanges Georges Ostrogorsky, 2 vols. (Belgrade, 1968)

Oxford dictionary of Byzantium, eds. A. Kazhdan, A.-M. Talbot, A. Cutler, T. E. Gregory and N. P. Ševčenko, 3 vols. (Oxford and New York, 1991)

Pachymeres, George, "Ekphrasis on the Augusteion," in L. Schopen, ed., *Nicephori Gregorae byzantina historia*, CSHB (Bonn, 1830), II, 1217–20

Palamas, K., *Apanta*, 16 vols. (Athens, 1962–9)

The king's flute, tr. T. P. Stefaniades and G. C. Katsimbalis, The Kostes Palamas Institute 4 (Athens, 1982)

Papadaki-Oekland, S., "The representation of Justinian's column in a Byzantine miniature of the twelfth century," *BZ* 83 (1990), 63–71

Paparrigopoulo[s], C. [= K], *Histoire de la civilisation hellénique* (Paris, 1878)

Paparrigopoulos, K., *Istoria tou ellinikou ethnous* (Athens 1860–74; 2nd ed. 1885–7); revised ed. P. Karolides, 5 vols. (Athens, 1925)

Istoria tou ellinikou ethnous [i proti morfi: 1853], ed. K. Th. Dimaras (Athens, 1970)

Pavlović, M., "Nadgrobnata plocha najdena vo selo German kaj Prespa", in M. Apostolski, S. Antoljak and B. Panov, eds., *Iljada godini od vostanieto na komitopulite i sozdavanjeto na Samoilovata drzava: zbornik na materijali od naucnata sredba odrzana vo Prespa od 10 do 15 oktombri 1969 godina* (Skopje, 1971), 73–93

Pavlovski, J. and M. Pavlovski, *Makedonija včera i denes* (Skopje, 1996)

Pervanoglou, I., *Michail o Palaiologos. Istorikon diigma* (Leipzig, 1883)

Pirivatrić, S., "Vizantijska tema Morava i 'Moravije' Konstantina VII Porfiro-geneta," *ZRVI* 36 (1997), 173–201

Samuilova država. Obim i karakter (Belgrade, 1997)

Politis, A., "From Christian Roman emperors to the glorious Greek ancestors," in D. Ricks and P. Magdalino, eds., *Byzantium and the modern Greek identity* (Aldershot, 1998), 1–14

Popović, M., *Beogradska tvrdjava* (Belgrade, 1982)

"Les fortresses du system défensif byzantin en Serbie au XIe–XIIe siècle," *Starinar* 42 (1991), 169–85

Popović, M. and V. Ivanišević, "Grad Braničevo u srednjem veku," *Starinar* 39 (1988), 125–79

Popović, V., "Catalogue des monnaies byzantines du musée de Srem," in C. Brenot, N. Duval and V. Popović, eds., *Etudes de numismatique danubienne: trésors, l'ingots, imitations, monnaies de fouilles IVe–XIIe siècle*, Sirmium 8 (Rome and Belgrade, 1978), 179–93

"L'évêché de Sirmium," in S. Ercegović-Pavlović, ed., *Les nécropoles romains et médiévales de Mačvanska Mitrovica*, Sirmium 12 (Belgrade, 1980), i–iv

Poppe, A., "The political background to the baptism of Rus'. Byzantine-Russian relations between 986–89," *DOP* 30 (1976), 195–244

"Two conceptions of the conversion of Rus' in Kievan writings," *HUS* 12/13 (1988/1989), 488–504

"The Christianization and ecclesiastical structure of Kyivan Rus' to 1300," *HUS* 21 (1997), 311–92

Poulter, A., "Town and country in Moesia Inferior," in A. Poulter, ed., *Ancient Bulgaria. Papers presented to the International Symposium on the Ancient History and Archaeology of Bulgaria, University of Nottingham, 1981*, 2 vols. (Nottingham, 1983), II, 74–118

Preger, T., *Beiträge zur Textgeschichte der* Πάτρια Κωνσταντινουπόλεως (Munich, 1895)

Prinzing, G., *Die Bedeutung Bulgariens und Serbiens in den Jahren 1204–1219 in Zusammenhang mit der Entstehung und Entwicklung der byzantinischen Teilstaaten nach der Einnahme Konstantinopels infolge der 4. Kreuzzuges*, Miscellanea Byzantina Monacensia 12 (Munich, 1972)

"Das Bild Justinians I," *Fontes Minores* 7, ed. D. Simon (Frankfurt am Main, 1986), 1–99

"Das Bamberger Gunthertuch in neuer Sicht," *BSl* 54 (1993), 218–31

"Zu Odessos/Varna (im 6. Jh.), Belgrad (1096) und Braničevo (um 1163). Klärung dreier Fragen aus Epigraphik, Prosopographie und Sphragistik," *BSl* 56 (1995), 219–25

Prokić, J., *Die Zusätze in der Handschrift des Johannes Skylitzes, codex Vindobonensis hist. graec. LXXIV. Ein Beitrag zur Geschichte des sogennanten westbulgarischen Reiches* (Munich, 1906)

Reallexikon zur byzantinischen Kunst, ed. K. Wessel (Stuttgart, 1966)

Restle, M., "Hofkunst und höfische Kunst Konstantinopels in der mittelbyzantinischen Zeit", in R. Laurer and H. G. Majer, eds., *Höfische Kultur in Südosteuropa. Bericht der Kolloquien der Südosteuropa-Kommission 1988 bis 1990* (Göttingen, 1994), 25–41

Ricks, D. and P. Magdalino, eds., *Byzantium and the modern Greek identity* (Aldershot, 1998)

Riley-Smith, J., *The first crusaders, 1095–1131* (Cambridge, 1997)

Rosenqvist, J. O., "The text of the Life of St. Nikon 'Metanoeite' reconsidered," in ΛΕΙΜΩΝ. *Studies presented to Lennart Rydén on his sixty-fifth birthday*, ed. J. O. Rosenqvist (Uppsala, 1996), 93–111

Roueché, C., "Byzantine writers and readers: storytelling in the eleventh century," in R. Beaton, ed., *The Greek novel A.D. 1–1985* (London, 1988), 123–33

Rozen, V. R., *Imperator Vasilij Bolgarobojca. Izvlečenija iz Letopisi Jaxi Antioxijskago* (St. Petersburg, 1908; repr. London, 1972)

Runciman, S., *A history of the first Bulgarian empire* (London, 1930)

Byzantine civilisation (London, 1933)

The Eastern Schism. A study of the papacy and the eastern Churches during the XIth and XIIth centuries (Oxford, 1955)

Šandrovskaya, V., "Iz istorii Bolgarii X–XII vv. po dannym sfragistiki," *Byzantinobulgarica* 7 (1981), 455–67

Schlumberger, G., *Sigillographie de l'empire byzantin* (Paris, 1884)

Un empereur byzantin au dixième siècle, Nicéphore Phocas (Paris, 1890)

L'épopée byzantine à la fin du dixième siècle, I. Jean Tzimiscès; les jeunes années de Basile II, le tueur de Bulgares (969–989) (Paris, 1896)

L'épopée byzantine à la fin du dixième siècle, II. Basile II le tueur des Bulgares (Paris, 1900)

"L'empereur Basile II à Athènes," *Le Gaulois*, 4 October 1913; repr. in his *Récits de Byzance et des Croisades*, 2 vols. (Paris, 1916–22), I, 50–8

Mes souvenirs 1844–1928, 2 vols. (Paris, 1934)

Schöpflin, G., "The functions of myth and a taxonomy of myths," in G. Hosking and G. Schöpflin, eds., *Myths and nationhood* (London, 1997), 19–35

Schramm, P. E., "Das Herrscherbild in der Kunst der frühen Mittelalters," *Vorträge der Bibliothek Warburg*, ed. F. Saxl, III. Vorträge 1922–3 (Leipzig and Berlin, 1924), I, 145–224

Seibt, W., "Untersuchungen zur Vor- und Frühgeschichte der 'bulgarischen' Kometopulen," *Handes Amsorya. Zeitschrift für armenische Philologie* 89 (1975), 65–98

Ševčenko, I., "The illuminators of the menologium of Basil II," *DOP* 16 (1962), 245–76

"Sviatoslav in Byzantine and Slavic miniatures," *Slavic Review* 24 (1965), 709–13

Ševčenko, N. P., "Illuminating the liturgy: illustrated service books in Byzantium," in L. Safran, ed., *Heaven on earth. Art and the Church in Byzantium* (University Park, PA, 1998), 186–228

Shepard, J., "The Russian steppe frontier and the Black Sea zone," *Archeion Pontou* 35 (1979), 218–37

"A suspected source of Scylitzes' *Synopsis Historion*: the great Catacalon Cecaumenus," *BMGS* 16 (1992), 171–81

"Bulgaria: the other Balkan 'empire'," in T. Reuter, ed., *The new Cambridge medieval history, III: c. 900–c. 1024* (Cambridge, 1999), 567–85

"Byzantium expanding, 944–1025," in T. Reuter, ed., *The new Cambridge medieval history III: c. 900–c. 1024* (Cambridge, 1999), 586–604

Smith, A. D., *National identity* (London, 1991)

"The 'golden age' and national renewal," in G. Hosking and G. Schöpflin, eds., *Myths and nationhood* (London, 1997), 36–59

Spanaki, M., "Byzantium and the novel in the twentieth century: from Penelope Delta to Maro Douka," in D. Ricks and P. Magdalino, eds., *Byzantium and the modern Greek identity* (Aldershot, 1998), 119–30

Spatharakis, I., "The portraits and the date of the Codex *Par. Gr. 510*," *Cahiers archéologiques* 23 (1974), 97–105

"A note on the imperial portraits and the date of Par. Gr. 510," *JÖB* 39 (1989), 89–93

"Three portraits of the early Comnenian period," in his *Studies in Byzantine manuscript illumination and iconography* (London, 1996), 18–40

"The proskynesis in Byzantine art. A study in connection with a nomisma of Andronicus II Palaeologue," in his *Studies in Byzantine manuscript illumination and iconography* (London, 1996), 193–224

Speck, P., "Konstantinos von Rhodos. Zweck und Datum der Ekphrasis der sieben Wunder von Konstantinopel und der Apostelkirche," *Varia 3*, Poikila Byzantina 11 (Bonn, 1991), 249–61

Stavrakos, C., "Die Vita des hl. Nikon Metanoeite als Quelle zur Prosopographie der Peloponnes im späten 10. Jahrhundert," *SüdostF* 58 (1999), 1–7

Steindorff, L., "Die Synode auf der Planities Dalmae. Reichseinteilung und Kirchenorganisation im Bild der Chronik des Priesters von Diocleia," *Mitteilungen des Instituts für Österreichische Geschichtsforschung* 93 (1985 [1986]), 279–324

"Deutungen des Wortes *Dalmatia* in der mittelalterlichen Historiographie. Zugleich über die Synode auf der *Planities Dalmae*," in N. Budak, ed., *Etnogeneza Hrvata* (Zagreb, 1996), 250–61

Stephenson, P., "Byzantine policy towards Paristrion in the mid-eleventh century: another interpretation," *BMGS* 23 (1999), 43–66

"The Byzantine frontier in Macedonia," *Dialogos* 7 (2000), 23–40

Byzantium's Balkan frontier: a political study of the northern Balkans, 900–1204 (Cambridge, 2000)

"The legend of Basil the Bulgar-slayer," *BMGS* 24 (2000), 102–32

"Images of the Bulgar-slayer: three art historical notes," *BMGS* 25 (2001), 44–66

Stevenson, H., *Codices manuscripti Palatini graeci Bibliothecae Vaticanae* (Rome, 1885)

Strobel, K., *Untersuchungen zu den Dakerkriegen Trajans. Studien zur Geschichte des mittleren und unteren Donauraumes in der hohen Kaiserzeit* (Bonn, 1984)

Swiencickyj, I., "Byzantinische Bleisiegel in den Sammlungen von Lwow," in *Sbornik v pamet na Prof. Nikov* (Sofia, 1940), 434–50

Syme, R., *Gedenkworte für Georg Ostrogorsky. Orden pour le merité für Wissenschaften und Künste. Reden und Gedenkworte, vierzehnter Band* (Heidelberg, 1978)

Tăpkova-Zaimova, V., *Dolni Dunav – granichna zona na vizantiiskiia zapad* (Sofia, 1976)

Byzance et les Balkans à partir du VIe siècle (London, 1979)

"Les frontières occidentales des territoires conquis par Tzimiscès," in H. Ahrweiler, ed., *Géographie historique du monde méditerranéen*, Byzantina Sorbonensia 7 (Paris, 1988), 113–18

"Quelques nouvelles données sur l'administration byzantine au Bas Danube (fin du Xe–XIe s.)," *BSl* 54 (1993), 95–101

Tashkovski, D., *The Macedonian nation* (Skopje, 1976)

Terzić, S., ed., *Kosovska bitka u istoriografiju* (Belgrade, 1990)

Thibaut, J., "L'Hebdomon de Constantinople. Nouvel examen topographique," *EO* 21 (1922), 31–51

Tinnefeld, F., "Die Zeit Basileios II. in neugriechischen Romanen und Dramen des 20. Jahrhunderts," in E. Konstantinou, ed., *Byzantinische Stoffe und Motive in der europäischen Literatur des 19. und 20. Jahrhunderts*, Philhellenische Studien 6 (Frankfurt am Main, 1998), 317–36

Tougher, S., "The wisdom of Leo the Wise," in P. Magdalino, ed., *New Constantines: the rhythm of imperial renewal in Byzantium, 4th to 13th centuries* (Aldershot, 1994), 171–9

Toynbee, A., *The Place of mediaeval and modern Greece in history. Inaugural lecture of the Koraes Chair of Modern Greek and Byzantine Language, Literature and History* (London, 1919)

The Western Question in Greece and Turkey. A study in the contact of civilisations (London, 1922)

Treadgold, W., *A history of Byzantine state and society* (Stanford, 1997)

Troebst, S., "IMRO + 100 = FYROM? The politics of Macedonian historiography," in J. Pettifer, ed., *The new Macedonian Question* (London, 1999), 60–78

Trypanis, C. A., "Greek literature since the Fall of Constantinople in 1453," in C. Jelavich and B. Jelavich, eds., *The Balkans in transition. Essays on the development of Balkan life and politics since the eighteenth century* (Berkeley, 1963), 227–57

Ursinus, M., "From Süleyman Pasha to Mehmet Fuat Köprülü: Roman and Byzantine history in late Ottoman historiography," *BMGS* 12 (1988), 305–14

Vasiliev, A. A., *Histoire de l'empire byzantin*, 2 vols. (Paris, 1932)

History of the Byzantine empire 324–1453. 2nd English ed. (Madison, WI, 1952)

Veloudis, G., "Jakob Philipp Fallmerayer und die Entstehung des neugriechischen Historismus," *SüdostF* 29 (1970), 43–90

Verouka, A., *I onomatothesia odon kai plateion* (Athens, 1995)

Vryonis, Jr., S., "Recent scholarship on continuity and discontinuity of culture: classical Greeks, Byzantines and modern Greeks," in his *Byzantina kai metabyzantina, I: The "past" in medieval and modern Greek culture* (Malibu, CA, 1978), 237–56

Wace, A. and M. Thompson, *The nomads of the Balkans. An account of the life and customs among the Vlachs of the northern Pindus* (London, 1914; repr. 1972)

Wahlgreen, S., "Symeon the Logothete: some philological remarks," *Byzantion* 71 (2001), 251–62

Wasilewski, T., "Le thème de Sirmium-Serbie au XIe et XIIe siècles," *ZRVI* 8 (1964), 465–82

"La genèse de l'empire de Samuel," in M. Apostolski, S. Antoljak and B. Panov, eds., *Iljada godini od vostanieto na komitopulite i sozdavanjeto na Samoilovata drzava: zbornik na materijali od naucnata sredba odrzana vo Prespa od 10 do 15 oktombri 1969 godina* (Skopje, 1971), 249–52

Wattenbach, W., *Deutschlands Geschichtsquellen im Mittelalter*, 2 vols. (Berlin, 1939)

Wentzel, H., "Das byzantinische Erbe der ottonischen Kaiser. Hypothesen über den Brautschatz der Theophano," *Aachener Kunstblätter des Museumsvereins* 43 (1972), 11–96

Whittow, M., *The making of Orthodox Byzantium, 600–1025* (London, 1996)

Wolff, R. L., "How the news was brought from Byzantium to Angoulême; or, the pursuit of the hare in an ox cart," *BMGS* 4 (1978), 139–89

Wroth, W., *Catalogue of imperial Byzantine coins in the British Museum*, I (London, 1908; repr. Chicago, 1966)

Xydis, S., "Medieval origins of modern Greek nationalism," *Balkan Studies* 9 (1968), 1–20

Yiannis, J., ed., *The Byzantine tradition after the fall of Constantinople* (Charlottesville and Oxford, 1991)

Yuzbashian, K. N., *Ellinisticheskii blizhnii Vostok, Vizantiia i Iran* (Moscow, 1967) "L'administration byzantine en Arménie aux XIe et XIIe siècles," *Revue des études armeniènnes* 10 (1973–4), 139–83

Zacos, G. and J. Nesbitt, *Byzantine lead seals*, II (Berne, 1984)

Zaimov, I., *Bitolski nadpis na Ivan Vladislav samodrzhets bulgarski* (Sofia, 1970)

Zaimov, J. [= I.] "Eindeutige und umstrittene Stellen in der Bitolja-inschrift des bulgarischen Selbstherrschers Ivan Vladislav (11. Jh.)," *Zeitschrift für Balkanologie* 13 (1977), 194–204

Zakythinos, D. A., *The making of modern Greece from Byzantium to independence* (Oxford, 1976)

Zambelios, S., *Vyzantinai meletai. Peri pigon neoellinikis ethnotitos apo 8 achri 10 ekatonaetiridos m. X.* (Athens, 1857)

Zlatarski, V., *Istoriia na bulgarskata durzhava prez srednite vekove*, 3 vols. (Sofia, 1927)

Index

Plate 1   Illuminated portrait of Basil II standing over kneeling subjects or enemies, from
his psalter: MS Cod. Marc. gr. 17, fol. 3r. Marcian Library, Venice.

These plates are available for download from www.cambridge.org/9780521158831

Plate 3   A modern reproduction of Basil's psalter portrait, commissioned for the National Historical Museum, Athens, Greece. An enlarged photographic reproduction of this may be seen in the Hellenic War Museum, beside six maps illustrating Basil's Bulgarian campaigns. Historical and Ethnological Society of Greece.

Plate 2   Imperial Silk showing mounted emperor receiving tokens of victory, known as the Bamberger Gunthertuch. This silk is now housed in the Bamberg Cathedral treasury, Bamberg, Germany. Bayerisches Landesamt für Denkmalpflege, Munich.

Plate 5   A Greek poster from the time of the Second Balkan War (1913), by S. Christidis, depicting a Greek soldier biting a Bulgarian. The caption reads Ο ΒΟΥΛΓΑΡΟΦΑΓΟΣ, "the Bulgar-eater." Historical and Ethnological Society of Greece.

Plate 4   The cover art of Penelope Delta, Τὸν Καιρὸ τοῦ Βουλγαροκτόνου (Athens: Vivliopoleion tis "Estias", 1911). The image is clearly inspired by Basil's psalter portrait.

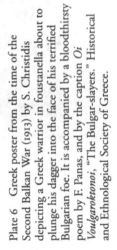

Plate 7 Greek poster from the time of the Second Balkan War celebrating the battle of Kilkis (21 June 1913). In the foreground, a Greek soldier is depicted blinding a Bulgarian. Historical and Ethnological Society of Greece.

Plate 6 Greek poster from the time of the Second Balkan War (1913) by S. Christidis depicting a Greek warrior in foustanella about to plunge his dagger into the face of his terrified Bulgarian foe. It is accompanied by a bloodthirsty poem by F. Panas, and by the caption Oi Voulgaroktonoi, "The Bulgar-slayers." Historical and Ethnological Society of Greece.